Science Fiction
in Classic Rock

Science Fiction in Classic Rock

*Musical Explorations of Space,
Technology and the Imagination,
1967–1982*

ROBERT MCPARLAND

CRITICAL EXPLORATIONS
IN SCIENCE FICTION AND FANTASY, 59
Series Editors Donald E. Palumbo *and* C.W. Sullivan III

McFarland & Company, Inc., Publishers
Jefferson, North Carolina

Library of Congress Cataloguing-in-Publication Data

Names: McParland, Robert, author.
Title: Science fiction in classic rock : musical explorations of space, technology and the imagination, 1967–1982 / Robert McParland.
Description: Jefferson, North Carolina : McFarland & Company, 2017. | Series: Critical explorations in science fiction and fantasy ; 59 | Includes bibliographical references and index.
Identifiers: LCCN 2017041520 | ISBN 9781476664705 (softcover : acid free paper) ∞
Subjects: LCSH: Rock music—History and criticism. | Science fiction in music.
Classification: LCC ML3534 .M472 2017 | DDC 781.66—dc23
LC record available at https://lccn.loc.gov/2017041520

British Library cataloguing data are available

ISBN (print) 978-1-4766-6470-5
ISBN (ebook) 978-1-4766-3030-4

Front cover image © 2017 iStock

Printed in the United States of America

McFarland & Company, Inc., Publishers
Box 611, Jefferson, North Carolina 28640
www.mcfarlandpub.com

Table of Contents

Preface

Science fiction and rock music have been involved in a dynamic relationship since the late 1960s. Rock's relationship with myth goes back even further, for myth has been a source of wonder and story in the human imagination since ancient times. The presence of science fiction imagery in psychedelic rock, progressive rock, and heavy metal has been part of the rock music experience of many listeners. Yet, few studies have explored the relationship between these popular arts, or have probed the mythical imagination of rock music. This book is a descriptive survey: a sketch of classic rock's engagement with myth and with science fiction. It begins with the premise that as we undergo significant technological change in our time we carry with us the ancient, the primeval, and indeed the mythical strands of human experience in a new social, technological, and cultural context.

The discussion that follows is presented in non-technical language, so that this book can be easily digested by readers who are not sociologists, musicologists, or cultural critics. This is a selective discussion, which is by no means an exhaustive inquiry into this subject. Nor is it intended as an analytical study of the compositions of the artists referred to here. My goal is simply to invite you to listen to and reflect upon the music, concepts, and imagery of a few commercially successful bands who have made use of myth and science fiction. These are bands whose most lasting work was created in the late 1960s, the 1970s, and the early to mid–1980s. The work of these artists has been amply documented and they have produced a good deal of critical and biographical information. With the exception of Hawkwind, or other early participants in the "space rock" genre, I omit cult bands and do not develop this discussion in relation to heavy metal or alternative music of the late 1980s into the 1990s and in this century.

1

Preface

Myth pervades popular culture: from rock music to television and from comics to film. A study of popular culture and its artifacts can provide us with insight into the social concerns and cultural thought and attitudes of a given time. Myth and science fiction motifs will likely continue to appear in the work of rock music artists and bands. This study investigates their assertion of imagination and individuality and the relationship of their music with mythology and with science fiction. It pursues an inquiry into how rock songwriters and performers utilize the mythical themes of heroism and journey and the monstrous or fantastic and how they direct their attention to social issues, technological wonders, and projections of the future.

Following an introduction, the first chapter provides a brief overview of some of the bands and artists who have created works that have engaged with myth or science fiction. The second chapter is a bit more theoretical and looks at creativity, the importance of myth, and at science fiction. Subsequent chapters deal with rock music artists who have utilized science fiction or myth in their work: the Jefferson Starship, ELO, Pink Floyd, David Bowie, Blue Öyster Cult, Rush, and the Alan Parsons Project.

I would like to invite you to listen to the recordings considered here and to read the science fiction texts that are mentioned. A bibliography will direct you to rewarding studies of these artists. While I was writing this book we lost David Bowie, Keith Emerson, and Paul Kantner. This book is written in thanks for their remarkable creativity and it is dedicated to science fiction readers and to avid rock music listeners, who can obviously say much more about how these fascinating artists, books, and recordings have touched their lives than I ever could.

Wishing you good listening.

Introduction

When the lights come up on a rock concert stage it is as if the sky has opened in a burst of solar energy. The sound of guitars rises over the long chords from keyboards, the pulse of a bass run, and the first sharp hits of the drums. Then a concert is born, like a moment of creation in cosmic thunder, and a voice breaks through to tell us a strange, mythical story. Rock and science fiction appear this way: as spectacle and sound, technologically driven music, imagery, and lyrics that refer to wondrous worlds.

So, buckle up. Put your headphones on. The countdown has begun. We are going to take off into imaginative journeys and speculative fiction with some of the finest rock acts in existence. Some of the most profound scientific questions about the nature of the universe appear in science fiction stories. Rock musicians and their fans are among the thousands of people who are fascinated with these stories and are asking these questions. Science fiction and mythological speculations appear in the work of Rush, Pink Floyd, the Electric Light Orchestra (ELO), Yes, David Bowie, the Moody Blues, Blue Öyster Cult, T. Rex, Hawkwind, Iron Maiden, Emerson, Lake, and Palmer, the Alan Parsons Project, Genesis, Muse, Motörhead, Brian Eno, Jefferson Starship, and many other bands. Rock music is part of the voice of our time and the work of these bands recognizes that our very fate as a species is bound up with science and imagination. Science fiction in rock is a fertile, creative subgenre that reminds us that the staggering advances of science and technology are now deeply connected with the human endeavor. These rock acts have absorbed science fiction in print or on film and have brought the imagery of science fiction to their songs, performances, and album imagery. We will look at how these rock music artists draw upon science fiction literature, film, and mythology to create their popular music.

3

Introduction

The science fiction genre has intersected with rock in one hit wonders like Zager and Evans' "In the Year 2525," popular hit singles like Elton John's "Rocket Man," and in dazzling instrumentals like Edgar Winter's "Frankenstein." In the age of the LP recording, science fiction imagery graced album covers, projecting the futuristic worlds of progressive bands like Rush and Yes, creating the androgynous Ziggy Stardust character of David Bowie, and visually expressing the imaginative vision of Boston and heavy metal bands like Iron Maiden. Science fiction may, likewise, be said to be in the sound of some of these artists. Conceptually, it registers in the expansion of keyboard sounds from synthesizers to the experimental lines of soaring guitars and throughout studio effects by which musicians and producers sculpt albums.

Rock artists have been drawn toward science fiction because it is one of the most progressive of fiction genres. Science fiction is rich in imagination. It supports the urge to envision possibilities. Stories of science fiction promote reflection and social critique. In this sense, science fiction is a voice of counterculture that is willing to break with convention and explore uniqueness, novelty, and the reaches of human consciousness. In this respect, it is parallel with the quest of some our world's most creative rock visionaries. These musicians are exploring the reaches of sound, image, recording technology, and the human story.

Rock musicians draw upon myths, which are the oldest form of human imagination. Science fiction is involved with myths and mythic patterns, while responding to modernity, or imaginative visions of the future. Science fiction seeks alternative realities and societal possibilities. There are rock performers who recognize how myth is used to construct future models of reality. With their propensity for imaginative vision, these rock composers borrow from myth. What are explored here are the science fiction themes and mythological themes that appear in the songs of these artists. In some cases, these come from their reading, or from their viewing science fiction movies, or from television shows that they have seen. However, it is wrong to say that these songs are simply derivative of such sources. Rather, these works of creative imagination arise from the unique talents of these artists, at times from an archetypal and mythological level of consciousness. They emerge from their music, their feelings and emotions, their personal experiences, and perhaps from hallucinatory drug use, in some cases. Open to cultural resources, including books and film, the rock musician makes culture as he or she seeks alternative worlds.

Mythology offers a rich repository of stories and images. Sir James Frazer, in *The Golden Bough* (1890), showed us that the stories and images which arise in these ancient myths have similarities across cultures. Myths and their heroes are something more than ways to dramatize natural phenomena that cannot be explained otherwise. They are expressions of cultural understanding, aspirations, and fundamental patterns of life. The psychologist Carl Jung believed that deep within the collective unconscious of the human race there are common images. These figures he referred to as archetypes.[1] The German ethnologist Adolf Bastian (1826–1905) asserted that the human imagination seems to be constituted in such a way that it works with certain shapes, images, themes, and elemental ideas. These archetypes continue to appear in our songs, in our imagery, and in our performance rituals.

The quest of a hero, exotic lands, alien beings, and strange places and characters make up motifs that appear in rock album concepts and lyrics. These worlds arise from mythological designs, whether the landscape is pastoral and agrarian, or highly technological. Joseph Campbell, in his fascinating study *The Hero with a Thousand Faces* (1949), identified the monomyth: a universal story pattern. In this story, the hero is called to adventure, experiences an initiation and rising fortunes, then faces what Aristotle called *peripeteia*, or a reversal of fortunes. Heroes face monsters, twisting plots, fierce conflicts, and they make thrilling escapes. When all seems lost, against impossible odds, the hero emerges. From imminent loss, constriction, or imprisonment he or she breaks free, rises to the challenge, and saves the day. The hero, Campbell pointed out, returns with a boon, or gift, to his society.

These figures that live in the roots of human consciousness appear in rock songs and performances. When a rock performer develops a persona he is dealing in archetypes and appealing to this kind of consciousness. In writing lyrics that dwell in fantasy, the rock songwriter is exploring these archetypal depths. The heroic fantasy figure, like the creative artist, is an adventurer, an explorer. At times, he or she is alone, possibly orphaned by society, or socially alienated. This character, however, has unique strengths of emotion, craftiness, or imagination. In this sense, the rock performer may project himself or herself into a heroic fantasy character, as Bruce Dickinson of Iron Maiden has done when singing of great cosmic duels, or as David Bowie has done with his hermaphroditic Ziggy Stardust. The rock performer creates alternative worlds and stages a fictional world in music and performance. The world that is created may seem quite tangible and real. In this respect, the rock music creator is much like the imaginative science fiction writer.

When science fiction themes and motifs have been incorporated into rock music these themes appear most obviously in the lyrics. Yet, they are also evident in the artwork that accompanies albums, or in concert appearances and performance styles. Musical composition, the aural space and the making of a record, as well as electronic effects, lines of melody, tempo, rhythm and key signature change in a band's music are all aspects of their musical art. In the art of the song, themes and motifs have to be considered musically, as well as lyrically. So too does each band's public image. So, make sure to consider these factors as you get hold of the albums, download the MP3s, and start your own exploration of the myths, sounds, and images of science fiction rock.

The variety of these bands is astonishing. Their sounds range from progressive rock to heavy metal and from alternative rock to space rock. What you will discover as you listen to them is a colorful palette of striking imagery and mind-stretching sonic textures. Since the late 1960s, science fiction themed songs have ranged from Pink Floyd's "Interstellar Overdrive" and "Set the Controls for the Heart of the Sun" (1968) to the identity and gender morphing of David Bowie's "Space Oddity" (1969) and from Alan Parsons' references to Isaac Asimov's *I, Robot* to Iron Maiden's use of Orson Scott Card's *Seventh Son* on their album *Seventh Son of a Seventh Son*. Science fiction rock has crossed over from epic length progressive rock forays from Rush, Yes, and Genesis to the heavy metal and alternative rock of the 1990s and 2000s. The Flaming Lips, Radiohead, the Verve, Flying Saucer Attack, Flowers of Hell, Comets of Fire, Angels and Airwaves, and many others have explored myth and sonic textures. The vitality of these bands shows that speculative fiction has been a potent contributor to rock music.

Connecting Rock and Science Fiction

Some bands have taken brief detours into themes of science fiction. Styx, which takes its name after the river of the Underworld, moved from Top 20 singles like "Come Sail Away" (1977) to "Mr. Roboto" (1982). Boston made use of the image of spaceship flying away from earth. Blondie sang "Rapture," the Killers sang "Spaceman," and Soundgarden recorded Chris Cornell's "Black Hole Sun" (1994). Science fiction references have crossed genres too. The Beastie Boys rapped "Intergalactic," singing about a pinch on the neck from *Star Trek*'s Spock. When a prominent funk band performed in 1976, the stage was aglow with a spaceship. This oversized prop represented the mothership, a U.F.O., and it had been created for the Parliament Funkadelic O-Funk Earth tour. Group members joined George Clinton in space outfits.[2] These are spectacles that draw upon science fiction imagery. For other bands, involvement with science fiction themes or mythological concepts has been more of a long-term commitment. Hawkwind played space rock for many years. They introduced their two-disc album, *Space Ritual* (1973), with a laser light show in their concerts. The science fiction escapades of Klaatu are legendary. (Someone started a rumor that Klaatu were The Beatles; the band immediately denied this. None of The Beatles were ever involved with this Canadian band and their space rock imagery.) Gong, an eclectic Franco-British rock band formed in 1967 by Australian Daevid Allen, a member of the band Soft Machine, has had a constantly changing entourage. The band Soft Machine took its name from a William Burroughs science fiction novel, *The Soft Machine*.

Science fiction imagery was alive when David Bowie transformed into Ziggy Stardust, exploring the boundaries of gender and identity. When Rush narrated a story of Cygnus X-1, they were bringing us to imaginative worlds, much like science fiction writers and filmmakers have done. These artists recognized that rock music, as a commercial art form, is very much about creating records that will sell, songs that will get downloaded, concert programs that will sell tickets. However, they also asserted that rock music is about play and rebellion and freedom. Rock is about energy, attitude, sound, and imagery. It breaks through the mundane and transforms the ordinary world, reminding us of magic, of instinct, and of mystery. Rock music's science fiction narrative, like science fiction itself, is about wonder, curiosity, and imaginative inquiry. It is a form of art that taps into the deep resources of mythology, music, theatre, and visual art.

When rock meets with mythology or with science fiction it offers musical expression that reminds us that humanity is fundamentally curious about origins and the mysteries and wonders of the universe. Science and the wide imaginative range of science fiction explore our sense of wonder; they express a curiosity that is a natural impulse within us. The astronomer Johannes Kepler once observed: "We do not ask for what useful purpose the birds do sing, for song is their pleasure since they were created for singing. Similarly, we ought not to ask why the human mind troubles to fathom the secrets of the heavens."[3] Musical imagination is at the center of rock music. It is stimulated by new sounds and creative performances, by stories and imagery. It is given shape in song lyrics and the imagery that artists bring to stage performances and videos. Mythology and the speculation present in science fiction thus have much to contribute to it.

The rock musician in the brave new world of digital technology has turned toward the speculations of science fiction to expand the range of his or her own expressive encounter with modern life. Rush's *Clockwork Angels*, Pink Floyd's *The Dark Side of the Moon*, the Alan Parsons Project's *I Robot*, or Brian Eno's *Another Green World* and *Before and After Science* are examples of rock creations that have stretched the boundaries of sound and music technology. Science fiction has provided them and acts like David Bowie with intriguing performance imagery that can imaginatively light up a stage, a stage persona, or an album concept. Science fiction imagination had been a colorful resource for rock music lyrics and album concepts for Blue Öyster Cult, Rush, the Jefferson Starship, Yes, Boston, and many other rock groups.

The Emergence of Science Fiction

The emergence of science fiction in the twentieth century predates the birth of rock music by several decades. In the first decades of the twentieth century, the pulp magazines of Hugo Gernsback, a scientist-entrepreneur, fostered modern science fiction in America. In the pages of *Amazing Stories*, "scientification" or "scientific fiction" reached a wide public in a seminal publication that was illustrated with imaginative covers by the artist Frank R. Paul. Today's Hugo Awards, science fiction's highest honor, are named after Gernsback. Science fiction imagery owes much to Frank R. Paul, an Austrian architect who tuned his imagination toward future worlds and created more than 150 spectacular magazine covers. The creators of LP album covers and the creators of films drew upon these images. The world of fantasy fiction, meanwhile, appeared in *Weird Tales*. While science fiction embraced the hard science of Gernsback, whose reflections helped to define the field, ancient myths and legends mixed with modern imagination in the realm of fantasy fiction as well. In the *Norton Book of Science Fiction*, Ursula K. Le Guin distinguishes science fiction from fantasy. Then she writes: "Science fiction behaves like fantasy ... in making things up which we know don't exist." Yet, how do we know for sure that they don't?[4]

In the 1930s, the renowned *Amazing Stories* was edited by John W. Campbell. This preceded the birth of all of today's rock music performers. However, some of them have read stories from the "golden age of science fiction" that included the fiction of Isaac Asimov, Robert Heinlein, Lester Del Rey, L. Sprague De Camp, Theodore Sturgeon, A.E. van Vogt and others. In the World War II era, science fiction appeared in the pulp magazines, which had been so popular in the 1930s and stories came to new audiences by radio, newspaper comic strips, feature films, and in motion picture serials. Rock performers who were born in the 1940s and 1950s absorbed juvenile serials and comic books and radio and they experienced science fiction as the field was advanced further by the advent of television, beginning in the 1940s and 1950s. Those born later, from the 1960s through the 1980s, have seen science fiction stories enter the literary mainstream and extend across the world in film. With the 1970s, science fiction, once a genre eschewed by many literary critics, gained further respect. It entered the classroom, appeared in anthologies, and was treated by scholars in critical studies. This book follows in this tradition, as science fiction meets with another highly popular cultural form that has gradually come to merit critical study: rock music.

Rock Heroes and Mythical Personas

Rock music asserts vitality. It also tends to resist conventionality. In several Rush songs, for example, Geddy Lee, the singer, is given lyrics by the band's lyricist and drummer, Neil Peart, that make assertions against a system that would deny a person's vitality. In one of their signature songs, "Freewill" (1980), he declares that he will assert his free will. For, as the Danish philosopher Søren Kierkegaard wrote in *Either/Or*, if one chooses not to decide one has already made a decision.

Rock performers play out personas; they engage in contrivance and their rock performances build upon artifice. At times, a listener may hear in the music a sense of conflict as the vocalist battles the mysterious forces that assault him. These tensions and dramatic conflicts are at the root of stories. The form of the fable is utilized to bring listeners to fabulous worlds. This fable veers away from traditional realism, often into fantastic places. Sometimes it explores a world of mystery with dark humor. The contemporary fable is a story at play; it is the enjoyment of story for its own sake, observes Robert Scholes. Meanwhile, the dark contemporary fable stares out into the wasteland with a recognition that may remind us of the satire of Jonathan Swift or Voltaire.[5]

The lead singer of a band, the rock music front man, is a mythical figure. That very visible figure onstage has at times been likened to a shamanic figure who casts spells. The singer enters the music and energizes an audience. The mythological potency of such performers can be examined through reference to symbolic rituals. These symbolic rituals have been investigated by Mircea Eliade (1907–1986), a Romanian mythologist and scholar of comparative religions. Eliade produced an important study of shamanism and numerous inquiries into ritual, myth, and symbols. He also wrote novels such as *The Forbidden Forest*, which presented an escape into mythical time. Along with Carl Jung and Joseph Campbell, he was one of the significant expositors of myth in the twentieth century. Eliade might see the glam-space rock David Bowie as a shamanic figure, dressed in spandex and makeup, shapeshifting across the boundaries of identity. When Iron Maiden's front man Bruce Dickinson (or, later, Blaze Bayley) sings bassist Steve Harris's adaptation of "The Rime of the Ancient Mariner" he becomes the haunted mariner who has shot the albatross and is chased eternally by ghostly demons. We find a quest into the unknown in songs like this, the kind of mystery that Eliade interpreted through metaphysics as he reached toward "a certain metaphysical valorization of human existence."[6]

Rock, Science Fiction and Wonder

Rock music is an exercise in wonder. When imaginative science fiction meets with rock music it reminds us of this. Rock music is a form of serious play and innovation, an act of rebellion and liberation. Of course, for rock music's business entrepreneurs rock is a business that sells recordings as commodities. The artists who make the music clearly appreciate the financial rewards of doing so. Rock rebellion gets co-opted, commodified, and sold. However, while the industry is about artifice for profit, for several musicians making music, songwriting, and recording continues to be about discovery and freeing the spirit. Mythology and science fiction motifs have been a feature of their musical exploration and a means for their audiences to explore their own creative capacity for wonder.

Rock music fans revel in that capacity for wonder and celebration of life. They know that rock is exciting and stimulating; it gets into the bloodstream and takes them beyond themselves. If you were to pick up a handful of sand you would be holding about 10,000 grains, Carl Sagan once pointed out. That would be more than the number of stars than we can see with the naked eye.[7] When Bob Dylan wrote "Every Grain of Sand" his song expressed the wonder that he and poets before him, like William Blake, had discovered in the tiniest particles of our world. Blake once wrote: "To see a world in a grain of sand/ And heaven in a wildflower." Similarly, people looking up at the night sky have felt wonder at the sheer magnitude of the reaches of space. Science fiction conveys this wonder and mystery of the cosmos and rock performers and their audiences likewise respond to this sense of awe.

The simple child's song about wondering at a star is amplified when a progressive rock band like Rush, for example, turns to science fiction to express their sense of wonder. They announce defiantly that their imaginative speculations and ambitious music making cannot simply be reduced to pragmatic requirements of a music business that emphasizes the manufacturing of hit singles and the creation of profits. Across more than thirty years, Rush has developed a large fan base. Today they are applauded when they take off on their speculative excursions into science fiction worlds. Yet, when they sing about a dark star, the Greek world of myth lies behind this. Our word "disaster" comes from the Greek meaning "bad star." You can see the word astral there and the "dis" prefix that we find in words like disgust, distraught, disturbed, or dysfunctional. We are thrown back to our connection with the ancient world of myth. Like that ancient Greek audience we too look at the universe with wonder.

Rock Music and the Power of Myth

An adventurous progressive rock song that is filled with mythical imagery is like a musical epic. It is recklessly long, filled with rhythmic shifts in time signature, and it allows for a narrative that can be based in the monomyth. The monomyth is an archetypal plot structure that was engagingly expressed in Joseph Campbell's insights in *The Hero with a Thousand Faces* (1949). It is a story that focuses upon a quest, or a journey, like Iron Maiden's "Run to the Hills" or "Rime of the Ancient Mariner." We find it in dozens of science fiction films. Campbell calls this pattern a single "consciously controlled" sequence that appears in myths and folk tales from all around the world. Called to adventure, the hero takes up the challenge to go on a journey and enters an initiation phase. He or she crosses a threshold into an unfamiliar setting. Then the hero confronts a series of trials. The hero encounters adversaries and obstacles and has to use unique abilities of courage, intelligence, strength, or character and is sometimes assisted by helper figures. The action proceeds to a climactic point at which the hero succeeds, or has a moment of revelation and realizes something. Then our hero returns with gifts for his or her society, which may be increased wisdom, insight, prowess, or strength of character. The hero may confidently venture forth, or be exiled, or tossed into the unfamiliar world.

Along the way there may be monster figures, troublesome terrain, or he may meet a temptress. The return may involve escape from certain doom, a flight from the strange world. In the return the hero finds the strength to push back across the threshold and become part of a change that may come to the society he returns to.[8]

For David Bowie's character Major Tom there is no return to society. Bowie sings the first person story of an astronaut who leaves his tin can of a spaceship to take a walk in space. Upon encountering complications, Major Tom is set adrift and becomes lost in space. In Bowie's song, where the stars are very bright, Major Tom is a doomed traveler.

Usually, the adventure of a hero suggests movement and transition, life-challenging encounters, and transformation. In the heroic quest archetypes are re-enacted. At the core of these archetypes are truths that express our humanity, universal figures which are relevant to all societies. We have seen these archetypes in films. *The Matrix* gives us an oracle, a figure derived from the ancient Greek oracle of Delphi. *Star Wars* unfolds the monomyth and a story of a quest for the father who is a dark figure. We are reminded that in our world of technological change the ancient and the primal is still with us. One cannot simply let go of the past. It lingers in the present.

The power of myth, as Joseph Campbell observed, is very much still with us. In Robert Silverberg's "After the Myths Went Home," a society believes that it can do without myth. Figures of myth are reincarnated through a time machine. But then the myths are put away and banished. Consequently, the society no longer has mystery or heroism. Like that society, we are sometimes forgetful of mythic power. A realistic and pragmatic world claims that myths are just stories. Yet, myths, from time immemorial, have always been a form of inquiry, a way to transmit values. "The world is too much with us," the poet William Wordsworth once lamented. "Getting and spending we lay waste out powers/ Little we see in nature that is ours/ We have given it away/ a sordid boon." Wordsworth's poem ends with the narrator's claim that he could be "suckled in a creed outworn" if only he could have the vision to see Proteus rising from the sea or hear Triton blow his wreathed horn. The surface of a world of commerce, labor, and business as usual is a world that hides the power of myth; it is a world that would call myth "not true." However, that perspective is one of a naïve realism that neglects other dimensions of human experience.

The rock performers who are discussed here revive mystery and the heroic in their songs, albums, and performances. They reanimate the world by returning mythological energy to our social imagination and discourse. The uses of enchantment, as psychologist Bruno Bettelheim once observed, bring new energy to life. What the rock musicians discussed here affirm is the power of story, the vitality of creative imagery, and the dynamic engagement of music with the human spirit. When rock turns to science fiction, or to myth, it is drawing upon deep psychic sources of imagery that are among the most potent collective resources of the human race.

Musical Creativity and the Myth of Dionysius

In 1969, the same year that David Bowie recorded "Space Oddity," the United States space program launched the Apollo rocket toward the moon. In Greek mythology Apollo was "the shining one," a god of light and sun, a god of rational order and symmetry. His curious counterpart was Dionysius. Whereas Apollo was neat and orderly, Dionysius was passionate and messy. Dionysius was the god of wine and revelry, earth, underground power and fertility: a god of intoxication. The philosopher Friedrich Nietzsche, in *The Birth of Tragedy from the Spirit of Music*, proposed that art itself was a dynamic interplay between the orderly power of the Apollonian and the destructive and creative chaos and ecstatic energy of the god Dionysius. The song and dance of the barbaric, the primal fire of rock, owes much to the Dionysian. Rock musicians are the progeny, the ancestors, of Dionysian passion.[9]

In the late nineteenth century, Nietzsche argued against the dullness, lack of courage, and mass-minded behavior that he saw around him in the Europe of his own day. He used a myth, the story of Zarathustra, to assert that the values that kept that society so enervated had to be transvalued. In his myth of Zarathustra he argued that a modern man needed to be heroic, like a man walking on a wire across an abyss. Later he said that one needed a will to power: a phrase that has often been misconstrued. Nietzsche meant not power over others but power within one's individuality. That was the uniqueness of the superman, the Übermensch. This idea has found its way into the poses of rock performers. The amplified power of guitars, the muscular energy and tribal pulse of drumming, the shrieking wail of a vocalist all mark the aspiration toward a Dionysian breaking through to transcendence.

Composer Richard Strauss took "Also sprach Zarathustra" as the theme for his powerful musical composition that became the familiar score for *2001: A Space Odyssey*, the science fiction film based upon Arthur C. Clarke's novel. The thunderous percussion and memorable musical motif of that composition was part of the German romantic heritage from which Nietzsche emerged. Nietzsche was deeply drawn to the music-drama of Richard Wagner, which had a strong influence on John Williams's music for *Star Wars*. Nietzsche's interest in music followed closely the philosophy of Arthur Schopenhauer, who posited that music is considered the highest of the arts. In his view, music can provide a moment of release from the inexorable power of the Will which courses through the world. Nietzsche, upon listening to Wagner, wrote to his friend Erwin Rohde: "Every fiber, every nerve twitched; for a long time I haven't had such a long lasting feeling of rapture."[10] Such words might echo the experience of a rock music fan emerging from a concert.

Nietzsche believed that the artist is an individual of rare sensitivity who can listen for the intimations of the world-soul. The musician feels the power of some unseen force and desires to bring this to the world. Nietzsche wrote: "To those real musicians.... Someone who [has] put his ear to the ventricle of the world's Will who [has] felt the raging desire for being a roaring river or as a most sublime creek pouring into all the veins of the world—and who would not immediately break."[11] The metaphor suggests that a stream of energy may flow through the musician. He or she can draw upon a powerful source of creativity or become a vehicle for sublime beauty.

Rock and Romanticism

What rock musicians have in common with Nietzsche, who composed music on piano, is their inheritance of a pose of rebellion against

Introduction

Enlightenment reason. In the 1980s Robert Pattison linked rock music with romanticism, which, in its English and German forms, countered an emphasis upon rationality with the reminder that we are also emotional, intuitive, feeling beings. Pattison called rock music "the triumph of vulgarity" and contended that rock refuses to submit to measures of good taste. He recognized "various Romantic myths of which rock is composed" and considered rock as a world of thought. The London based music critic Simon Frith, in his review of Pattison's book, *The Triumph of Vulgarity*, pointed out some of the shortcomings of this view. The romantic myths largely resided in what he called the "art school bands": the Rolling Stones, the Yardbirds, the Who, Cream and Led Zeppelin. (Eric Clapton, Jimmy Page, Pete Townshend, and Keith Richards all attended art school at one time. John Lennon did also.) Frith argued that Pattison's thesis that rock was black music, or the blues, meeting with white Romanticism failed to account for bohemian influences and sources of rock. Meanwhile, as a reviewer in *The Nation* (March 28, 1987) pointed out, in commenting upon rock music we cannot only "resituate [rock songs] on a high cultural terrain" in terms of traditional musicology. Our approaches have to be more varied. Rock is more than "an organic development of Western Romanticism expressed in the vulgar mode," as Pattison pointed out. Indeed, rock is this, in part, but it is also something more.[12]

The chapters that follow propose that the creations of science fiction are another way to look at rock's quest for freedom, wonder, and ecstasy. Certainly, the German romanticism of Novalis, Hoffmann, Holderlin, or Nietzsche and the British romanticism of Coleridge, Blake, and Shelley are precursors for the rock attitude that music is liberating, that imagination is to be celebrated, and that rebellion against confining norms is imperative. These poets and thinkers all sought to proclaim the power of imagination and dwelled in dark fantasies. They turned to the force of poetry and story. Rock music, likewise, in our age of science and technology, has combined these impulses with the imaginative resources of science fiction. Transcendence, which was so important to the romantics, is a feature of the science fiction genre. It is a significant feature of rock music as well. The choice to use science fiction motifs and concepts is an assertion of creativity. It provides a dream-world, a speculative wonder-world, or a way of critiquing present day assumptions about what is "real." It offers a way of storytelling and image-making that stretches the musical and visual imaginations of rock music listeners.

Listening to the Rock Universe

You and I are involved in what we listen to. You have your own unique way of listening, the way that you respond to different songs and rock performances. Your way of interpreting the songs and bands that follow may be different than mine. Two people listening to the same recording of music may hear it differently. Their perception of the same music event is different.

Imagine that the astronomers Johannes Kepler and Tycho Brahe are gazing up at the dawn. As the moments of dawn unfold, they look out at the horizon in the same direction. Surely, the distance between the horizon and the sun is increasing. However, they see different aspects of the same reality. Kepler, attuned to the Copernican theory of the universe, recognizes that the earth is in motion. Tycho, still holding to the Ptolemaic view that the solar system moves around the earth, sees the sun rising and in motion. Their interpretations of the same phenomena each reflect a way of seeing. That is just as true when we hear a rock music recording.[13] We are all individual listeners with our own interpretations.

The range of sound that a listener hears may be compared with the spectrum of light. That spectrum of light is the mix of the component parts of the white light of the sun. Isaac Newton, in 1666, cut a small hole in the shade by his window to let in a point of the daylight from the sun. He placed a prism between the light and the far wall of his room. Then he could see that the sunlight had dispersed into a spectrum of light. Like Isaac Newton, we see the phenomenon of light. When the refraction of light gives us a rainbow in the sky, this suggests to us that the spectrum of light is objectively there in nature. Yet, that phenomenon needs a beholder, a way of seeing. Likewise, there are thousands of recordings available around us but a recording needs a listener. When the MP3 or CD plays, or when a needle falls onto the turning LP vinyl record, those sounds come to us. How we listen in that moment is crucial to our experience of the music. Recordings need you, the listener, to engage your own interpretations.

A sound recording holds an act of the past, a voice that is caught in time, one that has been captured for posterity. Musicians know that music itself is restless and full of change. Music is heard by the man who stands on a platform, iPod in hand and earplugs in his ears, watching a train race by. It plays in his mind as he sees a woman on the train looking out. Her speed in time is relative to the man on the platform, as Einstein once pointed out.[14] His iPod plays Pink Floyd's clocks ticking into "Time." Her smartphone is playing futuristic rock. Do they hear the future? Does Rush's Geddy Lee's high tenor cut through the roar of the train to visions of Cygnus or the future of the earth? Does David Bowie's Major Tom imagine a tomorrow before that umbilical cord to his spaceship is cut and he drifts into space? What will rock music continue to borrow from science fiction? This book is about rock and roll memory. It is also about the future. And if the imaginings of rock music are any indication, what an incredible future that will be!

ONE

Rock Music and the Mythic Imagination

Rock bands play with fantasy. The power of myth resonates in their music, their images, and their performances. Rock has reached to Egyptian, Babylonian, Tibetan, and Norse imagery to create imaginative worlds. Haunting suggestions of the Underworld surface in stage spectacles, in song lyrics, and in the imagery created by Alice Cooper, Black Sabbath, Iron Maiden, Kiss, Nine Inch Nails and dozens of other bands. Mythology is recalled in many rock song titles. The Greek hero Achilles is mentioned in Led Zeppelin's "Achilles Last Stand" and in "Cry of Achilles" by Alter Bridge. Cream sings of "Tales of Brave Ulysses." Procol Harum opens "Pandora's Box" and Sinead O'Connor sings "Troy." Trivium is torn between "Scylla and Carybdis." Judas Priest turns to Nordic myth for "Halls of Valhalla" and Asia sings "Valkyrie." Dionysius lingers behind Third Eye Blind's song "God of Wine."

Rock music exercises wild imagination. It tears through convention, rebels against the commonplace, and conjures up figures from beyond the earth. Science fiction and myth cross rock genres: they appear in the shifting guises of David Bowie and in the progressive rock of Yes and Emerson, Lake and Palmer. They come onstage in the space-age stage shows of Parliament and George Clinton's funk. Medieval imagery abounds in heavy metal and hard rock, including in songs like "Neon Knights" by Black Sabbath and "Stonehenge" by Spinal Tap. Led Zeppelin sings of wonder in "Stairway to Heaven" and gestures toward the exotic, the mystical, and the occult with songs like "Kashmir." The album cover for Led Zeppelin's *Houses of the Holy* recalls

Arthur C. Clarke's *Childhood's End.* The wonders of mythology underlie *Led Zeppelin IV* which bears four symbols that represent the members of the band, symbols that have been traced to Egyptian, Celtic, Rosicrucian, Pagan and Wiccan symbolism.[1]

Myth, science fiction, and cosmic reflection have been a familiar feature of psychedelic and progressive bands. Psychedelia emerged in the late 1960s and brought key and time signature changes, modal melodies, surreal lyrics, and extended instrumental solos. The music accompanied a culture, in San Francisco and elsewhere, that embraced marijuana, peyote, mescaline, and LSD. The music intersected with notions of mind expansion and the thought emerging from figures like Timothy Leary, Alan Watts, Aldous Huxley, and Eastern sages like Paramahansa Yogananda. In America, psychedelia emerged in the music of the Jefferson Airplane, the Jimi Hendrix Experience, the Doors, and Santana. Psychedelia influenced the sounds of Pink Floyd, the Yardbirds, Traffic, and Soft Machine. These artists influenced other bands like the Moody Blues, who are sometimes considered one of the precursors of progressive rock. Psychedelia began to unravel and diminish around 1970 but it would influence many rock genres, including progressive rock, glam, and heavy metal.

The Moody Blues

Pop music met classical music and reflections on the cosmos in the creations of The Moody Blues, particularly on their *Days of Future Passed* (1967) album. On that recording the Moody Blues brought together British pop music and vocal harmonies with the range of a classical orchestra. Mike Pinder and Ray Thomas were central to the founding of the Moody Blues in 1964. The Moody Blues first single was "Go Now," which became a hit in 1964. Like the Beatles, they had been playing in Hamburg, Germany. The group's name emerged from Mike Pinder's recollection of Duke Ellington's "Mood Indigo," which he had heard as a child. They were playing the blues. Mitchells and Butlers (M&B), a brewery, owned many of the clubs in Birmingham. They hoped that M&B might fund them and get them onto the circuit.[2]

With a rich vocal sound and song titles that spoke of dreams, Mike Pinder, Ray Thomas, and Graeme Edge extended their music toward classical orchestration. They were joined by John Lodge and Justin Hayward in 1966 when Denny Laine left the band. Lodge was an engineering student in Birmingham at the College of Advanced Technology. Pinder helped to choose Justin Hayward, from Swindon, England, to replace Laine.[3] John Lodge and Justin Hayward created many of the group's most memorable songs.

The Moody Blues were an influence upon what has been called art rock, or progressive rock. Their song cycle in *Days of Future Passed*, emerging from reflection upon Antonin Dvorak's *New World Symphony*, became one of the first concept albums. The album included the Justin Hayward songs "Nights in White Satin" and "Tuesday Afternoon," which have become staples of classic rock radio airplay. Central to the album are Peter Knight's orchestral arrangements. Graeme Edge's opening and closing poems are recited by Mike Pinder, who composed "The Sun Set" and "Dawn Is a Feeling." The Moody Blues recorded with a symphony orchestra on *Days of Future Passed* (1967). The album cover featured a surreal abstract design.

The Moody Blues followed *Days of Future Passed* with *In Search of the Lost Chord* (1968). Among the songs on the album was Ray Thomas's contribution of "Legend of a Mind," a tribute to Timothy Leary which included Thomas's flute solo. They next produced *On the Threshold of a Dream* (1969), an album mixed in both stereo and quadraphonic. Exploring dreams, this concept album became the band's first #1 album on the British charts and entered the top 20 in America. It includes the group's response to Richard Strauss' "Also sprach Zarathustra," which serves as the theme for the science fiction film *2001*.

To Our Children's Children (1969) was inspired by the first moon landing. With a focus on space travel and children, the Moody Blues created a psychedelic album which included the single "Watching and Waiting." It is an orchestrated recording that is difficult to perform live. The next Moody Blues album, *A Question of Balance* (1970), pulled away from some of this orchestration, but *Every Good Boy Deserves Favour* (1971) returned to it.

The song "Lost in a Lost World" by Mike Pinder begins *Seventh*

Sojourn (1972) on a note of concern about racial tensions and revolution. Justin Hayward sings "New Horizons" of love, hope, dreams, and a quest. There is a lighter moment, with Ray Thomas's vocal on the lilting ballad "For My Lady." The first side closes with John Lodge's vocal on "Isn't Life Strange?" The album served up two successful singles: "Isn't Life Strange?" and the up-tempo hit "I'm Just a Singer (in a Rock and Roll Band)" by John Lodge. The re-release of "Nights in White Satin" also climbed up the charts.

The Moody Blues' world tour ended in 1974, and Mike Pinder left the band. From 1974 to 1978 the Moody Blues were inactive. Then Pinder rejoined them and they recorded *Octave* (1978). During this time, *Days of Future Passed* was taken aboard the spacecraft on the Atlantis Shuttle mission by its chief astronaut, "Hoot" Gibson. The astronaut enjoyed listening to "Nights in White Satin" and "Tuesday Afternoon." Meanwhile, Pinder found the band taking a more pop direction after he left the band in 1978. In an interview, Pinder recalls that he had planned to get together with Jimi Hendrix, but the date turned out to be five days after he died. They had planned to talk "about UFO's and things like that."[4]

Jimi Hendrix

The psychedelic music of the late 1960s served as a bridge to mythical themes, progressive rock, and the phenomenon of space music. Within this movement one of rock's most influential guitarists, Jimi Hendrix, built upon the blues and provided a passionate connection with speculative fiction. In *Jimi Hendrix: A Brother's Story*, Jimi Hendrix younger brother Leon Hendrix recalled his brother's interest in science fiction. They were interested in the Flash Gordon science fiction film serials that played in the activity center nearby in Seattle. Jimi Hendrix liked the actor's name, Buster Crabbe. The brothers liked the films *The Thing* and *The Day the Earth Stood Still*. They wondered where the universe had come from. Jimi Hendrix's cosmic thinking considered the constellations, ice ages, and the planets. Leon engaged in poetry and artwork that reflected an interest in the supernatural. He wrote a poem, "Star Child of the Universe," for his brother. Jimi

Hendrix wrote "Third Stone from the Sun" and "Up from the Skies." He wrote "EXP" with drummer Mitch Mitchell, wondering whether spaceships from distant planets exist.[5]

Hendrix has become almost mythical and legendary. His brilliant guitar playing awaits any listener to his recordings and remastered studio tapes. Turn on a radio or tap into Hendrix on your computer and you are bound to hear his singles: the bluesy "Hey Joe," the psychedelic "Purple Haze," or his treatment of Bob Dylan's apocalyptic "All Along the Watchtower." Dig a little deeper and you will find a thoughtful, speculative mind and an amazing creative gift for improvisation.

Hawkwind

Among the psychedelic bands to play "space music" and promote science fiction themes was Hawkwind. In 1972, Hawkwind performed their *Space Ritual* concert tour with lasers and a light show, costumes, psychedelic imagery, and Stacia, a nude dancer. Hawkwind's *Space Ritual* (1973) was a double album. It was "88 minutes of brain damage," said the ad for the recording. Hawkwind's space rock included Dave Brock's pentatonic scale riffs on guitar. Science fiction writer Michael Moorcock told biographer Ian Abrahams that Hawkwind was "like the mad crew of a long distance spaceship that has forgotten its mission"[6]

Hawkwind may be remembered for their 1972 single "Silver Machine." Dave Brock and Nik Turner of Hawkwind were fans of science fiction and they mentioned science fiction novels and films throughout their work. Brock (b.1941) grew up in Middlesex. Turner, a saxophonist, was born in Oxford. Turner has emphasized the band's interest in providing free music at festivals, such as the 1970 Isle of Wight Festival, during which they played outside the gates.[7] They participated in the first Glastonbury Festival in 1970 and the larger Glastonbury Festival in 1971, which included David Bowie and Traffic. Hawkwind was interactive with their audience, including invitations to their dressing room area after some shows.[8] They improvised extended solos. In his study of progressive rock, Edward Macan criticizes extended soloing by psychedelic bands, calling the long drum solo on Iron Butterfly's "In a Gadda Da Vida" mind-numbing.[9]

Hawkwind's *In Search of Space* (October 1971) made reference to "the ecology thing," according to Turner.[10] Brock's song "We Took the Wrong Steps Years Ago" sounds the warning about actions that have resulted in ecological disaster. "The Watcher" appears on *Doremi Fasol Latido* (November 1972), the band's third album. This is a character from a Marvel comics series who observes humankind from a distance. Lemmy sings above an acoustic guitar accompaniment.

"Sonic Attack" was performed in the *Space Ritual* tour from November 1972. These theatrical concerts were enhanced by a light show. The lyrics for "Sonic Attack" were written by Michael Moorcock and were spoken by Bob Calvert, who called the *Space Ritual* concerts "a mythical approach to what is happening today."[11] Moorcock lived in same area of London as the Hawkwind band members and he performed occasionally with the band.[12] His lyrics for "Black Corridor" on the *Space Ritual* album spoke of space. "Sonic Attack" offered a parody of the "four minute warning" for a nuclear attack, or sonic attack, insisting that listeners ought not to panic. In "Damnation Alley," lyricist Calvert turned to Roger Zelazny's 1971 novel of that title to address a world that has been devastated by nuclear war. A character who is sent to California from Boston fights off monster figures and storms.

"Choose Your Masks," co-written by Moorcock under the pseudonym L. Steele, sets up a situation in which people must choose which mask to wear. One represents chaos and the other represents law. The mask cannot be taken off until the individual is no longer involved in the war. Moorcock also writes "Note from a Cold Planet," a lyric that tells of people who survive in a world that is frozen. They live beneath the earth's surface and have to excavate through the ice to get firewood and to gather familiar supermarket brand items.

"The War I Survived" on the *Xenon Codex* album (1988) makes reference to "slaughterhouse five," suggesting Kurt Vonnegut's novel of the bombing of Dresden in the Second World War.[13]

Myth, Fantasy and Progressive Rock

Mythology and fantasy are closely connected with progressive rock. Edward Macan observes that "many of progressive rock's most representative lyrics draw on mythology, fantasy literature, science fiction."[14] Progressive rock is associated with the development of psychedelic music and space music. We find in progressive rock's various styles rock instrumental solo sections, the use of multitracking, reverb, echo, feedback, and ornate melody lines. With Pink Floyd, in the mid- to late 1960s, emerged the first wave of psychedelic rock. The Moody Blues may also be said to be part of the first wave of psychedelic rock. Their *Days of Future Passed* included a song cycle that reflected a working man's everyday experience. "The Day Begins" sets this theme for the album. In the Moody Blues' "Lost in a Lost World" by Mike Pinder, people search for an answer and wonder if they will be found by love.[15] Another band that contributed to this era was Procol Harum, with their single "A Whiter Shade of Pale" in 1967. In that song the Hammond organ adds an aura of cathedral-like mystery.

A second wave of progressive rock began to emerge with King Crimson, playing in minor keys, with acoustic and electric guitars and Mellotron, while making use of medieval images. Jethro Tull, Genesis, Yes, Gentle Giant, and Emerson, Lake and Palmer were part of this phase of development. In the 1970s, science fiction ideas and mythological elements appeared in the creative work of many progressive rock artists, also including Yes, the Moody Blues, Todd Rundgren's Utopia, and Nektar.

The progressive rock of the late 1960s and early 1970s has been linked with the counterculture or to hippie culture and "aspirations to a better society."[16] Far more was involved than "assigning a narrative" to the songs, Marianne Tatom Letts reminds us.[17] Edward Macan points to the initial association of progressive rock with psychedelic rock and the correlation between progressive rock and classical music in "continuous use of tone and instrumental virtuosity."[18] Other critics have pointed to the link with psychedelic rock's encouragement of synethesia: to see sounds and textures and colors of tone. LSD experience led to light shows by bands like Pink Floyd. Joe Gannon from the Hornsey College of Art brought his talent to Pink Floyd's stage shows. Extramusical props entered concerts by ELP, Pink Floyd, and Yes. The ELP world tour of 1973 was lavish in this respect. Keith Emerson's keyboards appeared as a massive array of technological gadgetry. When Carl

Palmer played his drums laser lights were synchronized with his solos. Genesis and Yes used fog machines and laser lights. Pink Floyd added props: dry ice and a falling waterfall for "Set Controls for the Heart of the Sun." Progressive rock first drew upon "the hermetic streak in psychedelia," Macan observes. It suggested "hidden meanings" for fans who were "insiders," meanings for which "outsiders would be oblivious."[19]

This visual aspect of concert performances was matched by the fantastic visual images created for LP records. The conceptual progressive rock album has always been enhanced by this imaginative cover art work which has often drawn upon surrealism. Science fiction and fantasy scenes are used frequently. These visuals have been described by Macan as "space scenarios, bizarre, futuristic machinery, or a combination of the two." Emerson Lake and Palmer's covers for *Tarkus* and *Brain Salad Surgery*, he suggests, represent "technology gone awry."[20] Examples of science fiction imagery on vinyl records include William Neal's cover for *Tarkus* and H.R. Giger's cover for *Brain Salad Surgery*. The latter ELP album's theme is human self-awareness and consciousness versus dehumanizing technology.

The Concept Album

Mythical imagery and fantasy concepts have contributed to the extended rock album. Progressive rock bands have often presented adventurous and lengthy compositions, or suites, with an emphasis on expression and theatricality.[21] The concept album can provide the appearance of unity with a subject or theme (*Days of Future Passed*, The Moody Blues, 1968), or a set of characters (*Tommy*, The Who, 1969). At times, entire albums are presented in concert performances. Pink Floyd played through its album *The Wall* in concert and the record can be listened to as a unified whole. Marianne Tatom Letts points out that such an approach as this might fit well with Joseph Campbell's concept of the hero's journey.[22]

The Beatles' *Sgt. Pepper's Lonely Hearts Club Band* (1967) is often seen as one of the pivotal concept albums which initiated the art of creating a thematic album. *Sgt. Pepper* creates the band as a character playing for an audience, which we hear applauding and laughing in delight on the first song. We are next introduced to the character Billy Shears, who claims that he is able to get by because of the assistance of his friends. The visual elements contribute to the notion of a concept album and the cover connects with the songs. The Beatles in colorful costumes become mythical uniformed and mustached characters. It seems that the songs could stand on their own. Yet, no singles were released from the album and this further reinforced the idea of a unified total production. The production of this Beatles album compelled multiple engagements in listening from its audience.[23]

Science fiction motifs and fantasy became pervasive in progressive rock album cover art. Roger Dean's outer space covers for Yes are a key example. On the cover of *Fragile* the earth is fragmenting. On *Yessongs*, issued two years later, there is a corresponding image. Yes offers the observation that they were seeking that "which we cannot wholly grasp; this is the material of myth." Macan writes that "for many, Dean's mythic landscapes became visceral symbols of progressive rock."[24] Other artists contributed their imagery: William Neal was associated with ELP and Paul Whitehead with Genesis. Hipgnosis, an art firm in London, was responsible for many Pink Floyd album covers up to *Animals* (1977). They created covers for Genesis, Renaissance, ELP, and Yes. The Yes album *Close to the Edge* had an inner gatefold landscape. Macan describes this image as stretching across a "foggy abyss": a surrealist landscape surrounded by fog and bordered by the sea. The "Close to the Edge" suite is based upon Hermann Hesse's *Siddhartha* and a spiritual quest for truth. So, the cover painting may suggest enlightenment: a quest across the visual landscape that is a spiritual journey.

In much progressive rock album art there is a juxtaposition of technology and nature. Macan points out that "much of the science fiction imagery depicts technology gone awry."[25] Visual artist Roger Dean presents an idealistic holistic society in "mythological, medieval, and Eastern subject matter." This contrasts with the nightmare totalitarian society we see being resisted in some songs (as in Rush). These opposites play out in the song lyrics. On Storm Thorgerson's cover for Pink Floyd's *Animals* we see a gray sky over London and the Battersea Power Plant coughing up soot as a pig drifts over it. This is factory

London: smoky and dismal, polluted and affected by the Orwellian animal farm of pigs, sheeplike followers, and power dogs.[26]

Rock music like that of Pink Floyd makes use of the fantastic to assert the resources of imagination, the energy of music, theatrical play, and the fusion of the visual and musical arts and performance. Since the mid–1960s rock has frequently employed mythological figures to emphasize this. Indeed, in heavy metal and in progressive rock some of this imagery and symbolism has become cliché. Rock songwriters continue to dig down into the archetypal consciousness: to that realm beneath wakefulness and ordinary reality.

The Quest for Imaginative Worlds

Rock music has often allied itself with science fiction motifs as part of a quest for escape from dullness or repetition: a break from the mundane world as it is. This is rock that stimulates imagination. Progressive rock, which was mostly a British development at first, is sometimes described as an extension of the counterculture. Its appeal to fantasy and myth and its connections with classical music contrast with the power chords, or bar chords played in open fifths, by American and British blues based rock bands like Cream, Deep Purple, or Alice Cooper. Some artists, like the multitalented composer and producer Todd Rundgren, in different phases of his career, have moved across this entire spectrum of rock music. However, most bands tend to be categorized by critics in the blues rock or progressive rock traditions.

In the 1970s album covers began to draw upon science fiction fantasy and surreal motifs. Progressive rock music "emerged in the wake of the counterculture" notes Macan, who remarks that it showed a "fascination with epic subject matter."[27] Brian Stableford argues, "The perceived countercultural links between rock music and science fiction may have been largely illusory."[28] More obvious, he says, are mythopoetic fantasy and the folk music tradition that lay behind much rock in the sixties and seventies. This critic has a valid point. However, there were indeed countercultural connections with progressive rock's attention to myth, imagination, and grandiose visions. Countercultural fascination with epic subject matter and mythopoetic fantasy are linked with some strands of science fiction.[29] The "hippie" subculture declined at the same time as the first wave of progressive rock began to wane in the late 1970s to early 1980s. The phenomenon of mythically based progressive rock and the counterculture may be seen as interconnected.

"Few styles of popular music have generated as much controversy as progressive rock," Edward Macan points out.[30] There was antagonism toward this genre from the rock music press. "Critical response to 1970s progressive rock was often brutal," writes John J. Scheinbaum. "Critics decried the genre's virtuosity, complexity and indebtedness to classical or art music as a betrayal of rock's origins."[31] The rock that has been often favored by rock critics is a minimalist chord-driven music that absorbs and assertively faces the grime of the earth. An alternative to this arose in forms like progressive rock that sought to re-enchant the world. However, claims of the authenticity in blues-rock by Dave Marsh, Simon Frith, and others have become matters of record.

It wasn't mythology or flights of fancy that the rock critics had an argument with. It was the break from the blues by these bands and their incorporation of classical music that the rock critics took issue with. Progressive rock bands may have sought a kind of prestige with their turn toward classical repertoire, as Robert Walser suggests.[32] However, the incorporation of classical style also offered an opportunity for virtuosity and musical expression. The Moody Blues connected their recording of *Days of Future Passed* with the London symphony orchestra in 1967. By 1972, Emerson, Lake, and Palmer began producing *Pictures at an Exhibition*, consciously drawing upon Mussorgsky's work. While Keith Emerson was displaying his musicianship by using classical resources, ELO's cover of Chuck Berry's "Roll Over Beethoven" again offered the advice that Tchaikovsky should be told the news of rock and roll's presence on the scene.

In the early 1970s, progressive rock was comprised mostly of British bands that used technological and sociological themes far more often than spiritual ones. Star Trek's William Shatner commented on this in an interview about his spoken word album *Ponder the Mystery*. "I think that prog rock is the science fiction of rock music," Shatner said.[33]

Emerson, Lake and Palmer

ELP was Keith Emerson (keyboards), Greg Lake (guitar and vocals) Carl Palmer (drums). The trio was a pivotal resource for progressive rock, according to Edward Macan, who meticulously analyzed the group through a musicological lens in *Endless Enigma: A Musical Biography of Emerson Lake and Palmer.* On *Tarkus* and *Brain Salad Surgery,* ELP were the creators of imagined worlds that contrasted the creative possibilities of technology with its dehumanizing downside. Yes, Jethro Tull, King Crimson, Renaissance, Gentle Giant and other bands were their contemporaries: part of the rise of the eclectic mix that has come to be known as progressive rock. In a review of Macan's book, Paul R. Kohl asserted, "The progressive rock movement of the 1970s is one of the most reviled musical genres of all time."[34] However, such a perspective may rest upon the preferences of those few previously mentioned major rock critics for blues-based rock and stripped down three chord songs played with attitude. Prog rock, in contrast, emphasized musicianship and musical virtuosity and made use of fantasy literary genres. The blues tradition relied upon guitars, bass, drums, and sometimes an organ or a harmonica backing a focused, grungy, sometimes seedy vocalist. The first wave of progressive rock, characterized by ELP, made use of obvious displays of technology, banks of amplifiers, and stages filled with synthesizers and vast percussion sets.

Those rock critics—Lester Bangs, Robert Cristgau, and Dave Marsh among them—let it be known that they favored blues-based rock and regarded rock as deriving in a lineal descent from the blues.[35] Marsh insisted that only rock based in the blues was authentic. Lester Bangs preferred the Velvet Underground, the Stooges, and the New York Dolls to complex keyboard figures by Keith Emerson, or the vocals of Jon Anderson and the musicianship of Chris Squire, Steve Howe, Bill Bruford, and Rick Wakeman of Yes. For some listeners, there was a vast gulf between Iggy Pop and the MC5, on the one hand, and the guitar pyrotechnics of Robert Fripp of King Crimson or Renaissance's Annie Haslam's three octave vocal range, on the other. Macan argues for a place for progressive rock's fusion of classical music and rock music and its appeal to mythological imagery.

Emerson, Lake, and Palmer were at the center of progressive rock's merging of science fiction themes and images of the fantastic. Their innovative music made use of complex guitar and keyboard runs, shifting time signatures, and the Moog or other synthesizers. Their album *Tarkus* (1971) included a 21-minute piece about fighting a war in the future. The album cover portrayed an armadillo and a First World War tank. The armadillo-like Tarkus, a cybernetic force, battles with Manticore, a mythical creature that is said to represent the counterculture and an idea of naturalness. This, Macan notes, represents a conflict between materialistic and mystic/Gnostic worldviews."[36] Macan argues that progressive rock's use of science fiction and fantasy was an extension of the hippie ethos of the late sixties that supported this argument against the system. (Kohl, in response, asserts that the merger of rock and classical music was an incompatible hybrid.) Macan points to Keith Emerson's interest in the music of Bela Bartok and the music of Alberto Ginastera. He asserts that ELP, employing the synthesizer and making it central to their sound, "were more responsible than any other band for shaping the progressive style."[37] They made "a truly idiosyncratic use of classical forms and techniques in a rock context."[38]

ELP's *Brain Salad Surgery* (1973) included "Karn Evil 9," concerning the earth's process from an ice age to the time of a future war that involved computers and humans. While this widely circulated record made a mark commercially, there was some critical resistance to this album. ELP's most notable recording, *Pictures at an Exhibition*, does not involve science fiction or fantasy themes. It underscores ELP's merger of classical and rock music. ELP brought vast technological stage sets from city to city for the concert tours that accompanied these albums. The rock critics decried this also.

Soft Machine's bassist, Hugh Hopper, saw the "rise of the keyboardist at the center" of progressive rock.[39] The keyboard player often substituted for piano, strings, and orchestra the Moog, the Mellotron, and the synthesizer. Robert Moog had developed the large Moog, which was adapted for the stage into a mini-Moog. The synthesizer followed, with its simulation of strings, horns, and guitar. The synthesizer is an electronic instrument that can be engaged in sound synthesis. RCA Victor created tone generators in the late 1950s. The synthesizer was further developed with the Moog and with the use of sequencers. Robert Moog and Donald Buchla created synthesizer manufacturing companies in 1966. They were soon followed by the Tonus firm and by EMS London. Synthesizers became portable and in the 1970s the synthesizer developed device control with a microcomputer. This was followed in the 1980s by digital techniques.

The incorporation of classical music figures on the keyboard made some of rock's guitar based blues fans upset. Keyboardists drew upon Bach, Liszt and Chopin and borrowed techniques from Bartok, Ravel, and Debussy. Audiences became familiar with Matthew Fisher's Hammond organ solo on Procol Harum's "A Whiter Shade of Pale" (1967). Harpsichord entered the Moody Blues' *In Search of the Lost Chord* (1968) and Procol Harum's "In Held Twas I" (1968). In the early 1970s, Keith Emerson sent his Hammond organ sound through a Marshall amplifier. He made use of J.S. Bach's Tocatta and Fugue in D minor for his organ solo in "Rondo." The rondo form is a basic form of classical music. The rondo has multiple sections. One of these sections, often the first, carries the tonic key. This tonic key section is contrasted with other sections, or episodes. (For example, ABACA.) There may be further complexities in this scheme. These sections introduce other tonal colors and themes. To many listeners, this just did not seem to be rock and roll.

Yes

The visual elements surrounding the band Yes's musical product reinforced connections with science fiction, myth, and fantasy. Roger Dean's artwork for the Yes album covers set forth a style for progressive rock imagery.[40] Rick Wakeman of Yes, recalling Roger Dean, said that "he'd become like a sixth member of the band."[41] Dean's visual iconography helped to create messages that linked with Yes's music, lyrics, and performances.

In Yes some folk elements and classical guitar met with "symphonic" progressive rock, complex vocals, keyboard arrangements, and electric guitar leads. This was matched with Roger Dean's album cover artwork on *The Yes Album* and *Fragile* (1971) and *Close to the Edge* (1972). Jon Anderson's soaring vocals were joined by other band members who also sang. Steve Howe and Chris Squire composed much of the music and contributed their musicianship on guitar and bass respectively. The talented Bill Bruford played drums with Yes. He would also make music with King Crimson, Genesis, UK, National Health, and with his own fusion band. Wakeman has noted that the members of Yes were all "technically gifted musicians" and that each individual was "entirely different" from the others.[42] Typically, Wakeman's keyboard skills complemented the tenor voice of Jon Anderson, the stirring drumming of Bill Bruford, and the complex guitar based work of Steve Howe and bassist Chris Squire. He was able to undertake his own musical innovations with *Journey to the Centre of the Earth* as a solo project and his record rose to the top of the album charts.

Mythical journeys like the one suggested by Wakeman's album were common figures in progressive rock in the early 1970s. It was a time period in progressive rock music that included Yes's *Fragile* (1971) and *Close to the Edge* (1972), Jethro Tull's *Aqualung* (1971), Renaissance's *Prologue* (1972), ELP's *Brain Salad Surgery* (1973), and Genesis' *The Lamb Lies Down on Broadway* (1974). In contrast with Yes, Emerson, Lake and Palmer developed their mostly electric style with multi-keyboard sounds. Jethro Tull created an eclectic mix of English folk song and rhythm and blues featuring Ian Anderson's flute playing.

In "Starship Trooper" (1970) Yes's Jon Anderson, Chris Squire, and Steve Howe created a dynamic composition that was given vague lyrics by Anderson that reflect his interest in mysticism and space. The title comes from Robert Heinlein's novel but the song lyrics do not correspond in any way with the book. The trooper is an expansive soul who has traveled across the universe. In one sense, the utopian society in Heinlein's story appears to be without racial discrimination or gender discrimination. In another, Johnny Rico learns that military code of duty carries a "controlled violence to enforce orders." The restriction of voting rights to those who have been in government service suggests a repression of democracy. Heinlein's *Starship Troopers* dramatized war and some readers saw in it a subtext that was political. Yes steered away from that controversy.

The song "Starship Trooper" has three parts: Life, Seeker, Disillusion. The opening motif is repeated often in the song's first section. The song is rich with melodic ideas. Steve Howe provides polished guitar playing over vocal harmonies. There is a bass melody by Squire at

1:41, a bridge at 1:51. "Disillusion" begins at 3:16. At 5:36 there is a descending three-note pattern (D to Bb, resolving on G) and the music winds around these three notes. The final section is carried by Anderson's vocals.

With their releases of *Fragile* and *Close to the Edge*, Yes became quite a popular progressive rock band. Like other bands, Yes went through changes in their sound across the next two decades. Bill Martin observed that the album *Talk* (1994) by Yes "took on the feel of science fiction."[43] The use of computers, Digital Performer, and what he calls "futuristic arrangements" reinvented the sound of Yes. Yes's Chris Squire noted the shift to using the new technology of Digital Performer in recording sessions.[44] Yes guitarist Steve Howe, who was so central to the band's earlier sound, did not like the new "futuristic Yes."[45]

Yes has sometimes been associated with classical music. However, most of their musical figures have little to do with classical harmony. They were inventive with their own musical patterns. *The Yes Album* (1971) was built around science fiction concepts and signaled the Yes sound. "Your Move," "Starship Trooper," "Perpetual Change," "Yours Is No Disgrace" became central pieces in the band's repertoire. *Fragile* (1972) incorporated science fiction and fantasy elements. Rick Wakeman's synthesizers, Mellotron, and organ—all quite costly—contributed greatly to their sound. "Roundabout," as an edited piece, became a single that brought Yes widely to public notice. *Close to the Edge* (1972) offered three tracks, with the lengthy "And You and I," "Siberian Khatru," and the side long title track. This became a top five album supported by a long international tour. By the time Yes released *Tales from Topographic Oceans* (1974) they had become popular and critics called this album overindulgent. The album was musically alive and Jon Anderson's lyrics hearkened to Eastern mysticism. The lyrical approach to the four songs was influenced, in part, by Anderson's reading of Swami Paramahansa Yogananda. Anderson looked through *Autobiography of a Yogi* while on tour in Tokyo. Yogananda's name is derived from *maha,* or great and *ananda,* or bliss. Anderson, on his spiritual search, knowing little about Hinduism, developed a cosmology and made a unique contribution. The album attempts to represent four interlocking *shastras* and to suggest a path to inner peace.

A few years later, Yes developed *Relayer* (1974). The band was now out of critical favor but remained popular. This recording alternates dense instrumental sections with vocal/chorale sections. Some critics wanted songs. The band was composing suites. They were also engaging in side projects. *Olias of Sunhillow* (1976) was Jon Anderson's concept album. His song "Sound Out the Galleon" expressed a fantasy in which an alien race is forced to abandon their planet and find another. The spaceship is the Moorglade Mover, operated by Olias. The album reflects Anderson's speculations in science fiction and his acquaintance with Eastern mysticism. Rick Wakeman created his album titled *Six Wives of Henry VIII* (1973) and *Journey to the Center of the Earth* (1974). Then he produced *The Myths and Legends of King Arthur and his Knights of the Round Table* (1975). For Yes's recording *Going for One* (1977) Wakeman returned to the band after a two year hiatus of reflection and rehabilitation. The content of this album was mystical and abstract on five songs. They were melodic, filled with Steve Howe's guitar work and with the band's vocal harmonies. Rick Wakeman played the organ at St. Martin's Church in Vevey, Switzerland. Their follow-up album, *Drama*, shifted the sound to harder rock. Howe played more electric guitar. John Anderson and Rick Wakeman were missing. Geoffrey Downes and Steve Howe joined the band they called Asia. Yes unraveled.

Jon Anderson continued to explore mythology. He incorporated neo-pagan elements into his lyrics and appears to have sought to express a sense of "presence" in nature: a pantheism and polytheism. His words "gravitate to ancient symbols and ancient myths," Margot Adler has observed. Jennifer Rycenga notes: "They are reclaiming these sources, transforming them into something new and adding to them the visions of writers of science fiction and fantasy."[46]

Klaatu and Nektar

Klaatu and Nektar were creative bands with big dreams and limited followings. Both bands created music that they connected with science fiction and space rock. Klaatu was formed in 1973 in Toronto by John Woloshuck and Dee Long and was named after the character Michael Rennie (and later Keanu Reeves) portrayed in the film *The*

Day the Earth Stood Still. The band later added Terry Draper on drums and Klaatu worked as a trio. They started recording in January 1973. Their work went on periodically for 2½ years. They decided to remain anonymous and let the music speak for itself. At first they did not do public relations bios or appear in public concerts. Their first album *3:47 EST* (named *Klaatu* in the United States) has been re-mastered by Peter J. Moore with Terry Brown sitting in. Drummer Terry Draper took the lead in starting their independent record company. Stephen Peeples interviewed them for promotion for the *Endangered Species* album. They listened often to King Crimson. The Beatles and ELO are cited as influences. (Jeff Lynne's songwriting and production with ELO is clearly Beatles influenced.) A Washington radio program director, Dwight Douglas at WWDC, came close to identifying their names. They were preparing their *Hope* album. Ted Jones provided the artwork for the album covers. The cover for *Endangered Species* appeared like *National Geographic* meets Audubon. When seeking a possible single, Terry Draper suggested writing about outer space rather than about love. "Dog Star" emerged with Hendrix influenced spacey guitar and feedback. They commented that they wanted to avoid the CSN preach to the crowd about save the whales, feeling that that was too sixties.

The progressive rock band Nektar produced several science fiction related titles. Nektar was Allan "Taff" Freeman on keyboards, Derek "Mo" Moore on bass, Ron Howden on drums, and Roye Albrighton, guitar/vocals, who left the band and was replaced by Dave Nelson on guitar/vocals. Mick Brockett provided an array of special effects and the lighting for the band's shows. *Remember the Future* (1973) told the story of a blind boy who communicates with an extra-terrestrial. The melodic progressive rock sound of Nektar on this album reached the top twenty. *Down to Earth* (1974) followed with a circus theme. It included the song "Astral Man." *Recycled* (1975) was Nektar's next release. It is a record that has been described as having a sound similar to that of the progressive band Gentle Giant. *Magic Is a Child* (1977) followed with the use of Norse mythology and the theme of magic. Nektar concluded the decade by preparing the songs for *Man in the Moon* (1980). The link between Nektar's progressive rock sound and science fiction imagination came through clearly in many of their titles for songs and instrumentals: "Astronaut's Nightmare," "Time Machine,"

"Void of Vision," "Desolation Valley," "Automation Horrorscope," "Man in the Moon," "Journey to the Centre of the Eye," "Cybernetic Consumption," "A Tab in the Ocean."

Space Rock-Glam: Todd Rundgren and Utopia

Todd Rundgren emerged as a creative force in recording in the early 1970s following his work with the Philadelphia group the Nazz. He came to public attention with his pop singles "I Saw the Light" and "Hello It's Me." A versatile musician, Rundgren combined creativity and virtuosity with comic satire and the skepticism of a scientist. He had soaked in the sounds of Gamble and Huff and Philadelphia groups and the musical figures of the Beatles and British Invasion bands. He was a fine guitar player, an innovative keyboard player, and an extraordinary background singer for his own vocals. He was also keenly aware of the of the New York rock scene that followed in the footsteps of the Velvet Underground. Patti Smith, soon to be instrumental in the new wave emerging from Max's Kansas City and CBGB's in lower Manhattan, was one of the rock music writers who praised his work. As Rundgen attended to the progressive sounds of Frank Zappa, Yes, John McLaughlin and others, he took on projects as a producer for the provocative New York Dolls, Badfinger, Grand Funk, and other artists. He developed his double-album *Something/Anything?* and his cosmic-tinged *A Wizard, a True Star*.

In this phase Todd Rundgren was perhaps more cosmic than mythological. He recognized the influence of David Bowie during the period when he was assembling and developing the music of his band Utopia. When Daryl Hall commented on Bowie's influence to Paul Myers he called the Bowie influence "all pervasive" and observed that while they did not imitate the music, they copied "the attitude."[47] Bowie had begun exploring his glam phase and orientation that led to his creation of the Ziggy Stardust character and his flirtations with science fiction based transformations.

Todd Rundgren's *Utopia*, released on November 9, 1974, was the product of Rundgren's musical explorations with Ralph Schukett, drummer Kevin Ellmann, Moogy Klingman, and John Siegler. "Utopia

Theme" was written by Rundgren and Dave Mason. While Rundgren was always at the center of the group, band members contributed their musical compositions and creativity to the overall output of Utopia. The space rock-glam phase included a stage show in which they wore spacesuits modified from welder's apparatus with visors. "International Feel" was sung by Rundgren in a space suit in 2009. Following *Faithful*, Rundgren and the musicians from Utopia (John Siegler, Roger Powell, and John "Willie" Wilcox) developed the playful instrumentals for *Disco Jets*. This was a comic parody, a response to then-current trends like *Star Wars*, CB radio, and disco and Rundgren's recasting of the *Star Trek* theme.[48]

Queen

The conspicuously operatic vocals of Queen combined with science fiction themes on their album *A Night at the Opera* (1975). It was a sure recipe for pop music magic. Freddie Mercury's vocals rested upon the layered guitar work of Brian May and were surrounded by the band's rich background harmonies. With those operatic vocals, Queen's *A Night at the Opera* offers a narrative of explorers in space: characters that set off and reach a new world. Upon their return only one year has gone by for them but a hundred years have passed.

The band's first album, *Queen* (1973), reflects the progressive rock of the period. *Queen II* (1974), containing fantasy themes and virtuoso musicianship, reached number five on the British album charts. It featured the single "The Seven Seas of Rhye" and the six-minute "The March of the Black Queen." *Sheer Heart Attack* (1974) showed experimentation with hard rock, heavy metal, ballads, and the English music hall tradition. The single "Killer Queen" suggested the layered music and vocal sound that would appear on their next recording. *A Night at the Opera* launched one of the most successful pop rock bands of its day. It contained the hit "Bohemian Rhapsody" (1977). *News of the World* contained the anthems "We Will Rock You" and "We Are the Champions."

Mythology and astrology underlie the Queen logo, designed by Freddie Mercury. The logo includes the zodiac signs for the four band members: two lions for Leo (Deacon and Taylor), a crab for Cancer (May) and two fairies for Virgo (Mercury). The lions wrap around the Q. The fairies lie beneath one of the lions and the crab sits above Q. A Phoenix rises above this. The design appears to represent the royal coat of arms of the United Kingdom, as much as the band it designates.

Much more than time was lost for Brian May of Queen when Freddie Mercury died and the world came toppling down for him. He retired from music for a while to get his life together and then returned to Imperial College to complete a Ph.D. in astrophysics. Before Queen was formed and shot up the charts he had been in Jim Ring's astrophysics group at Imperial College (1970–74). Physics lived alongside music for many years for May. Earlier, while at the university, he was playing in a band called Smile with Roger Taylor (1968–1970). They formed Queen with Freddie Mercury. John Deacon was soon added on bass guitar.[49] May let go of his focus on physics to work intensely with the band.

May is best known for his fluent and creative guitar playing and the precise guitar solos he has brought to Queen. His guitar sound is layered and has a distinctive tone. Brian May frequently plays a home built guitar, the Red Special. He sang the bass parts on "Bohemian Rhapsody." He is also a living example of a musician who has a deeply developed sense of the correlation between music and mathematics. His knowledge of sound waves, timing and distance contributed to studio work with Queen, such as on the clapping sequence on "We Will Rock You." The stomps were based upon prime numbers and "repeats at various distances." The use of delay created the effect of sounding as if many people were involved in the clap and stomp sequence.[50] May reflected upon the possibility of uniting the audience and developed the rhythmic ideas. The band worked this out in an old London church. This became an audience participation part of their shows, breaking down the distance between band on stage and the audience. Unexpectedly, it became a rousing pulse to build crowd enthusiasm in sports contests and is heard today in stadiums throughout the world.

May's academic work was on hold for the two decades that he was involved with Queen. He returned after 2000 to complete his degree in 2007. May's dissertation inquired into interplanetary dust. This has been described as "a survey of radial velocities in the zodiacal dust cloud."[51] The earth moves through this dust and he wanted to figure out the motion of the dust. Does this dust have anything to do with the origin of the solar system? His website brings together music and astrophysics. *The Guardian* noted May's discussion of "hyperbolic orbits or interstellar particles."[52] Brian May became chancellor at Liverpool John Moores University from 2008 to 2013. This was primarily a ceremonial role, noted *The Guardian*. Yet, the university is also a key site of ground-based robotic telescopes that are trained upon the stars. He has supported the John Moores University's Astrophysics Research Centre. He is an animal rights activist and is interested in photography. May also collaborated with the New Horizons Pluto mission.

Dark Imagery and Heavy Metal

Heavy metal makes use of myth and dark fantasy and it draws upon the horror genre. Bands have created albums with titles like *Demons and Wizards* (Uriah Heep 1972). They have worn tattoos depicting dragons and demonic figures and engaged in escapism and fantasy. Some bands have represented chaos and danger, suggested dark magic or occultism, or insisted upon the haunting imagery of snakes and daggers. Iron Maiden, for example, has drawn upon imagery that has ranged from dynamic mythical heroism and science fiction to gothic horror. Their public presence is filled with British cultural identity and their songs recall Greek mythological figures like the flight of Icarus and Odysseus and the Sirens ("Ghost of the Navigator"). They reference the beast of Revelation and their most familiar image is that of their 'mascot,' the cartoon zombie Eddie.

Metal bands crossing from the subcultural to the commercial draw from settings outside this world. Some appeal to the occult, to the supernatural, or to Norse mythology. Some have names that derive from classical sources: Aeon, Charon, Thanatos, Satirycon. They have addressed mythical forces of devastation. British heavy metal, born in the working class Midlands, seeks re-enchantment while grinding out its assertions against adversity. Black Sabbath and Judas Priest have both sung lyrics about dystopia and songs of concern about the future of the planet earth. The aggressive sounds of heavy metal may channel violence while offering a sense of freedom and catharsis, as Robert Walser and Deena Weinstein have suggested. The symbolism within heavy metal ranges across the fantastic images and sounds of speed metal, death metal, and black metal.

In their studies of heavy metal, Robert Walser and Deena Weinstein have each provided strong and distinctive justifications for the examination of a rock music genre that was rejected by some critics and "reviled" by others. Weinstein offered an insightful sociological approach and Walser set forth a theoretical and methodological approach which has been influential for subsequent investigators of the genre. In his study of heavy metal, Walser pointed to the uses of rock for people who have to come to terms with modernity.[53] Walser wrote that "metal has been ignored or reviled, not only by academics of most stripes, but even by most rock critics."[54] Yet, the fantasy and energy in this medium touches a chord with its core fans. Deena Weinstein argued that metal is the music of the global proletariat.[55] Other voices have joined the conversation. Harris Berger points out that "the world of metal has undergone enormous transformations."[56] Heavy metal has expanded beyond its working class roots. The heavy metal genre provides an array of voices that includes those of both male and female fans. This polyvocality spans the world.

Heavy metal has always "evoked power and potency," notes Walser.[57] Guitar distortion has become a key signifier in heavy metal and hard rock, suggesting power and intensity. Loudness and intensity are coupled with grandiose stances, threatening imagery, and fantasies of power. Terror and death (Anthrax, Poison, Megadeth, Slayer) or evil and blasphemy (Black Sabbath, Judas Priest) express heavy metal transgression. This is heavy metal's mythology. "By 1989 heavy metal accounted for as much as 40 percent of all sound recordings sold in the United States," notes Robert Walser, although "genre boundaries are not solid and clear" today.[58] The term heavy metal itself is contested. For example, Bruce Dickinson would never use it to describe all of Iron Maiden's output. Def Leppard and AC/DC reject the term, while Judas Priest wants to be classified as heavy metal.[59]

Anecdotal accounts suggest that heavy metal fans respond primarily to the sound, fantastic imagery, and energy of the genre. Deena Weinstein makes the observation that heavy metal fans are more inclined to respond to key phrases than to the entire lyric of a song. They listen to the overall sound of the music. The meanings conveyed by the lyrics may be secondary. She tells the story of meeting with Rush fans who knew every word of Rush's "2112" but had varying interpretations of the narrative. The singer of the song is, of course, on the side of the dreamer who found the instrument and does not at all side with the priests. In this song Rush declares their "romantic individualism" against any theocracy that would diminish this. However, not all of the fans who responded to Weinstein's questions about the song saw it that way. Curiously, "narrative was not these fans' strong point," says Weinstein, who explained the story to them.[60]

Of course, the perception of Rush as a heavy metal band might itself be contested by heavy metal fans. Most critics would identify Rush as progressive rock. Weinstein recognizes the variety of heavy metal and notes the fragmentation of metal in the 1980s. She distinguishes between heavy metal and what she refers to as lite metal. Heavy metal remained subversive, rhythmic, driven by power chords. Lite metal combined rock with heavy metal qualities and adapted itself to melodic lines and less heavy bass. With its embrace of romantic themes and MTV it gained radio airplay and a wide audience. Some metal fans would not characterize these bands, like Def Leppard or Bon Jovi, as metal at all. Resisting this trend was speed or thrash metal, in which bands like Metallica rose to prominence. Thrash or speed metal "contrasts with punk's simplicity and nihilism," observes Robert Walser. It brings together heavy metal with punk influences of aggressiveness, critical lyrics, and fast tempos. However, it displays more virtuosity and control.[61] It can be differentiated from the glam metal of Mötley Crüe and Quiet Riot and other bands that have drawn upon the androgyny set forth earlier by the New York Dolls and David Bowie.

Mythology is pervasive in heavy metal. In her sociological study, Weinstein distinguished between two key features of heavy metal: the Dionysian and chaos. Dionysius, the Greek god of wine and revelry, could be both destructive and creative. This was the god of ecstasy, the god of liberation and breaking through into wonder, pleasure, and heightened experience of the moment. Heavy metal seeks this vitality and transcendence. However, it is also characterized by the recognition of chaos, including elements of conflict, confusion, and violence, as

Weinstein points out.[62] The underworld, often viewed as a grotesque realm of apocalyptic horror, is one of its key images. This is an inversion of the sublime, experienced as terror and awe. It is expressed in themes of disorder, defiance, opposition, and destruction. This is a discourse, Weinstein notes, that embodies contradiction and includes images of monsters, the grotesque, mayhem and disaster.[63] With this discourse has come biblical imagery, particularly from *Revelation*, like Iron Maiden's "Number of the Beast." References to the devil connote disorder. Heavy metal also turns to Gothic and horror imagery to denote chaos and turns to sword and sorcery to explore the fantastic.[64]

Heavy metal bands may argue against contemporary forces of destruction, as in Black Sabbath's "War Pigs," or against those of conformity and diminishment of imagination, as Rush does in "2112." They may call for rebellion or change. Or they may simply delight in the imagery of the fantastic, the heroic, or the horrific.[65] Much like Dante once did in expressing the horrors of Inferno, these bands shake things up, challenge the apparent stability of daily life, and they remind us of our vulnerability. Or, like the angels of Milton's *Paradise Lost*, heavy metal offers symbolic rebellion. The dark images of heavy metal may reflect the anxieties and problems of the culture, as critic Robert Palmer has suggested.[66]

Led Zeppelin

Heavy metal's precursors Led Zeppelin and Black Sabbath turned toward what might broadly be called mythology. It is well-known that guitarist Jimmy Page was fascinated with occultism and Aleister Crowley. Page purchased esoteric books, including rare volumes, and he financed the Equinox book shop in Kensington. Led Zeppelin's fourth album includes symbols that are said to represent the four members of the band. Page has said that Led Zeppelin was the alchemy of the elements, a combination of Led Zeppelin's four members. The Hermit from the Tarot on the inner sleeve of *Led Zeppelin IV* has been identified as a variation of the Rider Waite. When asked if he advocates the hermetic tradition, Page has said that he does not advocate anything; he simply hopes that people will find things themselves.[67]

In Led Zeppelin's music, Jimmy Page's esoteric interests were matched with the mythical lyrics of Robert Plant. "Plant verbalizes his Viking and Lord of the Rings fantasies over Page's riffs," writes Theodore Gracyk.[68] Astrological interests also connect with Led Zeppelin's music, Chris Welch notes in an interview with Jimmy Page.[69] Page has a sense of talismanic magic, observes Theodore Schick.[70] He has been intrigued by the hermetic tradition and perhaps he is the hermit figure on the inside cover of *Led Zeppelin IV*: the hermit, the bearer of the lamp and light. Page, with embroidery on his stage clothing at that time, was a public figure, not a reclusive one.

Led Zeppelin provides "one expression of living mythology in contemporary culture and fan responses to this are a clear indication of the necessity of such mythology in people's lives," observes Susan Fast.[71] In her book on Led Zeppelin, Fast says that the band "consciously constructed a kind of mythology" and utilized "the spirit of mythological discourse by using "poetic, formal, or slightly archaic language."[72] She has conducted surveys in which the band's fans have referred to Led Zeppelin's "mystical" landscapes.[73] Their response, she observes, does not mean that the fans perceive "a coherent narrative" but that they do respond to suggestions of "big" or "epic" themes and images. Symbols and attitude are perceived by Led Zeppelin's fan culture and by rock critics, Fast says[74] "Mythology" here means discourse and imagery.

"Definitions of myth and epic are highly contested among scholars of this genre," Fast observes. "Myth" and "epic" are not readily distinguished by most rock fans. "Epic," for most, tends to mean length. Fast notes that what fans seem to be saying is that Led Zeppelin's lyrics, imagery, discourse, music may suggest "the sacred."[75] Fast then cites Paul Ricouer's view that the sacred and myth are linked. The "symbolic function of myth is its power of discovering and revealing the bond between man and what he considers sacred"[76]

In Led Zeppelin's songs we encounter lyrics that speak of darkness and light, illumination, angelic-power, and mystery. Ideas of magic and alchemy swirl through blues- based songs. On "Stairway to Heaven" Robert Plant sings of mystery that makes him wonder. There are lines in "The Battle of Evermore," "Misty Mountain Hop," and "Ramble On" that recall J.R.R. Tolkein's *The Lord of the Rings*. Mordor and Golum enter the lyric for "Ramble On." "Immigrant Song" suggests a world of primeval Vikings. Led Zeppelin presents fantasy-like production in songs like "The Song Remains the Same" and songs on *Houses of the Holy* like "Dancing Days." Archetypes appear in "All My Love," "The Battle of Evermore," "Kashmir," and "Achilles Last Stand." On side two of the original pressing of *Led Zeppelin III* we hear the phrase "So mote it be," which was used in rituals of *Ordo Templi Orientis* (The Order of the Oriental Templars).[77]

Led Zeppelin's output is filled with myth and fantasy:

- On *Led Zeppelin II*, "Ramble On" is a song about leaving and seeking an ideal woman. The lyrics recall the stories and imagery of Tolkein. The speaker laments that he was in Mordor's depth and darkness in the days when there was magic. The evil golem took his lover away.
- Opening with Plant's striking primal wail, the "Immigrant Song" on *Led Zeppelin III* invites us into the Nordic mythical imagery of Thor's hammer, the hammer of the gods, a land filled with ice and snow. The song pulses rhythmically through Viking imagery of threshing oars and a call to overcome war and rebuild the ruins in peace.
- Listeners have often commented on the evocative quality of "Stairway to Heaven" as it moves from the opening woodwinds through a ballad form to its energetic conclusion. After several verses, there is a pause and a bridge section follows. D chords descend to a C and overdubbed guitars. A Telecaster cuts in with a solo and echo, repeating a figure eleven times. The guitar rings out on suspended chords and the band blasts into the song's familiar Am-G-F conclusion: a rock pulsing section with Plant's vocal climbing and Page's guitar rising into a searing lead.
- "The Battle of Evermore," also on *Led Zeppelin IV*, begins in a pattern of A minor to G and A minor to C, followed by the D chord and it stays with this harmonic pattern throughout. The vocal melody then jumps to A, an octave from the note on which the song began. The lyric begins with an interplay of light and dark; there is a queen of light and a prince of peace. There are agrarian images of hoes, plows, and apples,

a rich and well cared for land that is spoiled by tyranny and war. The lyric tells us of a thunderous sound and waiting upon Avalon's angels: a mythic image of an ideal land. We are given an imagery of a castle, battle, bows and arrows flying, a dragon of darkness, magic runes and a world that must be brought back into balance.

This mythic aspect of Led Zeppelin songs has often been noticed by the many rock critics, academic writers, and fans who have commented on the band. The creative magic of musical performance by Led Zeppelin is discussed by Randall E. Auxier when he writes of "history and re-enactment" in their blues tributes. "The magic happens when a musician is playing" and is in the zone and is able to "get out of the way."[78] Auxier observes that "Page is a "creator of powerful archetypal symbols" and Plant is the force behind "poetic lyrical symbols."[79] He asserts that Led Zeppelin has "mythic power" and that past and present are connected by "symbolizing power." Auxier also points out that a belief in magic is one of many expressions of mythic consciousness that have "provided the basis for human civilization."[80] Susan Fast has pointed out that the Led Zeppelin audience felt a sense of unity and a "feeling of connectedness." She points to Victor Turner's reflections in *From Ritual to Theatre* on ritual and performing myth and "symbolic enactment."[81] Fast cites Christopher Williams's assertion that this is transformative experience for fans and is ritualistic.[82] Scott Calef discusses the band's use of symbols in *Led Zeppelin and Philosophy*. He remarks that he was bothered by their cover photo of a suburban family gathering around a kitchen table until he explored the possible meanings of the black obelisk at the center of the table. One interpretation is that this oddly placed figure is a hole, or nothingness, at the center of modern life. Perhaps it is a black hole in space.[83]

Black Sabbath

Black Sabbath has titled albums *Paranoid, Masters of Reality, Sabotage, Heaven and Hell,* and *Sabbath Bloody Sabbath.* In 1968, founding members of Black Sabbath Tony Iommi and Bill Ward had a band called

Mythology. When the band Rare Breed dissolved, vocalist Ozzy Osborne joined them and they named their band Earth, in fall 1968. This became Black Sabbath. Another band in England had the name Earth and Iommi, Ward, and Ozzy sought something that sounded more ominous. (Iommi played briefly with Jethro Tull and then returned to Black Sabbath.) Because of a factory accident, Tony Iommi created false fingertips. He later tuned down from E to E flat. He was joined in this tuning down by bassist Geezer Butler. They then began to tune down a minor third to D flat.[84] Boosting treble and distortion, Black Sabbath developed its own heavy, power chord driven sound. Tony Iommi's tuning down was to make the music darker. It could not really help him much with the tension on the strings, or the strain of playing, as a rumor suggests. Tuning down a third does not really help much with the tension of the strings. He had to have lighter gauge strings to gain the ability to bend the strings on his Gibson SG. The way to soften the action is to adjust the bridge and use lighter gauge strings.

Paranoid (1970) and *Black Sabbath* (1970) were recorded in standard 440 tuning. *Black Sabbath* was recorded October 1969. During the recording, left-handed Iommi changed from a Fender Stratocaster to a Gibson SG which he played upside down. The album provided the first expressions of paganism, the occult, H.P. Lovecraft-like horror. The first song begins on a tritone interval played on guitar by Iommi. This is three adjacent whole tones. Harmonically, this is often considered unstable.

In Black Sabbath bassist Geezer (Terry Butler) wrote the lyrics. These were often a satirical critique of humanity. The band appeared zombielike with mustaches and crosses. Musically, the guitar riffs of Tony Iommi led the way. Bill Ward was the percussionist who loved jazz as well as rock. Ozzy has iconic status but reality TV has diminished his credibility. Black Sabbath produced fantastic songs like "The Wizard," "Symptom of the Universe," "Electric Funeral," "Hand of Doom," the quieter "Planet Caravan," and "Iron Man" on the *Paranoid* album. An apocalyptic future war is imagined on "War Pigs" The song announces the power E chord. A siren sounds about thirty seconds into the song. Black Sabbath produces a bleak, desperate, and dark art that argues against the darkness in humanity. They contest "robot minds." In singing about darkness and evil, fantasy intersects with this critique. Robert Walser observes: "Osborne plays with signs of the supernatural mystery because they evoke a power and mystery that is highly attractive to many fans."[85]

The expansion and variety of heavy metal has continued across the past several decades. Motörhead brought together punk and metal. In the 1990s Metallica received frequent radio airplay as heavy metal became mainstream. Alternative bands like Pearl Jam and Smashing Pumpkins also moved center stage. Korn and Limp Bizkit drew upon a variety of heavy metal and other musical forms.[86] Death metal vocalists growl and scream, writhe and spit and vomit out words about death, misery, and decay. Speed/thrash grumbles alienation, assaults our ears with chaos, or vents against injustice over a throbbing bass and crashing drums. Metallica, Megadeth, and Anthrax built a distinctive, grungy sound. The genre continues its interaction with the power of myth.

Two

The Forgotten Language
Rock, Myth and Science Fiction

Myth and Dreams: The Forgotten Language

Mythic patterns and themes underlie narratives and imagery in rock music. Songs offer us heroes and action, important themes of journey, birth or rebirth. They present encounters with darkness or monstrous and demonic figures, sacrifice, honor, loss, and victory. Heroes seek the Holy Grail and young men, like Icarus in the Greek myth, fly too high. They drift away from contact with Ground Control and are lost in the heavens like David Bowie's Major Tom. Rock music enlists the image of the outlaw and the rebel. Heroes defeat the darkness and evil, or are swept up by it. In rock songs they face alienation, madness, deception, violence, disillusion and chaos.

Rock musicians offer us an emotional language of rebellion, self-expression, and mythical imagery. Mythical ideas have a great deal to do with how we approach and shape our world. Often our western view has held that discursive reason offers the most logical and reliable view of life. This perspective has often marginalized the counter-rationalistic and romantic, religious, or mythopoetic reflection that we find in rock, dismissing it as merely "imaginative." In contrast, comparative mythologists value archaic modes of experience and recognize humanity's access to myth as pre-reflective or intuitive. Rock, likewise, responds to the feeling, the dream, the ecstasy that some cultural critics say we have lost: the intuitive, somatic, and visceral aspects of life that have been repressed in Western culture. Rationalists have usually sought to replace mythopoetics with analytical thought, although these styles of thought are not mutually exclusive. The Enlightenment position is that mythopoetic thinking is the opposite of rational thinking. Much modern thinking, following the disposition of the Enlightenment, assumes that we have progressed beyond the 'primitive' notions of our ancient ancestors. Surely, their anxieties, perceptions, and ways of framing reality have been transcended and we are now enlightened and rational. Myths were common to those cultures. The modern mind assumes that we are able to toss away those myths that they used to explain their world. However, we still ask questions about those strangely illogical aspects of our world. We still create stories, sing songs together, go to concerts and participate in rituals and wonder what we are to make of those mysterious dark corners of experience. How are we to understand magical experiences of love? Stories, songs, or other art forms may express them. Symbols and metaphors point to them. Rock performers enter into this art of associations, into the ambiguities of poetry and myth.

When the rock composer draws upon a primordial image and makes use of myth that composer connects society past and present in images, emblems, ritual, and archetypes. Psychologist Carl Jung calls the archetype a primordial image. The collective unconscious, Jung asserts, is a repository of archetypal images. Throughout the world these archetypes and patterns appear. Among them are: earth, fire, sky, water, the circle, the road or path.[1] They have persisted in the human unconscious as remnants or vestiges of fundamental human experiences across the ages. In the mythological figures of rock songs, as in literature, these enduring memories may be found. The myth-making imagination is at work in both the creator and the listener to the song.

In her book *Musicians in Tune* (Fireside, 1992), Jenny Boyd explores rock music creativity with attention to Jungian perspectives by interviewing many well-known rock music performers. Included in this inquiry are discussions of archetypes (pp. 109–10, 119–20), dreams (pp. 102–03, 110, 255) and the figure of the hero (pp. 120, 136–37). Boyd considers the role of the unconscious in musical creativity, the perspective of a rock musician as an outsider, and the role of tapping the unconscious while performing. She explores creative communication in concerts (pp.174–181) and the audience-artist connection. Like psychologist Abraham Maslow, Boyd is interested in peak experiences and she offers an array of musician's comments that support her suggestion that creativity may be hindered by the rational mind. She quotes Jung: "The archetype is a force. It has an autonomy and it can suddenly seize you."[2]

A demonstration of the depth dimension of the human psyche and the drives in human instinctual life was Sigmund Freud's chief contribution in his psychological investigations. In Carl Jung's analytic psychology, Jung distinguished the personal unconscious from what he called the collective unconscious. We participate in the collective unconscious of the human race, Jung believed, and we draw upon archetypes or primordial images.[3] These archetypes are expressed in metaphors, and in the songs, imagery, and rituals that are central to the rock concert experience. The ecstatic experience lifts a listener out of the everyday world. The individuals that Deena Weinstein calls the "core audience" of heavy metal music seek this experience of "falling into the moment" in which the listener becomes one with the music and "time stands still."[4] The rock concert, she observes, has become a multi-media event that generates excitement. The band is loud. The lights flash. There is "sensory overload," Weinstein says. Loud sounds "raise adrenaline levels" and "strongly rhythmic music ... increases breath and blood-pressure rates."[5] The bodies of some audience members move in synchrony with the music: they thrust, punch, tap; they sway, nod their heads, and express emotion. Members of the audience become part of the collective consciousness that the sociologist Emile Durkheim has written about. They are engaged in the music, open to the performer's emotions, prompted to excitement by lights and special effects.

To view the concert experience through this perspective is to consider the links between celebration and ritual with myth and religion throughout our world. Recognizing heavy metal fans as a subculture, Deena Weinstein quotes Durkheim on "the bringing together of normally isolated groups to celebrate, and indeed create, their corporate existence.... For a society to become conscious of itself and maintain at the necessary degree of intensity the sentiments which it thus attains, it must assemble and concentrate itself."[6] From another perspective, the rock concert may parallel ritual and may be experienced as sacred in contrast with the everyday world. Weinstein suggests that such moments at concerts may be described by Mircea Eliade's term of hierophanies "in which sacredness is revealed."[7]

The imaginative rock musician may enter the realm of myths and dreams, which are expressed in a symbolic language. In ages past myths and dreams appeared in ritual and story. In recent times, rock music has provided us with mythical figures, suggestions of awe, power, and terror. Rock performances make use of symbol and myth in the ritual of concert experiences. Artists who play with these dreamscapes invite us to regain this knowledge that myth provides:. They seek to open these forgotten dimensions of the human mind.

The force of mythology is recognized by the philosopher Ernst Cassirer, who says that "it would be impossible to characterize the structure of myth as rational." Humanity is a symbol maker he tells us and symbols are not only signals; they are "part of the human world of meaning."[8] "Myth is non-theoretical," writes Cassirer. "It defies and challenges our fundamental categories of thought. Its logic, in its very meaning and essence, is incommensurate with all our conceptions of empirical or scientific truth."[9] While language is associated with reason, the philosopher observes, this discursive language is only part of the whole. "For side by side with conceptual language there is an emotional language; side by side with logical or scientific language there is a language of poetic imagination."[10] "Reason is a very inadequate term with which to comprehend the forms of man's cultural life in all their richness and variety," says Cassirer. "But all these forms are symbolic forms."[11] We must "unmask" the meaning that lies within its images and symbols.

Myths, Reason and Romanticism

Rock inherits the ancient legacy of myth and ritual. Myths, in preindustrial societies throughout the world, were models for living. They were integral to tribal life and society. Ancient societies believed in magic and practiced ritual. In the modern age, in the late eighteenth century and the early decades of the nineteenth century, Romantic poets held that our culture had been overlaid with an emphasis on reason and rationality. They held that myths still addressed core concerns in humanity. From William Blake, William Wordsworth, Percy Bysshe

Shelley, and John Keats in England to Ludwig Tieck, Novalis, E.T.A. Hoffmann, and Heinrich Heine in Germany, romantic poets argued that the modern Western world had absorbed the rational perspective of the European Enlightenment concerning what reality consists of. These poets declared that beyond these definitions of reason, emotion, feeling, and intuition are important in human experience and they turned to sources in mythology. Rock has inherited this perspective and, likewise, engages myth and expresses rebellion. It expresses raw emotion and feeling. In romantic terms, rock aspires to search beyond the mundane and it embraces the power of ritual in the concert and festival. To reanimate the world it taps deeply into the realms of myth.

The Greek myths developed across generations of storytelling. Mythology was conveyed through an oral tradition and Greek writing later began to be formulated, around 800 B.C. Edith Hamilton notes that Greek myths did not fully produce regions of terror, although there were mythical monsters: Hydra, Gorgon, chimeras and the Furies. The good place in the afterlife was Elysium, or Elysian Fields. The Eleusinian rites celebrated Demeter and Persephone. Images of these figures have come down through the ages. Charon is depicted by Michelangelo in *The Last Judgment* in the Sistine Chapel. Tartarus was situated beneath the underworld as a dark and fearful place for the truly evil ones. Passing the fierce, doglike Cerebrus, souls entered the Underworld. Hades was the name of the god who ruled there and he stole away Persephone, who had been gathering flowers, making her his wife.

"We tend to see the ancient Greeks as icons of rationality," writes William Broad in *The Oracle*. "[...] But their genius had another side, one of occult impulses and procedures far removed from the world of reason." The Greeks began to distinguish *mythos* from *logos*, or reason. The emphasis upon reason in the West is a legacy that left a lingering suggestion that myth was the equivalent of something illusory or unreal. However, a myth is a story seeking truth and a gathering of images that opens us to the unknowable. Myth, like rock music, is sensual, immediate, and emotional. Myth symbolizes hopes, dreams, fears, dreams and aspirations.[12] Myth also expresses dimensions of human experience and ways of thought and feeling that the modern mind may have subordinated to rational, "left-brained" thinking. This challenge to the conventions of rational thought may lie behind David Bowie's fascination with myth, archetypes, visual imagery, and books like Julian Jayne's *The Origins of the Bicameral Mind.* Jaynes speculated that the "voices" of the Oracle of Delphi could once be heard in a now neglected region of the mind.[13] When Jenny Boyd proposes that creativity may be hindered by the rational mind, the voices of the rock musicians she has interviewed concur, as they offer their testimonies about synchronicity and their "a-hah" experiences.[14]

Without myth, the philosopher Friedrich Nietzsche once claimed, humanity is rootless. The "forgotten language" of dreams and myth provides modern people with a path to a new story.[15] This forgotten language surpasses the limits of philosopher René Descartes' dualism between mind and matter to acknowledge broader imaginative knowledge. This was also the argument of the English Romantic poets Wordsworth, Coleridge, and Shelley. Samuel Taylor Coleridge compared the poet to an Aeolian harp through which blows the wind of inspiration. Making use of this figure, Percy Bysshe Shelley called upon the West Wind to infuse his spirit with poetry and to drive his thoughts across the earth. William Wordsworth wrote that the world is too much with us. We lay waste our powers in getting and spending, he wrote. We see little in nature that is ours. We have lost access to the forgotten language of myth. In his poem he muses that if only he could reawaken the power of myth within himself he could see Proteus rising from the sea and hear old Triton blowing his horn. Vital imagination could be revived within him and renew the world.

Rock musicians make a similar affirmation. The symbols, images, and narratives of rock reawaken this romantic sensibility. Modern audiences rediscover in rock the imagination to create new myths. The shaping spirit of Imagination constructs and invents, re-creating our sensations and experiences, as Samuel Taylor Coleridge affirmed in prose in his *Biographia Literaria* (Chapter XIII) and in poetry in "Dejection: An Ode." He wrote of "the willing suspension of disbelief" that we allow for when we stretch our capacity to enter an experience of fiction and fantasy. The fantasies of rock music call upon us to suspend disbelief. We need what Coleridge called "poetic faith," or what Keats called "negative capability": the ability to live with uncertainty and doubt without having to grasp for reason and fact.

Rock music's inheritance from Romanticism is clear. Myth and emotion, imagination and intuition, pervade rock genres from progressive rock to heavy metal. Rock, likewise, inherits the rich mythical traditions we also find in Western classical music. Orpheus, the musician of Greek mythology, appears in the plots of numerous operas. (Orpheus has been the subject of more than sixty operas, including works by Monteverdi, Gluck, Offenbach, Telemann, Rameau, Rossi, Peri, Caccini, and Milhaud.) Robert Walser points out that Orpheus, like a heavy metal vocalist, must sing with a rhetorical effusiveness that could undermine his masculine identity.[16] This "flamboyant display of his emotions" is a feature of power and expression by some heavy metal vocalists.

The rock poet is open to mystery. The poet T.S. Eliot once commented that he believed that the poet has a mind which is "much more important than his own private mind." The poet realizes that he or she is part of human experience throughout time and recognizes the fusion of past and present. It is within this larger mind or consciousness that archetypes are formulated and conveyed in poetry.[17]

Archetypes and Adventure

Rock music draws upon myth in its use of archetypal imagery. Beneath the images of a song of the fantastic is often an archetype. For example, the king or pharaoh in Iron Maiden's *Powerslave*, or the sea in The Who's *Quadrophenia*. The word archetype derives from the ancient Greek word *eidos*, from which we get the word "ideas." The mythical story involves heroes, the creation of a world, complications and the transformation of the hero. The story presents conflicts and thresholds that the hero encounters: doorways and staircases, mirrors and reflections (the catoptric), the oracular, the astronomical, and geometrical shapes. There may be a threatening terrain, monstrous figures, and strange unknowns. These are the figures of fantasy and myth. When a rock performance makes these gestures it is engaging the fantastic and the mythical.

"The tale of adventure—of great courage and daring, of battle against the forces of darkness and the unknown—has been with the human race since it first learned to talk," science fiction author Leigh Brackett wrote in 1975 as she introduced a science fiction story collection. "It began as part of the primitive survival technique, interwoven with magic and ritual, to explain and propitiate the vast forces of nature with which man could not cope in any other fashion." She pointed out that science fiction ["the space opera"] is the folk tale and the hero tale of our time.[18] Other writers of science fiction have said things that sound similar. C.S. Lewis spoke of myth as "a real though unfocused gleam of divine truth falling upon human imagination."[19] When the theorist of popular culture John Cawleti addressed the functions of myth and folklore he recognized that the myths performed the important role of articulating and reaffirming the primary cultural values "in earlier more homogeneous cultures."[20] Following this line of thought, we can say that myths hold societies together. They transmit traditions, encourage heroism, offer cautions, and move people to action. Myths attempt to explain the universe. Joseph Campbell once commented to Bill Moyers that myths are often learned in childhood and then integrated more deeply in adulthood.[21] "The first function of a living mythology ... is to waken and maintain in the individual an experience of awe, humility and respect," Campbell wrote in *The Masks of God*. Mircea Eliade writes: "Myth assures man that what he is about to do has already been done."[22]

The archetypal critic, following the ancient patterns of myth, recognizes that much symbolism in storytelling arises from the archetypal structures within the unconscious mind. When the art of rock songwriting meets with science fiction it also draws upon these sources. The mythical style ranges across hero myths and legends, monster figures, the exotic, the paranormal, the fantastic, the mystical, and the sublime. Rock songs that draw upon myth employ a symbolic language. We hear Led Zeppelin sing of the hammer of the gods in Norse mythology and we may recognize J.R.R. Tolkein's characters in their song "The Battle of Evermore." Iron Maiden sings of the flight of Icarus. Heavy metal bands beckon toward the underworld.

In mythology, the quest (from *quaere* in Latin) is a purposeful journey filled with ordeals. In *The Odyssey*, Homer tells us the story of Odysseus seeking his home in Ithaca, while his son Telemachus grows into maturity and ventures out to the world in search of his lost father. In the Greek myths we see Jason gathering the Argonauts to pursue the Golden Fleece. Medieval texts from Chretien de Troyes and others recall the adventures of King Arthur and his knights as they seek the Holy Grail. In modern literature, Herman Melville's *Moby Dick* brings us the dark, obsessive quest of Ahab to assert revenge against the mysterious white whale.

The plots of many myths are familiar to us. A hero or heroine is called to adventure and sets forth into new surroundings. The hero becomes a stranger in a setting of wonder that becomes one of fear, or awesome foreboding. After struggling with the shadow the hero at last gets free and returns to the familiar world. These story patterns appear in ancient and biblical literature, in Greek and Roman stories. In the Hebrew Bible Jonah rejects the call to preach to Nineveh and he is swallowed into the belly of a whale, only to return later to his mission. In late medieval literature we encounter Dante's trip to Inferno and through Purgatorio to save his soul. Journey stories repeat often in tales of voyage in the age of discovery. In the 1700s Daniel Defoe created the character of Robinson Crusoe who is shipwrecked on a deserted island and becomes self-reliant. Robinson Crusoe feels isolated but then he sees a footprint and realizes that he is not entirely alone. There is an alien about and he realizes that he must protect himself. Before long he has met Friday and is recruiting him and a small band of followers. In Jonathan Swift's satirical *Gulliver's Travels*, Lemuel Gulliver awakens to see that he has been tied down by the Lilliputians. Then in Borbindignag he becomes a curiosity for the giants and the box in which he is contained is picked up by an eagle and plunged into the sea from which a passing ship rescues him. In Voltaire's *Candide* the protagonist is kicked into a puzzling environment which Dr. Pangloss insists is the best of all possible worlds. Neil Peart of Rush remembered that story when he was devising his narrative for *Clockwork Angels*.[23]

Rush and Iron Maiden have been attracted to the Gothic and surreal tales of Samuel Taylor Coleridge from the late eighteenth century. The fantastic hallucinatory imagery of Coleridge's "Kubla Kahn" was adapted by Rush in "Xanadu." The haunted tale of *The Rime of the Ancient Mariner* is a ghostly ballad by Coleridge that the heavy metal band Iron Maiden has adapted. The albatross has been shot and forever is the mariner pursued by a curse. A ship approaches filled with death and the mariner witnesses the ghosts of his shipmates dying of hunger and thirst. He is entranced by the sight of the sea-snakes and calls a blessing over the water. The wind carries the ship toward home but it is devoured and sinks into the sea and the mariner is wrested from the dark sea half-drowned and must eternally repeat his story.

Rock musicians have also been fascinated by the legendary underworld. In the dark dreams of myth we see characters that must make journeys into the underworld, like Orpheus seeking Eurydice, or Odysseus seeking Tiresius. Orpheus looks back over his shoulder and loses his love. Odysseus and Aeneas find the residents of the underworld difficult to communicate with. Dante must face monsters and the souls of the damned. He may lean upon Virgil, his guide, but he must face tests and episodes in learning so that inner growth can occur. The dark phase of Inferno is only bearable if there is some vaguely discerned distant prize that he may one day realize.

Science Fiction, Rock and Mythology

Myth and science may seem to be at odds with each other. After all, science can dispel superstition and demythologize the world. Science provides us with answers and descriptions about how the natural world operates. We do not live in the world of our ancient ancestors who heard in the thunder and the inexplicable storm the voice of the gods. However, pure science, based in our drive to know and to understand, is engaged with curiosity and wonder. There is a dialogue between the empirical world and the world of scientific imagination, as science fiction writer Samuel R. Delany observed. When Yevgeny Zamyatin, the Russian writer of the dystopian novel *We*, wrote on H.G. Wells in a 1922 essay, he called him a writer of "urban fairy-tales." He noted the apparent contrast between "exact science and fairy tale, exactitude and fantasy." However, Zamyatin added: "After all, myth is always, whether explicitly or implicitly, connected with religion, and the religion of the present day city is the exact sciences, so that there is the most natural connection between the latest urban myth, the urban fairy tale, and science."[24]

The author J.G. Ballard has suggested that stories of outer space are projections of inner space, or psychological experience. David Bowie offered the same insight when he reflected in 1997 interviews about his song "Space Oddity" and his other space figures: "They were metaphysically in place to suggest that I felt alienated," he concluded.[25] Bowie told the *Los Angeles Times* in 1974 that "Space Oddity" was "quite personal" and that he used "science fiction patterns to put forward concepts, ideas, and theories" and to explore creative possibilities.[26] Songs like "Space Oddity," "Life on Mars," "Starman" and his Ziggy Stardust persona "insured that he would be forever associated with the planets, space, the moon, and the stars," wrote biographer Wendy Leigh.[27] Bowie brought this interior dimension of his creativity into connection with visuals, music, and his continual revision and recasting of himself. "An outfit is much more than something to wear," he once told an interviewer. "It's about who you are, it's a badge and it becomes a symbol."[28] His inner life was expressed outwardly in chameleon fashion and many of his musical narratives might be likened to speculative fiction.

Speculative fiction, the term Robert A. Heinlein offered in 1947, broadens the scope of the quest through the unexplainable to include the wonder of the visionary that is seeking possibilities. Imaginative speculation in rock music concept albums, song lyrics, performances, album covers, and stage design has intersected with scientific imagination, fantasy and psychological experience. Rock's musical and theatrical innovation appeals to the human sense of wonder that has drawn many people toward science. Its artists have appealed to creative and innovative uses of technology, while stretching, with the mythology of its stories and images, toward possibilities.

Some forms of rock have sought to mythologize, to create theatre, music, and imagery that will re-re-enchant the world. Some bands have turned toward imaginative sources in science fiction. Gary K. Wolfe has observed that science fiction demythologizes "the cosmos into quantifiable concepts" but is also involved in "creating new arenas for myth." Thus, a genre which prizes scientific rationality "has become more closely associated with the secret centers of consciousness represented by myth than any other popular genre."[29] Scientific rationality focuses upon the cognitive, the rational, the empirical, the skeptical, and the systematic. There is a tension between romantic wonder and mysticism on the one hand and agnostic rationalist materialism on the other. One might say that C.S. Lewis, for example, represents the anti-scientific position and Isaac Asimov represents the scientific position.

In "On Science Fiction" Lewis connects his sense of science fiction with mythopoetic fantasy. C.S. Lewis writes: "Nor need the strange worlds, when we get there, be at all strictly tied to scientific probabilities. It is their wonder, or beauty, or suggestiveness that matter."[30]

Science Fiction and Mythopoetic Fantasy

The emergence of science fiction in the twentieth century predates the birth of rock music by several decades. In the first decades of the twentieth century, the pulp magazines of Hugo Gernsback fostered modern science fiction in America. His *Amazing Stories* magazine was illustrated with imaginative covers by Frank R. Paul. Science fiction imagery owes much to Paul, an Austrian architect who created more than 150 spectacular covers. The creators of rock music LP album covers and the creators of films drew upon these images.

Science fiction embraced the hard science of Hugo Gernsback, whose reflections helped to define the field. Meanwhile, ancient myths and legends mixed with modern imagination in the realm of fantasy fiction as well. In the *Norton Book of Science Fiction*, Ursula K. Le Guin distinguishes science fiction from fantasy: "Science fiction behaves like fantasy ... in making things up which we know don't exist...." Yet how do we know for sure that they don't?[31]

Rock musicians, of course, make things up. They draw upon art, comics, movies, and previous rock music, as well as blues, folk, jazz, and classical music. Its performers who were born in the 1940s and 1950s and after absorbed juvenile serials and comic books and radio and they experienced science fiction. Some artists, like Neil Peart of Rush, David Crosby of Crosby, Stills, and Nash, or Lenny Kaye of the Patti Smith Group read science fiction books and fanzines. In the World War II era, science fiction appeared in the pulp magazines, which had been so popular in the 1930s and stories came to new audiences by radio, newspaper comic strips, feature-films, and in motion picture serials. In the 1930s, *Amazing Stories* was edited by John W. Campbell. This preceded the birth of all of today's rock music performers. However, some of them have read stories from the "golden age of science fiction" that included the fiction of Isaac Asimov, Robert Heinlein, Lester Del Rey, L. Sprague De Camp, Theodore Sturgeon, A.E. van Vogt and others. Rock musicians like David Bowie took cues from William S. Burroughs, the author of *Naked Lunch* and a member of the Beat movement of the 1950s, whose transgressive writings had particular appeal in the psychedelic era of the late sixties and early seventies. Rock musicians who were born from the 1960s through the 1980s have seen science fiction stories enter the literary mainstream and extend across the world in film. Songwriters like Eric Woolfson of the Alan Parsons Project or Steve Harris of Iron Maiden were inspired to lyric writing by these films and they read other fantasy literature as well. Wolfson, for example, was a lifelong fan of the Gothic-tinged work of Edgar Allan Poe, some of whose works might be seen as precursors to science fiction. Harris, Iron Maiden's bassist and principal lyricist, draws upon movies and reads science fiction, history, and horror genre books.

Popular Culture, Science Fiction and Rock Music

Science fiction has a curious partnership with rock music. Often it is more like an occasional visitor than a member of the family. Yet, some might say that science fiction concepts have been visiting rock and roll ever since Bill Haley called his group the Comets. Rock music is a form of discourse and that discourse has included dozens of reflections upon time, future societies, and the stars. Lyrical suggestions of outer space appeared in the Rolling Stones' "2000 Light Years from Home" (1967). We have seen that Jimi Hendrix improvised songs around cosmic themes and that the era of psychedelic bands mutated into progressive rock, heavy metal, and glam. David Bowie gave us "Space Oddity" (1969). Marc Bolan with T. Rex created what he called cosmic rock in "Ballroom of Mars," "Venus Loon," and "Spaceball Ricochet." The pop music world of the 1970s was filled with music like "Rocket Man" (Elton John), "Venus and Mars" (Paul McCartney), and "The Dark Side of the Moon" (Pink Floyd). Kraftwerk's instrumentals on *Man Machine* (1978) and *Computer World* (1981) suggested science fiction progressive music to some listeners. Justin Hayward of the Moody Blues contributed vocals to Jeff Wayne's interpretation of H.G. Wells' *War of the Worlds* (1978). In the 1980s, Rush appeared with albums rich in science fiction themes. Toto reflected upon Frank Herbert's

Dune (1984) and the mythically named band Styx cast a robot in a song that told us that "Kilroy Was Here" (1983). More recently, Radiohead, Muse, Angels and Airwaves, and Thirty Seconds to Mars have called upon science fiction motifs and Nine Inch Nails has recorded *Year Zero* (2007) with a dystopian theme. Listeners have also gotten into the act. In May 2013, astronaut Chris Hadfield of Canada sang Bowie's "Space Oddity" on a You Tube video while on the International Space Station. "Sympathy for Vengeance" by Flowers of Hell was played by staff members at the Kennedy Space Center.

Science fiction offers us the fantastic by using the imagination of modern science and it gives us the modern myths of our technology-rich society. Science fiction reflects and comments on the world and suggests possibilities. It makes use of the terms of science and rationality to invent new mythic structures. For some of its audience science fiction may restore a lost enchantment. In 1969, Leigh Brackett argued that the worst loss of science fiction was its "loss of splendor."[32] When science fiction retains its splendor and its capacity for wonder, it recalls science as a quest, an inquiry, and a journey of discovery. *Scientia*, or knowledge, is cognition that involves separating one thing from another through analysis. Science fiction connects science with the fictive, or the imagining of possible worlds. This reconnection of science and the humanities is crucial for our future. Today science, in its connection with technology, is at the center of society. Science has become one of our chief ways of understanding reality. Science is now, as the philosopher of science Alfred I. Tauber points out, "constitutive to our very selves."[33] Science fiction stretches our understanding and recasts reason in a post-positivist age.

The connection between rock music and science fiction becomes most obvious to us when rock bands use the imagery of spaceships, create lyrics that speak of robots, produce a musical ambience that suggests the expansiveness of space, or fashion narratives like Bowie's "Space Oddity" and images like the cosmic aura of his Ziggy Stardust persona. The popular arts of science fiction and rock music merge when Rush's Neil Peart collaborates with the science fiction writer Kevin Anderson, or Blue Öyster Cult's Eric Bloom works with Michael Moorcock. Rock performers and songwriters are affected by their reading of science fiction, and they are often inspired by films. Those encounters of rock music with science fiction are a form of contact between texts and art forms that we can call intertextual. When a rock songwriter draws upon the science fiction film medium, for example, that songwriter is participating in an "interart" creativity. The work that emerges is intermedial. That is, it moves between media. Films are not only constructed from literary sources but they are imagined also through visual art, drama, and music. The adaptation of a science fiction text to film or to a recording is engaged in this intermediality. It is on this visual and auditory dimension of film, videos, and recordings that rock performers most often have drawn.

Rock musicians are most influenced by science fiction film and television. Some of them, like Peart and Geddy Lee of Rush or Bloom of Blue Öyster Cult, are also avid science fiction readers and have working relationships with science fiction writers like Kevin J. Anderson and Moorcock. The stories of Isaac Asimov, Robert A. Heinlein, Frank Herbert, and Ray Bradbury are vividly in their memories, as are television scripts of Rod Serling's *The Twilight Zone* or Gene Roddenberry's *Star Trek* and dozens of films. These stories, films, and television shows have been resources for their songs and albums. Verbal meanings "make up only a fraction" of what rock music audiences care about, observes Robert Walser.[34] When a band makes use of suggestions of science fiction those suggestions exist in the sound of the music and the imagery surrounding the band, as well as in whatever the lyrics might convey. Science fiction is a path to expanding the palette to offer colors, moods, and ideas that spark imagination.

The literature of possibility lifts imagination and challenges our world-view. In science fiction we are given fantastic social and technological developments that can be explained rationally within a scientific world-view. In mythic heroic fantasies we are given adventures in which the laws of science are suspended in strange worlds filled with magic. Such stories break through our narrow pictures of reality and animate our capacity for wonder. They tell a new story, one that challenges us and stimulates our quest for meaning and our place in the world. Walt Whitman saw the significance of this startled wonder at the universe when he wrote of the learned astronomer:

> When I heard the learned astronomer
> When the proofs, the Figures, were ranged in

Columns before me
When I was shown the charts and diagrams, to add
Divide and measure them
When I sitting heard the astronomer where he
Lectured with much applause in the lecture room
How soon unaccountable I became tired and sick
Till rising and gliding out I wandered off by myself
In the mystical moist night air, and from time to time
Looked up in perfect silence at the stars.

Popular Culture

Science fiction and rock music are expressions of popular culture. To suggest that they can tell us something about contemporary life is to take popular culture quite seriously. Pat Cadigan, who is often advertised as the queen of cyberpunk, offers the recognition that "[p]opular culture in general is a reflection, warts and all, of what of going on in society."[35] One might, for example, consider how rock's space imagery intersected with the sixties counterculture and psychedelics and was further highlighted by the 1969 Apollo mission to the moon. David Bowie's story of Major Tom in "Space Oddity" was released to coincide with that space mission. Countercultural visions of utopia and dystopia were projected into songs by members of the Jefferson Airplane and other bands.[36]

Science fiction and rock music, during the past few decades, have both been embraced as subjects worthy of critical attention. Science fiction first appeared in the United States in periodical publications and it was regarded as popular pulp fiction. For most literary critics, it did not fit into critical formulations of the literary canon and it was generally not a subject for scholarly literary discussion. Rock music emerged as a popular form of music arising from fifties rock and roll that drew upon rhythm and blues and country western roots. It was regarded as a popular music form that did not merit the attention of serious musicology. However, as Bob Dylan once sang, the times they were a-changing and so were attitudes toward science fiction and toward rock music, especially among critics who had come of age listening to rock music and viewing science fiction film and television. Today both science fiction and rock music, with their strong subculture fan bases, remain thriving aspects of popular culture. Increasingly, science fiction is considered in literary terms and rock music is approached through musicological analysis. Science fiction and rock music are also addressed sociologically. Yet they have seldom been brought together within studies of popular culture.

Science fiction audiences and rock music audiences participate avidly in these popular culture forms and the popular arts stake a claim upon our attention. Where the popular forms of science fiction and rock music meet is in the realm of ideas, the sharing of images, and in the often synthesized aural textures that suggest technological innovation and space or expansiveness. If popular culture has taken our dreams, packaged them, and sold them back to us, says Richard Maltby, "it is also the achievement of popular culture that it has brought us more and more varied dreams than we otherwise could have ever known."[37]

A study of science fiction alongside rock brings together these two significant forms of popular culture. In *Future Shock*, Alvin Toffler wrote that "Science fiction is held in low regard as a branch of literature, and perhaps it deserves this critical contempt. But if we view it as kind of sociology of the future, rather than as literature, science fiction has an immense value as a mind-stretching force for the creation of the habit of anticipation."[38] Of course, Toffler's view is mostly based upon the pulps he was familiar with. Science fiction has developed since the 1970s in a variety of ways and many writers have generated texts that may be called literary. Writers from Margaret Atwood to Doris Lessing to Ursula K. Le Guin have written masterful works that are science fiction. This mind-stretching force is also present in rock music speculation.

The British cultural critic Raymond Williams has offered four possible definitions of popular culture: (1) Works that are well-liked by many people. (2) Works that are not as artistically crafted as certain higher art works. (3) "Work deliberately setting out to win favour with the people." (4) "Culture actually made by the people themselves" (1983). The creative expression of science fiction may fit with some of these definitions, as may rock music. Popular culture may be contrasted with the formal complexity in high culture art, although Pierre Bourdieu has argued that such distinctions are ideological matters of taste that support class differences. Bourdieu writes that "the consumption of culture is predisposed, consciously and deliberately or not, to fulfill a social function of legitimating social differences."[39]

Science fiction and rock music have each become part of "the documentary record" that Raymond Williams has spoken of. They are among the enduring practices and texts of imaginative work. Williams says that "culture is the body of intellectual and imaginative work, in which, in a detailed way, human thought and experience are variously recorded."[40] Williams has pointed out that one goal of cultural studies is to understand what "a particular community of experience" is experiencing and expressing. This, he observes, reflects a particular way of life and "structure of feeling."[41] The artifacts of science fiction or of rock music and their fan cultures constitute aids to cultural memory. There is historical value in considering these forms side by side. What we recall of the science fiction culture of the 1930s and 1940s is part of the documentary record of that time that is present in periodicals, books, and illustrations. Likewise, the rock music culture of the 1970s or the 1980s is present to us now on vinyl LP's and in other recorded formats, as well as in images, interviews, and critical commentary. Science fiction may "reveal a complex codification of many of the beliefs and values of an increasingly technological culture."[42] Rock music culture, likewise, reflects where we have been across the past sixty years and may offer suggestions about where we are going.

Science Fiction's Value

Popular science fiction and popular rock music both participate in myth, romance, epic, and fable. Both have gradually gained critical currency. Science fiction has sometimes been dismissed by literary critics as ephemeral and has sometimes been presented as uncritically consumed pulp fiction. However, science fiction can also be viewed not merely as a diversion but also as a literature of ideas. Science fiction, in this sense, is a repository of creative scientific and political ideas. This suggests that there are many science fiction readers, or listeners, who are prompted to think, reflect, and arrive at their own views. Science fiction is a particular kind of discourse, as Samuel R. Delany has pointed out. It offers us "fictional case studies or conceptual experiments," observes Nicholas D. Smith.[43] Approached sociologically science fiction can be viewed as a cultural phenomenon, a commercial product, and a communication with a message. Social issues are hiding behind science fiction masks, Michael Berman has pointed out. A reader may learn to allow that topic to gradually appear, to "sneak up on you ... with metaphor and disguise, at a distance, through parable ... inviting you to think in depth."[44]

Science fiction and rock music both participate in a literature of the fantastic that is grounded in myth and mythopoetic consciousness. There are several literary precursors to science fiction. Mary Shelley's *Frankenstein* focused upon the creation of life in a laboratory. The creature that emerged was estranged, or alienated, and the emergence of this distorted figure can be read as a cautionary tale, a warning about the detached empirical mode of inquiry that isolates itself from life. If we look back across American literature, we can see that there was scientific romance in Nathaniel Hawthorne's "The Birthmark" (1843) and "Rappaccini's Daughter" (1844). Edgar Allan Poe is a precursor to science fiction with "The Great Balloon Hoax" and in "The Unparalleled Adventure of One Hans Pfall" (1835), which speaks of "the application of scientific principles to the actual passage between the earth and the moon." Poe emphasized ratiocination in his detective stories like the "Murders at the Rue Morgue." Robert A. Heinlein speculated in "Realistic Future Science Fiction" that science fiction would be "realistic speculation about possible future events, based solidly on adequate knowledge of the real world, past and present, and on a thorough understanding of the nature and significance of the scientific method."[45]

Rock music songs have also occasionally speculated about the future. (More often, they evoke feelings and thoughts about relationships and places here and now in the present.) Michael Moorcock, who edited *New Worlds* magazine, was among those who realized the connection between science fiction and the rise of rock music by writing lyrics for bands like Hawkwind and Blue Öyster Cult. *New Worlds* was a resource for the New Wave in British science fiction, as were the *Dangerous Visions* anthologies edited by Harlan Ellison. James Blish, meanwhile, encouraged science fiction to develop with scientific inquiry and literary quality.[46]

When rock music meets with science fiction it encounters a medium that is engaged in presenting the apparently unexplainable and one that makes use of imagination to convey a sense of wonder, a moment of awe, an aura of mystery. Rock and science fiction are related in their uses of myth, fantasy, and archetypal imagery. Of course, some science fiction writers, like Samuel R. Delany, distinguish fantasy from science fiction by suggesting that science fiction deals with the possible, with what has not happened, while fantasy deals with the impossible. Science fiction may have character action that is "in accord of what we know of the physically explainable universe." For this Delany coined the word subjunctivity. Following this idea, science fiction writer Joanna Russ affirms science fiction's connection with actuality and possibility as "one of its chief pleasures."[47]

Fan Culture: Rock as a Mass Cultural Phenomenon

Rock music and science fiction are interesting to study in tandem because they both have large fan bases. Rock has become a mass cultural phenomenon. The images and practices of rock popular culture have become part of a public dream or fantasy. Rock music artists, appealing to imagination and fantasy, have made extensive use of science fiction motifs and mythological resources. Science fiction likewise has a large fan base and has a pervasive presence in film and popular television programming. Producers are quite aware that appeals to imagination and the fantastic sell products. Bands signed to contracts likewise know that the imagery of science fiction and fantasy is shaped into a product and that their record companies approve of a rock song that gains life in the market economy. However, many bands that practice the science fiction edge of rock appear to have made a commitment to asserting that imaginative creation can transcend such commercialization.

Bands recognize that each audience is a particular interpretive community. Rock audiences appropriate songs and images and their responses reflect the kinds of interests that their listeners bring to the music. Among heavy metal fans, for example, there are those who embrace one band enthusiastically while vigorously rejecting another, as both Robert Walser and Deena Weinstein have pointed out in their studies of the genre. Across the variety of rock music genres there are publications, zines, web chatrooms, conventions, clubs, and concerts that become interpretive spaces. This phenomenon is similar to the fanzines and conventions of science fiction fans.[48]

The relationship between audience and performer, often lost with industrialization, is revived in science fiction reader culture and in rock fan cultures.[49] American science fiction and rock music both are engaged in the deliberate construction of fandom. This sense of interaction with audiences goes back to the original dissemination of rock on records and the periodical distribution of science fiction. When science fiction emerged in the pulp magazines of the 1930s and 1940s, Gernsback and Campbell included letters by readers in their magazine publications and they encouraged science fiction fan meetings. As a result, a subculture developed. (Market distribution keeps storytellers in contact with the expectations of the audience and publishers. This tends to encourage formula.) The fan base of rock music has developed through concerts and airplay. Audiences become fans of particular bands and merchandising runs parallel with this.

Rock music fans and science fiction fans both develop a keen knowledge of the codes and signals of their genres.[50] Literary critic Robert Scholes has pointed out that a reader must know codes that are used in a genre. The reader recognizes that fiction differs from nonfiction and knows how to assemble narrative elements "into a coherent story." This reader must have enough cultural information to make sense of a story's language and images and cultural and historical reference points have to be understood.[51] This is also true of avid rock music listeners.

The rock music fan is immersed in the songs, images, stage-theatrics, and press commentary surrounding the band that he or she follows. Some fans participate in conversations, or the online chatter of blogs. They wear concert t-shirts, engage in file sharing of songs, collect memorabilia, or imitate the visual images and styles that resonate with them. This occurs across a wide spectrum of different musical styles and sub-cultural rock communities. Science fiction, likewise, offers an unpredictable variety, as Brian Atteberg and Veronica Hollinger assert. There are influences, conversations, shared materials and intertextuality. A new concept, like Isaac Asimov's three laws of robotics, is quickly taken up by other writers who try out alternatives. Samuel R. Delany describes science fiction reading as unique since readers draw upon their knowledge of the figures in past science fiction stories. Science fiction requires a new way of reading says Delany: a use of knowledge from outside the text that often comes from previous exposure to science fiction texts and films. Information sets off a chain of associations in such a science fiction reader. When the references are not quite explicit a keen reader immersed in the genre will pick up the nuances.[52]

This intertextual practice is similar in rock music, where imitation of styles, sounds, and musical approaches may lead to creative breakthroughs. William Tenn (Phillip Klass) viewed science fiction writers as artists who act like jazz musicians riffing on each other's work.[53] Rock musicians work similarly, listening to each other's work and developing their own sounds and ideas amid the hooks and clichés of the genre. The rock music listener learns the codes that are used in heavy metal, blues rock, or in progressive rock. The listener can relate what he or she is hearing to a band's history of recordings, to comments in the rock press, or to conversations among rock music fans.

In science fiction, Atteberg and Hollinger point out, there are recurring images that are emblematic of the concerns of the genre, images that "become iconic through repetition."[54] They remind us that stories have used a variety of tropes and genre conventions ranging from the experiment gone wrong (*Frankenstein*) to the lost colony (James Blish's "Surface Tensions") and from the alien invasion to the cosmic gadget. Science fiction stories have explored utopias and dystopias, virtual reality, the stranded alien (E.T.), post-apocalypse and the new Eden, and the Galactic Empire (Asimov's Foundation Trilogy). One might link aspects of modernism with science fiction's probing of social issues and the trials and tribulations of modernity such as exploitation, recession, war, genocide, totalitarian repression, or violence. A rock band like Rush, for example, will address such themes within science fiction narratives.

Science Fiction Themes

When science writer and novelist C.P. Snow delivered the Rede Lectures in 1959 he identified a rift between science education and literary learning in Britain that he called "the two cultures."[55] Aldous Huxley, likewise, writing *Literature and Science,* recognized that scientific rationality and myth have often operated on separate tracks. Huxley could look back to his own ancestors for clues to how to heal this apparent divide between literary art and science. His grand-uncle was the poet Mathew Arnold and his grandfather was Thomas Henry Huxley, "Darwin's bulldog," the great exponent of scientific education. In the latter part of the Nineteenth-Century, positivism, following the lead of August Comte, consigned the mythical to some archaic and primitive past that had been left behind by scientific advancements. Yet, neither of Huxley's progenitors bought into that view. Arnold believed that culture would triumph over anarchy and he asserted that there was a great future for poetry as a source of myth and hope as the appeal of religion waned in a secular society. T.H. Huxley remained a staunch Darwinian and he did not subscribe to Comte's views or to a reductive science. As the twentieth century began, science uncovered the mysteries of relativity, quantum, and radioactivity. Aldous Huxley and his brother, the biologist Julian Huxley, frequently discussed advances in science and Aldous Huxley fashioned his science fiction dystopia *Brave New World* (1932). In the twentieth century scientists went on to explore the atom and nuclear fission, the cell and DNA, and other wonders. Huxley wrote *The Perennial Philosophy,* suggesting that myth and mythopoetic thinking is not far away from creative scientific thinking. More recently, speculative scientists like Freeman Dyson have discussed imagined worlds. Physicists recognize the curiosities of physics. Cognitive scientists explore the complexities of consciousness. Science fiction writers bring together the arts and the sciences in their fictional dreams.

Nearly a century ago, in *Daedelus, or Science and the Future* (1924), J.B.S. Haldane turned to myth when he asserted that "the physical inventor is always a Prometheus."[56] The researcher, like the mythical hero, is engaged in a quest. So too is the creative artist: the musician, or the science fiction writer. "The unknown is an overwhelming presence in science fiction," observes Gary K. Wolfe, who refers to the "dialectic of the known and the unknown" in the genre. He points out that the transformation of the unknown into the known is central to science fiction narrative and often "accounts for its conventions and formulae."[57]

The future is something that is unknown for all of us, and it is often a subject of science fiction. Yet, science fiction is also very much about now. Neil Gaiman, in his foreword to an edition of Samuel R. Delany's *Einstein Intersection*, asserts that the view that science fiction is "fundamentally predictive" of the future is a misconception. Rather, science fiction is often concerned with the present. A story may reflect, react against, "or illuminate the prejudices, fears, and assumptions of the period in which it was written," he observes.[58] Gaiman discusses how Delany weaves myth into his work and his use of the figure of Orpheus. He sees the novel as "an examination of myths and of why we need them, and why we tell them."[59] Myth becomes a resource for critiquing technology, imagining future cities, speculating on whether it would be possible to communicate with life from distant planets. It becomes a means for interrogating society. Critics like Larry McCaffrey have argued that transformations in science fiction appear to have a relationship with cultural dislocations and technological changes. This includes multi-media, information as a key global resource, ads, spectacle, simulations and copies.[60]

Science Fiction and Social Critique

Science fiction has often taken on the role of interrogating society. Considering the work of Wells, Huxley, and Orwell, the writer Doris Lessing once suggested that writing with reference to the future was "the only lever to nudge the present in a better direction."[61] Science fiction performs this cultural work when it boldly questions social assumptions. In *New Maps of Hell* (1961) Kingsley Amis described science fiction's role as "a means of dramatizing social inquiry [...] a fictional mode in which cultural tendencies can be isolated and judged."[62] This mode of inquiry has made science fiction a useful resource for rock music social satirists like Frank Zappa and for social critics like Neil Peart, who critiques totalitarian control and asserts the importance of liberty, creativity, and individuality.

Science fiction enters the realm of social criticism by making use of myth and anticipations of the future. One may recall that Mary Shelley's *Frankenstein* begins with a reference to the Promethean myth. Her story brings this ancient myth into connection with medical science, chemistry, anatomy, and galvanism. Ultimately, the novel questions how mankind seizes the fire in the act of investigation and creation and then isolates its creation. In *Frankenstein* the creature is without nurturance and moral sensibility.[63] Frankenstein, of course, most often represents the monstrous because of Boris Karloff's film adaptation. The creature of Victor Frankenstein's bold experiment has been interpreted in a variety of ways. When Edgar Winter created his instrumental "Frankenstein" he was tapping into a figure of innovation and energy in a piece with synthesizer effects, guitar riffs, and his multi-instrument virtuosity. David Bowie, Ozzy Osborne, and others have tapped into the sense of alienation and monstrosity and in their transformations they have challenged conventional social norms.

Bands like Black Sabbath, Judas Priest, and Rush have appealed to apocalyptic and dystopian narratives. The dystopian novel is a precursor to today's cyberpunk and the dystopian narratives of punk and metal bands. Yvgeny Zamyatin's *We* or Ray Bradbury's *Farenheit 451* are social critiques that are as laced with angst as was the grating grunge of Kurt Cobain and Nirvana. Aldous Huxley's *Brave New World* provided an expression of the Twentieth Century age of anxiety. In a letter to Ketheran Roberts, Huxley wrote that *Brave New World* was "on the horror of the Wellsian utopia and the revolt against it."[64] Iron Maiden has evoked this spirit of revolt on *Brave New World*, their last album to achieve gold in the United States.

The first wave of rock musicians grew up during and after the Second World War, when there were many apocalyptic stories. This was a time, observes Gary K. Wolfe, "in which survivors struggled to revive and build some semblance of civilization." The "novels of the period were designed as warnings," Wolfe points out. "The focus of science fiction almost seemed to shift from its essentially optimistic vision of a conquerable universe to a darker, nightmarish vision of demonic forces being unleashed by an unwitting human race."[65] Novels turned toward existentialism or concern about the nuclear age, as in Pat Frank's novels of the 1950s, *Forbidden Area* (1956) and *Alas Babylon* (1959), and Nevil Shute's *On the Beach* (1959). Brian Aldiss points to the "new pessimism" of the genre in stories in *Astounding*.[66] There were atomic warfare apocalypse stories and catastrophe-natural disaster stories.

Science fiction as social criticism emerged forcefully in the magazines of the 1950s. It pointed to a time of new technologies, advertising, and the development of the computer.[67] Kurt Vonnegut's *Player Piano* and Kornbluth and Pohl's *Space Merchants* (1958) are examples. There were fables of power like James Blish's *A Case of Conscience* and Arthur C. Clarke's *Childhood's End*. The images that came along with these critiques were material for fertile imaginations of the rock musicians and their listeners who read science fiction stories and watched science fiction films. The parodies and pastiche of Frank Zappa and David Bowie are examples of imaginative uses of science fiction's capacity for social critique.

The dystopian theme has appeared often in rock music. David Bowie turned toward Orwell's *1984* as he developed his album *Diamond Dogs*. Judas Priest created many songs with dark, apocalyptic themes and other heavy metal bands have followed likewise. However, the sharpest social satire came from Frank Zappa, who jested and jousted with the abuses of authority and power in society, government and the music industry. Zappa offered a comment on our world through irony and parody.[68] This creative maven's intertextuality drew from film, art, television, commercials, pop music and other media and science fiction became one of his vehicles for social commentary. *Joe's Garage, Act I and Act II and Act III*, utilize satire and a quasi-science fiction narrative for social critique. Joe plays in a garage band. His girlfriend Mary runs off with the road crew of a rock star and their bus leaves her stranded in Miami, where she has to participate in a wet T-shirt contest to earn money for a bus home. Meanwhile, Joe has an encounter with Lucille, a girl at a fast food place, and he contracts VD. The song's narrative begins to move toward science fiction dystopia as he joins Ron Hoover's "church," a thinly veiled reference to L. Ron Hubbard's Church of Scientology. Here he meets the Central Scrutinizer, an information collector, and he is taught about sexual fulfillment through machines. Joe has sex with Model XQJ-37, Sy Borg. He destroys the device and is sent to prison, where he is sodomized by record executives. The Central Scrutinizer blames the music for Joe's demise. Joe gives up music for work in a pastry kitchen. In Zappa's lyrics the George Orwell image of Big Brother appears in the Central Scrutinizer and reflects concern about government surveillance and social management that is done by machines.

Technology

Progressive rock musicians make much use of technology. In fact, they have been criticized for burying their acts in rows of synthesizers, an array of pedals, and stacks of Marshall amplifiers. Yet, from ELP to Rush, rock artists have responded negatively to any encroachment upon individuality by mechanism. Creative artists generally do not respond well to visions of a totalitarian state that would stifle their individuality and creativity. We have seen how on ELP's *Tarkus*, human creativity and expressiveness is contrasted with an oppressive machine-culture. In Rush's work, technology is appreciated but individualism appears to be the higher value.

Science fiction frequently has shown an avid embrace of technology and a marked emphasis on technological innovation. However, science's close connection with technology has aroused some critics. Michael Polyani, for example, called for a quest to rediscover knowledge in myth and religion as a balance to technological society and scientific vision. For technology/science, he wrote, "has become the greatest source of dangerous fallacies today."[69] Lewis Mumford also critiqued technology and science in *The Pentagon of Power* (1970), calling quantifiable science "a religion."[70] Mumford opposed optimism about scientific progress, scientific methods, and the assumption that everything is quantifiable and can be predicted and controlled by humans. Dystopian fiction repeats this theme.Some non-fiction writers on technology have also urged caution. Victor Ferkiss has suggested that the human dependence of humanity on machines might become anti-evolutionary.[71] With the image of the robot a science fiction icon, has arisen the fear of automation that has persisted from Fritz Lang's *Metropolis* and its chromium robot and underground work-force through Norbert Wiener's cybernetics.

The City of the Future

Rock music celebrates the city and mythologizes it. Rock is often a creature of the urban world. Rock music scenes begin in cities: folk/rock in L.A., heavy metal in Birmingham, new wave punk at CBGB's and Max's in New York City, grunge in Seattle. Rock bands tour city to city and sing of "London Calling," New York nights, "Detroit Rock City," "L.A. Woman." Songs address the harsh reality and mystique of New York, London, L.A., Chicago, Cleveland, and dozens of other places. In some of its more imaginative moments the places rock mentions are literally out of this world.[72]

The cultural theorist Raymond Williams saw science fiction as responding to "the crisis of metropolitan experience" initiated by industrialization.[73] He cautioned that control and planning of the human environment could be a source of dehumanization. David Ketterer points out: "Science fiction cities tend toward Babylon rather than toward the New Jerusalem."[74] Theodore Roszak offered a similar critique in *Where the Wasteland Ends*: "The supercity alone guarantees the utmost in artificiality, which is the unquestioned goal of progress."[75] Rock has both reveled in the city and rebelled against it.

In Rush's *Clockwork Angels* the city and country opposition appears in a science fiction context. Owen, from rural Barrel Harbor, lives a pre-planned life in the domain of the Watchmaker, the overseer. One day, Owen hops on a steamliner bound for Crown City. He encounters Chronos Square and Poseidon City and the Seven Cities of Gold. The cities of legend are disappointing and not how they seemed to him in storybooks. Yet, they have their own character. Even so, Rush's *Clockwork Angels* suggests a pervasive aspect of the city and the oppressive centrality of the Watchmaker, who represents the kind of rationalized control that the English poet William Blake once called "mind forged manacles." The Anarchist calls for a break with this stifling control.

What cultural critic Raymond Williams referred to as "metropolitan experience" is a fact of many of our lives. John Naisbitt's *Megatrends* speaks of "Bosnywash," or a continuous corridor between Boston, New York, and Washington. In "The Roads Must Roll," Robert A. Heinlein looked toward a future of urban sprawl from Chicago to St. Louis that "met near Bloomington, Illinois," and William Gibson, in *Necromancer*, depicts an urban society that extends from Boston to Atlanta.[76]

Cities in science fiction include: the technological city, the city in space, the imperial city, according to one classification.[77] Gary K. Wolfe sets forth a series of characteristics of the city in science fiction narratives: The city is centralized, collective, xenophobic, authoritarian, unnatural, of the past, regressively technological, superfluous, chaotic, mythic.[78] Add to this overpopulated Babylon and the dangers of over-populated "hive" cities in Samuel Delany's *Dahlgren* (1975), Asimov's mechanized city of *The Caves of Steel*, and those of Arthur C. Clarke's *The City and the Stars* (1958). Descendants of E.M. Forster's *The Machine Stops* are works that deal with automated cities in which people do little but involve themselves in games. Or, one may look back at Fritz Lang's *Metropolis* (1926), which offers a powerful film portrayal of a subterranean city. In the film we see impoverished workers who toil while a utopia exists above. *Metropolis* recalls images in Wells' *The Time Machine*.[79] In Wells's novel the year is 802,701 and the Morlocks and Eloi are in a limited world atop the ruins of what was London. Wells parodied William Morris's utopia in *News from Nowhere* (1891) and he developed the city image into a "call for reform."[80] Raymond Williams pointed out that H.G. Wells' *The Time Machine* presented an evolutionary dimension to class divisions in the city, projecting them into the future.[81] In Rush's *Clockwork Angels* Neil Peart and Kevin J. Anderson position the creative action of the Anarchist against the totalitarian social structures of the Clockmaker. The ideal city that Owen has read about presents him with new challenges.

The city has appeared in a great variety of forms in science fiction, including descriptions of futuristic cities of other planets. A few examples are:

- Samuel R. Delany's *The Fall of the Towers* (1970) was conceived as a three volume work. The third novel is *City of a Thousand Suns*: a communal utopia.
- James Blish's *Cities in Flight* (1955–1962) is a tetralogy of novels about imperial cities that were collected into one volume in 1970. Blish's story might be described as an epic space opera. *A Life for the Stars* (1962), the last of four novels written, provides a more detailed look at the flying cities. *The Triumph of Time* is the last novel in the sequence.
- *The City and the Stars* (1953) by Arthur C. Clarke is set a billion years in the future in a city called Diasper, a technological city. This city is managed by the Central

Computer and none of its inhabitants venture outside to a barren planet Earth. The protagonist, Alvin, learns of Lys, a more pastoral environment and a fierce battle that took place in the past. A spaceship that was buried long ago can still be used. The stars of the title suggest the desire to transcend the city and to explore the universe.

- J.G. Ballard wrote a series of space adventures and disaster novels focused upon inner states of perception rather than the outer space of much previous science fiction. Ballard veered away from the typical materials of science fiction and addressed the dehumanizing aspects of the city in *Crash*, *Concrete Island* (1974), and *High Rise* (1975). In the latter novel the residents of a high rise apartment building revert to a primitive state as things go wrong in their building. The floors of the building- lower, middle, and upper- begin to designate a stratified society of warring classes.

Rock songs frequently bring us to cities and approach them with hard-nosed realistic descriptions or with fantasies. Rock songs sometimes bring us on highways to hell or into nightmares. Such songs open out expansive horizons and transform into chilling enclosures like heartbreak hotels. There may be the wonder of new vistas sharply followed by constricting traps. Indeed, this may be a metaphor for the music business itself, as in the Eagles' "Hotel California." In the Eagles' song the dark desert highway is open to the breeze and a light is up ahead. However, tiredness, heaviness, and dimness soon set in and the narrator, entranced at first by enticements, is pulled into an underworld from which he can never leave.

We are reminded by rock songs like this that myths and folk tales have long influenced narrative. Behind the modern city lie long traditions of ancient experience and myth. Following myth critics like Northrup Frye, we might see rock music's romance as mediating between myth and contemporary forms. Frye described science fiction as "a mode of romance with a strong inherent tendency to myth." He asserted that the hero of romance travels through a realm where ordinary laws of nature are suspended.[82]

In the rock concert ordinary reality is suspended. The rock vocalist is a romantic figure, raising a microphone like a talisman, strutting among guitar wielding associates and a mad drummer creating fire. The ordinary laws of life are indeed set aside as their song breaks forth with images of ogres, witches, and wondrous cities, bringing us to those places where the mundane world is re-enchanted.

THREE

The Jefferson Starship Takes Off

The San Francisco Scene

Rock music was a crucial resource for the sixties counterculture. Myth and magic came along for the ride. Rock coalesced with lifestyle choices and personal expression. Lengthy hair, bright colored clothing, flowers, beads, jeans, miniskirts, hats, and glasses became sign-systems indicating participation in this relaxation of cultural conventions. Jefferson Airplane was at the center of this movement. They took these signs and turned them into signifiers: images that showed their participation in a mythic, idealized, alternative community. Grace Slick joined vocalist Marty Balin when her band the Great Society dissolved. Paul Kantner and Jorma Kaukonen and Jack Casady soon joined them. They drew upon folk music and the blues and their music unified youthful audiences into a subculture in the San Francisco Haight-Ashbury scene.[1] Jefferson Airplane was the first San Francisco band to sign with a major record label, RCA, and they broke upon the national scene with Grace Slick's plaintive vocals on "Somebody to Love" and "White Rabbit," their drug-culture song recalling *Alice in Wonderland*. Jefferson Airplane was involved with hallucinogens and the quest for alternate lifestyles that brought the counterculture into contact with psychedelic rock. The folklore of the people that J.G. Frazer writes about in *The Golden Bough* (1890) seemed to be at the center of Jefferson Airplane's communal message. The concert became like a sacred rite for the fans of the San Francisco area bands the Jefferson Airplane and the Grateful Dead. In 1970, Jefferson Airplane broke up. Kaukonen and Casady started the blues band Hot Tuna. Paul Kantner's science fiction interlude, *Blows Against the Empire,* launched the band in new directions. Then these musicians reconstituted their musical identity as the Jefferson Starship and evolved into a popular recording group in the 1970s.

Notions of shamanic art were at the center of the explorations of the Jefferson Airplane and the Grateful Dead, as drummer Mickey Hart has pointed out. If we look at J.G. Frazer's second chapter of *The Golden Bough,* we read about the king of sacred rites, or shaman, a role that these bands adopted. Frazer proceeds to specify categories of magic: sympathetic, contagious, or "contact," and homeopathic, or healing. The ethos of the Jefferson Airplane and the Grateful Dead implied that music and community ritual were all of these. In 1967, audiences became entranced by the outpourings of the Jefferson Airplane, the Grateful Dead, and other San Francisco area bands. In the San Francisco scene, rock's base in the working class persisted, particularly in the blues rock stemming from the British invasion bands like the Rolling Stones, the Who, the Kinks, and the Animals. Meanwhile, psychedelic bands like Pink Floyd, Procol Harum, the Moody Blues, and the Nice created a basis for progressive rock between 1966 and 1970. Blues and folk based groups like Jefferson Airplane and the Grateful Dead would continue to foster one brand of hippie consciousness and music, while the emergence of British progressive rock would follow with Emerson, Lake and Palmer, Yes, Genesis, Gentle Giant, Renaissance, and Jethro Tull between 1970 and 1975. The work of Jefferson Airplane is part of this psychedelic phase and exemplifies the musical quest and mythical quest for freedom and transcendence that was vitally present in sixties counterculture.

Jefferson Airplane, in their hallucinogenic, creative outpourings on *Surrealistic Pillow* appeared to be the Dionysian band *par excellence.* Greek mythology speaks of Dionysius, the wine-god, as a force of creativity, destruction, and renewal. In the Greek drama *Antigone,* the Chorus of senators lifts their hands and voices in appeal to Dionysius for healing and transformation for the city of Thebes. Rock music has been linked with the Dionysian by some of its fiercest critics, from Allan Bloom in *The Closing of the American Mind* (1986) to Robert Pattison's *The Triumph of Vulgarity.* Yet, this creative impulse toward breaking free and remaking the world is also one of rock music's strengths. The Dionysian consciousness expresses itself in radical novelty, a willingness to risk ecstasy and chaos. The ancient Greek drama *The Bacchae* by Euripedes warned against having emotion overcome reason. The chorus in *Antigone* indeed appeals to Dionysius as the patron of Thebes but also counsels against humans who dare to exceed the boundaries of moderation.

Rock is immoderate: it seeks highs of ecstasy and wonder and it plays with illusion. Science fiction soon came into the group's songs and album concepts as singer Grace Slick and guitarist Paul Kantner sang about a group of people escaping earth in a hijacked starship in *Blows Against the Empire* (1971), an album nominated for a Hugo Award (but no award was given that year). Kantner imagined spaceships and wrote "Let's Go Together" and Grace Slick opened side two of *Blows Against the Empire* by singing of sunrise, as if of a new age dawning.

The makeup and stage shows of David Bowie and Alice Cooper and dozens of progressive and heavy metal bands are theatrical play and expressions of imagination, Eros, and breaking out of "straight" society. They challenge inherited modes of perception and seek a non-repressive social order. Play, spontaneity, and fantasy challenge conventional boundaries of order with a kaleidoscopic variety, a sensuous immediacy in which improvisation is allowed to happen. The creative rock band oscillates between work and play, thinking and feeling, fantasy and realism, concept and imagination. It lives within musical structure and ventures to break out musically and sometimes theatrically, wandering into strangeness or tempest and passion. Rock bands often seem to defy order.

Myth and science fiction in the Jefferson Airplane catalog appear to be allied with a search for transcendence. The late 1960s brought a turbulent period of countercultural resistance to the Vietnam War characterized by student protests, calls for change in the social imagination, and drug-induced quests for transcendence. The "sixties," a period that several sociologists suggest extends from about 1965 through the early 1970s, was a time of idealism and socio-political restlessness. The youth culture realized a close connection with rock music. For some listeners, rock music became associated with drugs, sex, spiritualism, or a quest for higher consciousness. With this idealism arose progressive movements in civil rights, feminism, environmentalism, justice and equality, and opposition to war.

Paul Kantner's science fiction recordings suggest a sixties spirit that sought Avalon, an ideal of a mystical place, a new consciousness that would reconstitute society.[2] In effect, the narrators of the songs on Kantner's *Blows Against the Empire* wish to escape, to sail away to create a new world. Theodore Roszak viewed the counterculture as a loose collection of people who felt disaffiliated. Timothy Leary believed that spiritual development could come from LSD and consciousness-raising. Todd Gitlin, observing America through a sociological lens, observed that the counterculture sought pluralism and pursued issues with political resonance and a sense of community free from the mainstream. Science fiction writers veiled social and political concerns in their stories. The vision of some writers, like Paul Kantner, or Michael Moorcock in Britain, fit well with these counter-cultural approaches.

The Jefferson Airplane rose amid a series of cultural symbols that expressed for some people an "anything goes" freedom. Rock supported an ethos of rebellion. It coupled with a negation of convention and "the system." The rock counterculture was never a united, monolithic group. Some of its listeners sought what the counter-cultural attorney Charles Reich, in his book *The Greening of America*, called "Consciousness III." Others fiercely declared their independence and sincerely wished to change the world. They became involved in civil rights, woman's rights, or in social and political concerns. Some rock fans simply enjoyed the music. Evidently, some of the Jefferson Airplane's audience were more interested in listening to music and getting high than in fostering the transformation of society. They protested what they felt to be repressive and then participated in hedonism and expressive indulgence. Indeed, some individuals likely wanted to step out of the society altogether. Others stayed on in their communities, spending time with family and friends, working their jobs, or attending school. Meanwhile, they listened as the Jefferson Airplane pointed toward mythical consciousness and toward new possibilities for the culture. America persisted through the years of the Nixon administration and Watergate, years that saw Woodstock, Altamont, the rise of progressive rock, folk-pop singer-songwriters, and the growing vitality of Motown rhythm and blues.

These were years of change for the Jefferson Airplane, as they morphed into the commercially successful Jefferson Starship.

Blows Against the Empire was an experimental concept album, and Kantner and Slick came up with what they called the Planet Rock and Roll Orchestra. The *Sunfighter* (1971) album followed. Jefferson Starship appeared in 1974. "Miracles" on the *Red Octopus* album was a huge single, reaching number one on the *Billboard* charts. The band's *Earth* (1978) album offered another of their biggest hits, "Count on Me," which reached number eight, and the hit song "Runaway."

In a *Creem* review that began by insulting ELO (Electric Light Orchestra), Jefferson Starship's music was called "faceless, expert and bland."[3] The suggestion in the *Creem* article is that a quality of "seriousness" may be embraced in the lyrics of Bob Dylan, Elvis Costello, Michael Stipe of REM, or in Peter Gabriel and some Neil Young, while one ought to disparage the "vapid" fantasies of other artists. However, the rock of Jefferson Airplane was valued for its relationship with the cultural underground.[4]

Transformation

The years during which some of the members of the Jefferson Airplane reinvented themselves as Jefferson Starship were a time of seeking. Some seekers turned East, quite seriously exploring meditation and spirituality. They pursued alternatives in Eastern religions and theosophy and followed the encouragement of figures like Ram Das (Richard Alpert) to "be here now."[5] Rock musicians like George Harrison, Pete Townshend, and John McLaughlin turned East for Enlightenment. For others, sitars were exotic and talk of chakras was trendy. Esotericism and new age approaches could be co-opted by capitalist entrepreneurs as marketing strategies. Hallucinogenic drugs were tools for a spiritual quest for some people and recreational escape for others. Questioning of authority came with questioning the reliance on technocratic culture and a desire for communal relationship rather than atomization. Many individuals sought peace but had to deal with an often unsuspected undertow of violence present in the counterculture and the wider society. Myth or mythopoetic awareness offered a narrative that was different from conventional daily life in Britain, or in America. Some psychedelic bands, or progressive bands, seized upon these alternatives.

The Jefferson Airplane and other San Francisco bands entered psychedelic music in explorations of human consciousness. Nancy Reid refers to the "maintenance of a healthy mythic imagination."[6] She provides a quote from Jerry Garcia in which he says that when the band gets onstage what they want is "to be transformed from ordinary players into extraordinary ones, like forces of a larger consciousness."[7] The ritual aspect of a Grateful Dead concert was compared by Joseph Campbell to a Dionysian festival. Reid mentions that the band generates "controlled trances" and says: "These shifts in consciousness may be experienced as metaphoric deaths or journeys to a mythic world."[8]

Paul Kantner's turn toward science fiction concepts came during the days that band members were drifting away to other concerns and Jefferson Airplane was dissolving. Kantner had grown up reading science fiction. As a teen, Kantner was fond of C.S. Lewis's *Prelandra* and *Out of the Silent Planet*. He also read novels by Robert Heinlein, like *Methuselah's Children*, which serves as a basis for the story line in his album. (Kantner asked for permission from Heinlein for the use of his images and Heinlein readily agreed.) Kantner developed the project with Grace Slick during a time in which their romance brought pregnancy and a child, China Kantner. The idea of new birth intersects with dreams of a counter-cultural utopia. They will free their child from government and realize a life of freedom. *Blows Against the Empire* was the first recording to make use of the Jefferson Starship name. The record was a silver LP with Russian art on the album cover and a collage inside. The record reached #20 on the *Billboard* album charts.

The transformation of Jefferson Airplane into Jefferson Starship was a gradual process. Paul Kantner's work on his record began after the departure of drummer Spencer Dryden from Jefferson Airplane. Kantner's album was recorded at Pacific High Recording Studios and at Wally Heider's recording studio in San Francisco. Phil Sawyer was the recording engineer. They brought Jack Casady and Joey Covington into the sessions, along with Jorma Kaukonen and Peter Kaukonen, at a time when they were involved with their band Hot Tuna. Also contributing to the recording were members of the Grateful Dead, Jerry

Garcia and Mickey Hart, David Freiberg of Quicksilver Messenger Service, and David Crosby and Graham Nash, who often recorded at Wally Heider's studio. Graham Nash, in his autobiography *Wild Tales*, notes that David Crosby was involved with the Jefferson Airplane members and with Grateful Dead members in a group they called the Planet Earth Rock and Roll Orchestra.[9]

The musical collaborations that developed during this time unfolded in a variety of directions. Crosby, Stills and Kantner wrote "Wooden Ships," which appeared on *Volunteers* (1969). The song was recorded again for *Crosby, Stills and Nash* (1969) and *So Far* (1974). "Wooden Ships" is apocalyptic. After a nuclear war the wooden ships seek shelter. This group would sail away to freedom—not on a spaceship this time. They are leaving and not needed by the culture they will escape from.

Paul Kantner's enthusiasm for science fiction was matched by David Crosby and Graham Nash. David Crosby writes in his autobiography *Long Time Gone* (1988, 2007) that he "soaked up huge amounts of science fiction."[10] He added: "if you want an education, read." Graham Nash mentions reading Ray Bradbury's *The Silver Locusts* while traveling and being held for his papers at the airport by immigration officials in Vancouver.[11] Returning home, he wrote a song on the cover pages of the book. Nash's self-education, however, has primarily been in photography and visual art, Beat poetry, and social-political concerns. He studied the art of M.C. Escher and Expressionist art and he has practiced the art of photography for many years[12] Nash claims that his songs are simple and do not approach the complexities of some of the songs written by Crosby or by Stephen Stills.[13]

Blows Against the Empire

They gathered to produce an improvised free-form rock on songs that were mostly created by Paul Kantner, alone or in collaboration with others. Kantner's acoustic guitar and his banjo playing on his cover of Rosalie Sorrel's "Baby Tree" contributed to the folk music inspired edge of the album. Grace Slick's piano playing served as one of the musical centers for the recording and it seems that her shimmering multi-tracked vocals on her own composition, "Sunrise," took the album to the higher dimension toward which it aspired. The overall theme was one of countercultural idealism typified by a breaking away from the constraints of earth. The power and harmonies that Grace Slick achieved on that song certainly seemed to transcend what one of Shakespeare's characters, Lorenzo, once called "this muddy vesture of decay." Likewise, the vocal harmonies on "Have You Seen the Stars Tonite" are another highlight of the album.

The free-flowing jam quality of the record is a clear match with the freedom sought by this collective. The story line says that they seek to break free of the oppression of Uncle Samuel. "Mau Mau (Amerikon)" begins the album with Kantner's vocal out front and a raggedy proto-grunge sound. There is an admonition to celebrate and play and to come alive. "The Baby Tree" offers a folk song played on banjo that brings us to an imaginary island where the babies grow on trees and fall to earth into the loving arms of happy couples. With "Let's Go Together" the collective joins together in an energetic ensemble that sounds like a live performance. The energy created by acoustic guitars supports characteristic chorus vocals. Kantner's singing is joined by those of others and Grace Slick's voice cuts through on top of them, holding out notes. In "A Child Is Coming" the group gathers before dawn, tripping on acid, wondering at the possibilities of the break of dawn and a new day. Kantner introduces the image of the park and claims that he will be the diplomat there. We hear a guitar chords-driven song with bright lead guitar lines. Slick's vocal rises in the background, echoing the lines sung by Kantner. David Crosby joins his vocal with other vocalists on this song and on "Have You Seen the Stars Tonite" on Side Two. Graham Nash mixed the second side of the *Blows Against the Empire* album, while "acid drenched."[14]

On Side Two, Grace Slick's powerful female vocal almost reshapes the texture of the album, piercing into the sunrise. She sings both vocal parts, overdubbed. "Have You Seen the Stars Tonite" adds to this vocal peak of this record and Kantner's 12-string guitar drones out octaves and fifths in an unusual alternate tuning in open C. Background vocals are overdubbed and processed. Sound effects suggest engines and the starship in flight. There is an inserted audio piece from a George Pal *War of Worlds* film from 1953 in which a woman cries out to get free and get out and a ray gun fires. The sound effects contribute to the narrative which continues on Side Two. Once Grace Slick's vocals take flight on "Sunrise," the song blends into the narrative of "Hijack." The group seizes a transport to the orbiting starship and then ventures off into space. They leave orbit in "Home" and this leads into "Have You Seen the Stars Tonite." The ship's engines are prepared in "X-M." A mutiny is fought for control of the spaceship. The idealists question if they ought to surrender or keep going. The idealists win the struggle. A gravity sling-shot propels the ship around the sun and out of the solar system.

Meanwhile, the band's transition to Jefferson Starship was under way. Vocalist Mary Balin, who had left Jefferson Airplane, would return later to Jefferson Starship and record the hit "Miracles" on *Red Octopus*. Jorma Kaukonen and Jack Cassady formed Hot Tuna. In 1971, *Sunfighter*, was released by Kantner and Slick. It included an ecologically-centered song, "Earth Mother," written by Jack Traylor, who was an English teacher and a friend of Kantner.

Jefferson Starship was more mainstream commercial than Jefferson Airplane. They took off on the *Billboard* charts in 1975. They played a free outdoor concert in New York's Central Park that year, as their *Red Octopus* album was released. That recording, with the hit single "Miracles," became a platinum album, selling thousands of copies. Of course, today you can purchase CDs or downloads of virtually all of the band's commercial output. The *Blows Against the Empire* recording has been remastered and issued with bonus tracks, such as Kantner's seven minute acoustic demo of "Hijack." In 1992, *Tales from the Mothership* emerged as a double-album recorded live at Roswell, New Mexico. The album included musicians Mark Aguilar, Jack Casady, and Papa John Creach. In 2008, *Tree of Liberty* included Jefferson Airplane and Jefferson Starship material. Cathy Richardson provides vocals in the absence of the retired Grace Slick. The new band includes David Frieberg, Danny Baldwin, and Jude Gold, replacing Aguilar.

Starships and Spaceships

The name Jefferson Starship calls to mind one of the iconic images of science fiction: the spaceship. When Jules Verne wrote his science fiction story *From the Earth to the Moon,* about sending space voyagers toward the moon, he indicated that rockets might be propelled by gunpowder. In 1970, NASA scientists anticipated that chemical propulsion rockets could travel at about 40,000 miles per hour. That July, American astronauts Neil Armstrong, Buzz Aldrin, and Michael Collins achieved the successful Apollo mission in which men walked on the moon. However, starships that could reach Alpha Centauri, over four light years away, remained a dream. NASA designed other missions to space, such as the Space Shuttle. There were the failures of the *Challenger* and of the *Columbia.* Satellites were sent into space at greater distances. To reach deeper points in space scientists needed to create ion thruster engines and plasma engines. Even so, these do not have enough propulsion to aim at the stars. To reach even the nearest of the stars would require further designs and a costly expenditure of fuel. Science fiction writer Robert Heinlein once said that if one could surpass 160 kilometers above earth one could extend that more easily to points in space more distant. As physicist Michio Kaku points out, that first 160 kilometers is the most expensive part of a launch, when a rocket ship is pushing upward against gravitational force.[15]

So, is a starship possible? The television series *Star Trek* popularized the idea, beginning in the 1960s. The Starship *Enterprise* was able to achieve warp speed and trace rapidly across space, "the final frontier." The Jefferson Starship imagined possibilities like that. They were a band in the spirit of late sixties revolution, yearning for social transformation. More than pointing toward any kind of technology, the starship idea suggested something cosmic, or the hope of transcendence. At first, this hope for cultural and personal transformation emerged in the context of the Kantner concept album, which was filled with the vision of science fiction.

As an avid reader of science fiction, Kantner knew that the spaceship had become an iconic image throughout the genre. When scientists began addressing the possibilities of rocket propulsion, science fiction writers began to use the image of the rocket frequently. In rock music iconography, the spaceship may be a symbol for launching and taking off, departure from convention and norms, or the aspirations of a band. In Kantner and Slick's science fiction-themed recording they recognized that a spaceship is also a habitat, or something like a house in which a group of like-minded people could travel in search of a new way of life.

The starship could be a universe unto itself. *Star Trek* provided a crew with something like a comfortable middle-class home that was often disrupted by hostile forces in the universe. In the 1950s, James Blish, one of the contributors to that series, wrote a series of novels in which cities of Earth are launched into space by using antigravity devices. Gene Wolfe, in his *Book of the Long Sun* series, has featured a spaceship that carries medieval city-states. Frank Herbert's *Destination: Void* (1966) presents spaceships managed by human brains, or Organic Mental Cores. The story suggests that artificial intelligence may one day operate the spaceships. The spaceship image continues to be familiar in recent fiction, television, and in Oscar nominated films like *The Martian* (2016).

The image of starships repeated throughout the 1970s in popular rock music album cover graphics with the bands Boston and Electric Light Orchestra (ELO). Starships burst into battle in George Lucas's *Star Wars* and carried voyagers to other solar systems in film, television, and science fiction novels. However, NASA was no closer to creating an interstellar rocket. In 2005 the Prometheus nuclear rocket was funded at $430 million but funding was sharply cut to $100 million the next year. Scientists had envisioned a nuclear propelled rocket in the late 1950s into the early 1960s. The Limited Nuclear Test Ban Treaty of 1963 curtailed that. The project ended largely because it was considered too dangerous. The British Interplanetary Society pondered the idea of a nuclear rocket in the 1970s, Project Daedelus, but this remained a speculative exercise filled with technical problems. For a spaceship to "go where no man has gone before" it will have to travel the speed of light. When NASA sends out space probes they may be sent into the orbit of a planet to boost their velocity, observes Michio Kaku. An example is the Voyager spacecraft that was directed toward Neptune. A slingshot effect "whips them around" the planet.[16]

The Jefferson Airplane could easily be constructed as the Jefferson Starship: a musical unit of talented musicians that could extend the creative work that had begun in San Francisco in the 1960s. Building an actual starship is quite another matter. One of the technical problems involved in constructing a starship is the great size of the space vehicle. It has been suggested that nanotechnology could reduce the size of spaceships; they need not be the massive size of a Starship *Enterprise*. However, the image of the large spacecraft persists. Consequently, scientists have proposed that such a project of starship construction should be performed in the weightlessness of outer space. There heavy objects could be lifted and moved far more easily than they ever could be under the weight of gravity. However, building the International Space Station and sending space shuttle launches to assemble it is tremendously costly. Scientists have explored the idea of a "space elevator" as a means to reduce the cost. Science fiction writers Arthur C. Clarke, in the *Fountains of Paradise* (1979), and Robert Heinlein, in *Friday* (1982), introduced the idea, but the idea stalled until about 1999, when NASA reconsidered the idea. As Michio Kaku explains in *Physics of the Impossible* (2008), the reconsideration of the space elevator idea was stimulated by the development of carbon nanotubes by a Japanese chemist, Sumio Iijuma. Lighter but stronger than steel cables, nanotubes can withstand pressure and hold fast a ribbon-like space elevator to transport materials (Kaku 167). However, it remains a technical difficulty to produce nanotubes that are sufficiently lengthy to make this operation successful. Also, as Kaku points out, "microscopic impurities ... could make a long cable problematic" and "atomic scale defects could reduce the strength of the nanotube cable."[17] Meanwhile, because satellites near the earth rotate there would be the potential of collision with the space elevator.

Space travel is further complicated by radiation, shifts in temperature, and weightlessness, which has many impacts upon the human body. This was evident in the recent experience of astronauts who returned to the Earth's atmosphere after having been in space for a year. There is also the matter of time. It would take many years in earth-time to reach distant stars. A single human life would not have the longevity necessary to complete the trip. It would require some form of intergenerational crew that could one day realize the arrival of the mission.

Even so, a rocket may be a bridge between worlds. It may carry passengers from our world into an unknown world. Or, it may bring the alien into our world. Psychologist C.G. Jung compared the spaceship with a mandala. For Jung, a mandala is a mythical figure which holds out the hope of unity; it is an "individuation symbol" or an "archetype that has always expressed order, deliverance, salvation, and wholeness."[18] The rocket and spaceship has been a primary image of American technology since "the new frontier" and space program initiated by John F. Kennedy.[19]

The spaceship of Paul Kantner's design was one of a self-contained society that had developed its own perspective. He dreamed that the break of this spaceship community from the larger society could lead to renewal. Robert Heinlein's *Methusalah's Children* provided the basis for this counter-cultural vision. Heinlein's "Universe" and "Common Sense" appeared in *Astounding* in 1941 and they were reprinted as *Orphans of the Sky* in 1963. The spaceship society that Kantner presented led directly to the Jefferson Starship. They are the spaceship family.

Robert A. Heinlein's story "Universe" provides the theme that a spaceship might carry people forth on a multi-generational mission into space. *Orphans in the Sky* (1963) collected this story with its sequel. Hugh Hoyland and his companion live on a spaceship, an interstellar world in motion, on which many generations have lived and died. A mutant reveals to him the night sky and its stars and planets beyond the spaceship: a universe he has never seen. The story pulls together the pieces of a back story that recalls that there was a mission to a star that was expected to last for sixty years. There was a mutiny and there was a destructive time that wiped out the memory of the mission. From this Kantner drew the theme that a family-like group of companions might escape the socio-cultural limitations of 1960s America and dream of creating new possibilities.

Similarly, Ray Bradbury's *The Martian Chronicles* (1950) has "family rockets." They are sent on leisure adventures to the moon. Of course, Bradbury, like Kantner, was utilizing science fiction to critique his society. In the linked stories of Ray Bradbury's *The Martian Chronicles* humanity is exploring Mars. The Martian population has been destroyed and the planet is being colonized. Meanwhile, the Earth is under the peril of thermonuclear warfare. Bradbury critiques the frontier thesis of historian Frederick Jackson Turner, who asserted in the 1890s that the American frontier had closed. It was the Western frontier that had provided opportunity, Turner theorized. The frontier was pivotal in American history: fostering democratization, encouraging vigor, calling for the transformation of America. In Bradbury's stories, his characters that colonize Mars come to think of themselves as Martians in this new landscape. In "The Million Year Panic" a father promises his children that they will see some real Martians. However, the Martian population has been decimated and when they arrive he points to a canal in which they see their own reflections.

Like Kantner in his songs, Bradbury explored contemporary society through his stories and dealt with social issues that were significant during the time during which he was writing. On Earth, a scarcity of resources prompts international conflict. Transnational corporations have become more powerful than governments. One entrepreneur leaves Earth for Mars and seek financial gain. In "The Offseason," a colonizer opens a hot dog stand on Mars, expecting that more people will come from Earth and make him wealthy by buying his hot dogs. Then he sees the Earth explode in atomic devastation and he knows that he will never see any customers. In "Way in the Middle of the Air" a racist store owner in the American South is annoyed when the African American population flees the area and moves to Mars.

Heinlein's *Methuselah's Children* (1958) shows the departure of a group of families to space so that they can escape the persecutions they experience on earth. (They are thought by the people on earth to have the secret of immortality.) Gary K. Wolfe notes the gender divide: the women teach school and have children while the men take care of the voyage.[20]

Women in Rock

Grace Slick is one of the most memorable women in rock music history. Some attention to her role as a key member of Jefferson Airplane and Jefferson Starship will remind most readers that the space in which we find a merger of rock music and science fiction has often been a field dominated by men. Women have developed fewer expressions of science fiction rock fantasy. Readers may recall that Patti Smith wrote a song that appeared on her album *Horses*. "Experiment IV" by Kate Bush on her album *The Whole Story* is another notable exception.

It is about a secret military project to create a sound that will kill people. However, many female artists have utilized fantasy or goddess mythology rather than science fiction.

Of course, some vocalists themselves have become mythic or legendary. Slick, Janis Joplin and Patti Smith are regularly cited as being within the rock pantheon. The Wilson sisters of Heart have also achieved similar Rock and Roll Hall of Fame recognition.[21] Perhaps one might say that these women have established their own myths. However, mythology has not been a frequent resource for other female rock artists. Blondie made occasional references to science fiction images. However, they are absent in the music of the Pretenders, Melissa Etheridge, Joan Jett, Pat Benatar, and others. Only occasionally has something mythic or science fiction oriented come through.

Patti Smith, in May 2005, told the British publication *The Guardian* that she turned to art, poetry, and music while feeing a sense of disconnection or feeling alien: "What I wanted to do in rock 'n roll was merge poetry with sonic-scapes."[22] On *Horses*, Patti Smith offers a science fiction reference when she imagines that the son of Wilhelm Reich hallucinates that his father is at the controls of a spaceship. In her androgynous "raggedy glory," said the *Guardian*, her fusion of Rimbaud and rock marked a pivotal movement in the mid to late 1970s that continues to be memorable and influential. That sense of feeling alien and finding mutual connection with others appears to have been crucial to the art that emerged from New York's underground rock scene.

Musician and rock critic Lenny Kaye, guitarist in the Patti Smith Group, has pointed to science fiction's connection with rock. "A lot of the sci-fi fans became hippies," he writes. "You could see these new trends oozing into science fiction; the sense of the counterculture started to break it out of its insular thing." There was a new sense of open possibility and the science fiction imagination connection with rock began moving into the culture. Kaye described himself as "a devoted reader of science fiction," one who collected hundreds of fanzines and read the "double novels" published by Ace. Science fiction was about crossing boundaries. It was a way to imaginatively break out of what he called the "monochrome" fifties and early sixties. As a science fiction fan, he says, "I didn't feel alone in my Otherness."[23] In the

2015 anniversary celebration of the Patti Smith Band's album *Horses* he brought guitar-work again to "Distant Flight," "Birdland," and other songs.

Even with iconic figures like Patti Smith, one might make a case for alienation among women in the rock music industry of the 1960s and 1970s. Since 1990 there has been an increase of attention to women in rock. In "Girls and Subcultures," Jenny Garber comments on a perception of females as consumers of pop music and men of rock music. The claim has been made that females in American culture are closer to consumerism and consequently are more inclined toward pop music than rock.[24] Several female rock acts resist this, although they clearly have entered the pop category. Joan Jett, Pat Benatar, Chrissy Hynde, Melissa Etheridge, who are all commercially popular, have maintained their rock edge.

A question arises: Why do not female rock performers make further use of mythology to assert feminist perspectives or to transform cultural consciousness? Myths may disclose "a level of reality quite beyond any empirical or rational comprehension," observes Mircea Eliade.[25] Christine McVie and Stevie Nicks of Fleetwood Mac brought "Rhiannon" to the pop charts in the 1970s, and Lady Gaga, in her various guises, has appealed to the image of Venus. However, the resources of myth have been tapped more frequently and more notably by male performers than female rock vocalists and musicians.

In Western mythology, there are several models of the goddess. Aphrodite, a goddess of love and sexuality, was honored in the Homeric hymns for her attractiveness, charm, and seductive power. The ancients also called her Ourania, or the sky goddess. For us, she may be both beauty and vanity, the adornment that fuels the cosmetic and fashion industries. She is grace and decoration, Eros and allure. Different images emerge when we look to Athena. She was honored widely and the great city of Athens is named for her. Athena, in *The Odyssey*, is the protector of Odysseus and his son Telemachus. She is a dynamic goddess who stirs them to action. Artemis, known in Roman myth as Diana, was a huntress, a virgin goddess, a figure of purity and moral rectitude who represents nature. Her daughter Daphne was chased by Apollo, who desired her. Yet, the moon is also associated with Artemis (or Diana), the moon goddess. Phoebe, likewise, is a name that is derived from Phoebus, god of the moon, whose name means brilliant and shining. This name is associated with Apollo, as one in whom there is no darkness. Selene (or the Roman Luna) is also a goddess of the moon.

Rock's women have often chosen rebellious and transgressive stances. Some, like Joan Jett, will dress in leather, suggesting urban toughness. Others adopt imagery that underscores that they are experimental, Dionysian, edgy, and bold. They express a dark Eros, an urban savvy, and the soul-power of Hera, Kali, or other poetic figures. They break through bias, chauvinism, and limited viewpoints with their art.

Performers of rock music have also adopted androgynous images, weaving male/female. Consider Patti Smith, wearing a white shirt and dark tie, or David Bowie in jumpsuit and dyed hair. The comparative mythologist Mircea Eliade points to divine androgyny and says that this was often expressed in biological terms, including bisexuality. Such androgyny expresses the coincidence of contraries. He writes: "We must simply note that the divinities of cosmic fertility are, for the most part, either hermaphrodites or male one year and female the next."[26] Eliade lists Attis, Adonis, Dionysius, Cybele the Great Mother, Purusa in the Rig Veda, and Siva Kali. He points out that the gods of Scandinavian mythology, Odin, Loki, Tuisco, and Nerthus retain elements of androgyny.[27] Some traditions hold that the "primeval man" was a hermaphrodite.[28] Perhaps Janis Joplin at her grungiest may suggest this androgyny. But it is the members of Queen, or the New York Dolls, Alice Cooper, or Bowie in whom this androgyny is more apparent.

Gender has been involved in the arguments of some rock critics against "soft," "weak," "light" music. This light pop sound has been identified by some critics as "feminine."[29] These critics favor blues rock with a lack of adornment and critically reject "slick" production, or overproduction. That, on the face of it, may appear a reasonable distinction. However, a problem arises when this becomes gendered into a simple dichotomy that hard rock is male and soft rock and pop is female. Viewed from this perspective Grace Slick seems to be caught within a cultural quandary. One would expect that critics of this disposition would favor the "authentic" blues and folk of the Jefferson Airplane and Hot Tuna to the commercial singles on Jefferson Starship's *Red Octopus* album. The Jefferson Airplane would be viewed as tougher and grittier and Jefferson Starship as lighter pop. Kambrew McLeod observes how rock critics have employed these terms within the discursive space of reviews and asserts that this "tells a story."[30] Such criticism associates tougher and grittier blues rock with masculinity and positions the feminine with the non-progressive, McLeod says.[31] This is the rock critic's sense of the serious, authentic, raw elements of rock versus what the critics consider formulaic fluff.

Some feminist critics of rock have pointed to the masculine posturing of heavy metal bands. Deena Weinstein, among others, rejects the claim that the mythical stance of some heavy metal bands is all that misogynistic. In contrast, Harding and Nett (1984) have called rock blatantly misogynistic. Gottlieb and Wald have viewed rock as deeply masculine. Norma Coates has written of "a constant process of reiteration and the performance of masculinity." Mimi Schippers has argued that "rock culture has relied upon and reproduced quite mainstream ideas about gender and sexuality and in these terms it does not live up to its rebellious counter-cultural image." Schippers points out that songs have often presented stories of the exploitation of women. Coates concludes that some rock songs create an "ultimately fictive masculinity." A stereotypical masculinity is "in play discursively and psychically," Coates says. Deena Weinstein observes that heavy metal celebrates masculinity and Robert Walser notes how it inscribes femininity.[32] Heavy metal masculinity embraces the heroic image, as in the stance of Iron Maiden's Bruce Dickinson and his mythological narratives about heroism and valiant fighting.[33]

However, the goddess figure, the female rock performer—often a vocalist—voices another dimension that is powerful. Grace Slick is one of the forerunners who evoked this power. Grace Slick performed at the 1967 Monterey Pop Festival wearing a flowing white tunic. Psychedelic rock gave attention to visual performance. They sought new world and sang songs with themes of alienation, culture crisis, dissent in relationships, social racial and sexual alienation. They called in "Volunteers," a song written by Balin and Kantner, for a revolution that would be peaceful. Whether Grace Slick, Paul Kantner, and crew were able to create change with their call to revolutionize America is open to question. They became Starship and were successful on the pop music charts with their album *Red Octopus*, which featured the hit single "Miracles." Perhaps, in the end, it can at least be said that they bravely used science fiction and myth to gesture toward the miraculous.

FOUR

The Electric
Light Orchestra
Science Fiction
with Strings Attached

With their album *Time* (1981), ELO—the Electric Light Orchestra—connected science fiction and the pop song. They joined the gallery of radio singles like Zager and Evans' "In the Year 2525," David Bowie's "Space Oddity," and Elton John's "Rocket Man." ELO emerged from the British band the Move in the early 1970s when Roy Wood imagined a rock orchestra in which rock guitars and drums met with violins and cellos. On July 12, 1970, Wood added multiple cellos to a track.[1] He was joined by drummer Bev Bevan, guitarist and songwriter Jeff Lynne, Bill Hunt on horns and keyboards, and violinist Steve Woolam. Jeff Lynne, from the Idle Race, would become the leader of ELO as Wood moved on to solo work and recording with his band Wizzard.

The science fiction themed *Time* is among the most popular of ELO's albums. It was a pivotal recording in the career of a band that would have twenty top 40 singles and sell more than 50 million records globally.[2] ELO emerged from Birmingham, where blues and rock were popular. From the industrial city came the Move, the Moody Blues, the Spencer Davis Group, Traffic, Judas Priest, Black Sabbath, and members of Led Zeppelin. Birmingham has been described as "the cradle of all things heavy" and has been called a birthplace for heavy metal. The ELO concept was to orchestrate a pop/rock sound with string instruments. In contrast with some of the Birmingham bands, ELO would be a pop singles oriented band. The rock and roll based Mersey beat was important to ELO and their tuneful creations launched them increasingly in a pop direction. The imagination of Roy Wood pushed them toward myth and the fantastic. Jeff Lynne would move ELO toward the science fiction concepts of *Time*.

While developing their first album, ELO played their first gig at the Greyhound Pub in Croydon, Surrey. Their first single "10538 Overture" may sound like a date in the future but it concerned the number of an escaped prisoner. During the recording of their second album Wood left ELO and formed Wizzard. Lynne and Bevan reconstituted the band with Mike Edwards (cello), Wilfred Gibson (violin) and Richard Tandy (bass and synthesizer). The "Electric Light" in the group's name appeared as a light bulb on early album covers. "Electric" meant electric orchestral instruments, plugged in. A "light" orchestra was one with only some instruments: in this case, mostly cellos and violins. Rich harmony vocals and large orchestration proved to be an effective combination. The debut record was initially released in America as *No Answer*. There would be eleven studio albums between 1971 and 1986. Lynne, Bevan, and Tandy remained at the core of the band, which brought in an array of string players and other musicians.

The second ELO album was to be "The Lost Planet": a clear reference to science fiction ideas. It was released as ELO II (1973) with cover art by the Japanese artist Shusei Nagaoka that featured a spaceship. ELO had begun to engage in science fiction reflections on space and the cosmos, time, and robotics. The record featured the single "Roll Over Beethoven" and the science fiction cuts "From the Sun to the World" (Boogie #1) and "Kuiama." The album was followed by *On the Third Day* (1973) and *Eldorado: A Symphony* (1974). Jeff Lynne became the creative center and director of *Eldorado*, which included the single "Can't Get It Out of My Head." The songs on the album create the image of a dreamer who gets lost in a dreamworld that becomes his life, in a way that is similar to the fictional character Walter Mitty.

Face the Music (1975) brought the hit singles "Evil Woman" and "Strange Magic." During the course of the third album, ELO again made personnel changes. The band grew in popularity as they received wide airplay and began to place single after single on the charts. There were colored lasers for the concerts that supported ELO's next album, *A New World Record* (1976), which featured the single "Telephone Line," and "Do Ya," a remake of the Move song with its repeating D-A-G power chord pattern. ELO remained hot on the charts with "Living Thing." *Out of the Blue* (1977), which followed, is a double-album with a cover by Shusei Nagaoka that bears the ELO logo of a jukebox which has become a spaceship. ELO made use of this spaceship design for their stage set for concerts. Curiously, there were no science fiction themed songs on the album.

Time

With *Time*, ELO clearly entered the realm of the science fiction concept album. Set in the beginning of the twenty-first century, the lyrics are framed by a story about a man who falls in love with a robot. This provided an opportunity to note some references by science fiction writers and scientists to robotics. ELO added a heavy use of synthesizers to its layered choral vocals for this album. In 1980, immediately before beginning work on *Time*, Jeff Lynne had been asked to compose music for the film *Xanadu*. Bev Bevan had recently produced his memoirs, *The ELO Story* (1980). The science fiction concept album emerged alongside the idea of bringing a further progressive rock edge to ELO's sound. Synthesizers, like the DX7, were coming into use at this time and they contributed an electronic futuristic sense to the album.

ELO also largely replaced the big string section that they were noted for. Some strings were added to the mix in the studio. However, this was a progressive rock album with Louis Clark's synthesizers and vocals, Dave Morgan's guitar, synthesizer, and vocals, and Mik Kaminski playing on his blue violin. The album brought songs with this new approach: "Hold on Tight," Twilight," "The Way Life's Meant to Be," "Here is the News," and "Ticket to the Moon." Fred the Robot voiced the Prologue and Epilogue on the band's tour.

The changes on this album were striking. Along with the narrative concept of a man's startling passion for a robot there was the obvious shift in the band's sound: a stronger emphasis upon synthesizers, guitars, and choral vocals. We hear songs like "Golden Age," which uses science fiction as a basis for inquiry into the future and to create a musical suite. The album begins with synthesizer chords in "Prologue."

A robotic distorted voice breaks through the music and points to fantasy and a message from another time. The up-tempo pulse is accompanied by lyrics that provide suggestions of dawn visions and twilight dreams. ELO's characteristic vocals are featured prominently but the ELO sound has clearly become dominated by synthesizers rather than by a symphonic string section. This is a keyboard saturated overture with a driving beat. ("Twilight" would later be used for a Daicon IV science fiction convention in 1983.) "Rain Is Falling" follows, with its opening passages washed with the sounds of rain. The sound effect of thunder is met by the lead vocal and high chorus vocals. The drums maintain a regular 4/4 time and violins pulse. The vocalist/narrator says that despite his intentions, goals, and dreams, he stays in the same place. The vocal comes to us underneath the higher tones of the keyboards.

On "Yours Truly, 2095" a distant boys-choir sound is covered by music that races along and the muffled, robotic voice we heard in "Prologue" returns. The theme of time is stated by the lead vocalist who declares that he has sent a message to some other place in the future, to another time. Then he begins to critique a female figure that is described as cold and mechanical. She is similar to you, he tells the listener, but she's an IBM wearing a jumpsuit. She is cool like the most up-to-date technology but watch out for that stone-cold heart. The music romps along in double-time with keyboards and chorus vocals singing above the melody line.

"Here Is the News" gives us a lead vocal that in answered by a studio-compressed vocal and spoken news reports that are surrounded by layered chorale vocals. The up-tempo energy is propelled by the drums and the keyboards simulate the higher melodic and harmonic figures of strings.

"Ticket to the Moon" is a ballad introduced by piano and a solo voice. The vocalist-narrator tells listeners that he will be traveling to the moon and has to get ready for the journey. He would prefer to stay home, looking into his lover's eyes and at the sunrise he sees there. This song moves into a strong vocal chorus in which there is melodic movement. At times the music suggests a sense of drifting in space, a sense of floating that is supported by the orchestration. "Ticket to the Moon," with its often repeated title, may be likened to a small orchestral suite.

"The Way Life Is Meant to Be" begins cinematically. Guitars support the vocal narrative in which the speaker, landing in a strange territory, recognizes that he is a stranger. The band plays music that is fairly predictable, utilizing pop chord patterns reminiscent of Spanish/Latino music. This proceeds toward "Another Heart Breaks," an instrumental that begins with Bev Bevan's drums. The bass guitar joins in and a keyboard pattern begins over this. The album's hit song "Hold On Tight," a top ten single, offers sounds out of late 1950s rock and roll with a vocal that is suggestive of Roy Orbison. (Jeff Lynne would later work with Orbison in the first incarnation of The Traveling Wilburys.) The lyric adds some French into the mix. The tune is catchy and the song is rhythmically infectious. It probably would serve for a good workout in an aerobics class. With its rockabilly atmosphere and positive message it is a simpler composition than many of the others on this album.

"From the End of the World" is a song that is based in synthesizers and it ramps up with a running bass line. The vocal is filled with reverb and joins straight ahead drumming, synthesizer, and ELO's characteristic high vocals. On "Twenty-First Century Man" a solo vocal tells the story of what it is like to live in the twenty-first century. What will it be like to be a man holding a suitcase and flying off to work? The experience is one of being a hero one day and completely down the next. Perhaps this is the life of a rock star who is acclaimed one day and a critical cast-off the next. There is a luxurious slide guitar break in the bridge of this song. One might imagine John Lennon singing the vocal with the Beatles, post–*Abbey Road*. ELO flies into the future with a suggestion of that musical past and what it might have become. These songs were familiar to their audience as ELO took them on the road.

The ELO entourage traveled a great deal on their tour and they experienced the ups and downs of their twenty-first century man within a music industry filled with changes. Their album spoke of humanity's interaction with robots and of a ticket to the moon. Yet, *Time* flew further in its implications. Music itself is within time. Its melodies, harmonic and rhythmic patterns flow as an art of time.

In 1905, Albert Einstein gave us a new concept of time. His landmark discovery appeared in his essay "On the Electrodynamics of Moving Bodies." Einstein held that if the speed of light is consistent for each of two observers in motion at a constant velocity space and time are not separate. Einstein later developed the General Theory of Relativity and published three consequential papers in November 1915.[3] The mystery of time or time travel to the stars that opened before humanity in the twentieth century lay behind ELO's speculations about twenty-first century man. The song recognizes that we are limited in relation to the speed of light and that the stars are light years away. A person might go to the moon but could one ever travel to the stars? One would have to travel near the speed of light to reach those stars within the span of a lifetime. Might there be another way?

Our ideas about time have changed over the centuries. Isaac Newton once called time absolute and universal and for him time was everywhere the same in the universe. ELO's twentieth-century man knows otherwise. Einstein challenged the Newtonian perspective and revolutionized our sense of time. The rate of time's passage is different for two observers who are in motion. Those two observers do not feel time passing at the same rate. Einstein showed that the passage of time depended upon the strength of the gravitational field in which the observer stood. In Pink Floyd's "Time" on *Dark Side of the Moon* (1973) a variety of clocks sound simultaneously. In ELO's *Time*, songs explore the arrow of time and romance in up-tempo pop.

Time was ELO's last album to go platinum. Their albums *Eldorado* and *Discovery* did well commercially but ELO could only have limited staying power into the 1980s. Jeff Lynne sought to follow this effort with a double album. Lynne was stretching out with his music production abilities. The band continued to be popular and its fans probably would have responded well to the double album. CBS, the band's record company, said no. It would be too expensive, they concluded. Instead, the next project became *Secret Messages* (1983). The band had not yet let go of its science fiction motifs. "Out of the Blue" turned a logo into a spaceship flying saucer. In many respects, ELO began to dissolve thereafter.[4]

Roy Wood's Wizzard

Roy Wood, meanwhile, played a role in glam, psychedelic, and progressive rock. His solo albums included *Boulders* (1973) and

Mustard (1975), with vocal appearances from Annie Haslam and Phil Everly. The band's name suggests musical magic. They performed their first concert at Wembley stadium on August 5, 1972, and then went on to play at the Reading Festival.

As ELO became the consummate pop singles band, Roy Wood took a different direction. Wood costumed his glam rock act. *Wizzard's Brew* (1973) was a jazz inflected recording. Wizzard's next recording, *Introducing Eddie and the Falcons* (1974), was styled more commercially. Wood also released his solo albums *Boulders* (1973) and *Mustard* (1975). Wizzard dissolved in 1975. Warner Bros., their record company, found the recording *Main Street* was not commercial enough and the record languished. In 2000, *Main Street* finally was released. Wizzard produced several non-album singles: "Ball Park Incident," "See My Baby Jive," "Angel Fingers," "This Is the Story of My Love," and "I Wish It Could Be Christmas Everyday." Wood had clearly taken a progressive and less commercial direction with his music, away from the pop orientation of his former band mates with ELO.

ELO's sheer pop music popularity may have caused some grumbles from people who rejected formulaic pop or shallow escapism. Yet, they were accomplished musicians with a strong sense of vocal harmony. They emphasized studio production and arrangements that some people found overblown. Rock musicians may dissociate themselves from pop music, regarding what they do as a separate art. At an MTV activity Axl Rose of Guns N' Roses, in 1992, declared: "This has nothing to do with Michael Jackson."[5] He might have added that his band's music had nothing to do with bands like ELO either.

A Note on Recording

ELO kept up with changes in recording techniques and varied their sound as they moved into the 1980s. Most recordings shifted from analog to digital during the 1980s. ELO, as a pop singles band, was by then ripe for re-mastering into greatest hits compilations. Digital recording and computers began to change the industry. The digital computer processes numerical information. A Pro Tools system in a recording studio casts a dance of colored bands of light that may be interesting to watch but a great deal is going on that does not meet the eye. The computer handles symbolic information by using binary digits known as bits. The data processing elements are in the integrated circuits that make up the microprocessor. The computer has data storage and or memory. A compact disc will store millions of sixteen bit "words" on a recording. Several progressive rock producers and performing musicians, from Alan Parsons to Todd Rundgren to Geddy Lee, have become extremely savvy about how to get sounds from technology in the concert setting as well as in the studio.

Musical acoustics remains an ongoing issue for rock musicians who are plugged in as well as those who are "unplugged." This is an area of acoustics that deals with musical instruments and how sound reaches the listener. Of course this is particularly important for a band's use of acoustic guitars, or ELO's cellos, or Ian Anderson's flute playing with Jethro Tull. It is also quite important for drums and percussion and for vocals. In the case of ELO's cellists, the musician puts energy into the vibration of the strings. The flow of energy exists within a vibrating system. In the case of Ian Anderson, he plays the flute with breath and the input valve is flow controlled. Musical sound has volume, pitch, timbre, and the duration of the notes that are played. Pitch is the tone low to high that we usually associate with a musical scale. Timbre is associated with tone color. It is a quality that depends upon the overall pattern of sound, waveform, and sound pressure. The instrument and the room sound will affect what is heard. The piano is a string instrument that produces music through vibration. It is also a percussion instrument because keys are struck by the player. When the acoustic piano is played the "room sound" in which the instrument is played is significant.[6]

Seeking a spacious, contemporary sound, ELO transitioned from acoustic instruments to synthesizers. Electronic instruments produce tones that are available for amplification. The electric guitar will sound thin and tinny unless it is plugged in. Then, with the aid of a variety of effects, it can become a monster. In the 1960s organ sounds were joined by Moog keyboards. Synthesizers developed based on frequency modulation using oscillators. With the 1980s came digital sampling, which involves playing back recorded material and manipulated sound. ELO was one of many groups that showed that synthesizers can achieve a wide variety of sounds. However, it is often difficult to reproduce the sounds of many of the acoustic instruments ELO played with great fidelity. Some programs reflect the sounds of acoustic piano remarkably well. However, solo woodwinds and bowed string instruments are difficult to imitate precisely, as this requires a lot of memory in the system.

Jeff Lynne, Alone in the Universe

Jeff Lynne remained a productive pop music innovator throughout the 1980s and 1990s. He took on musical collaborations, producing George Harrison's *Cloud Nine* and other recordings. He produced the Traveling Wilburys, a playful collective, in which he made music with Bob Dylan, George Harrison, Roy Orbison, and Tom Petty.[7] ELO's *Flashback* (2000) reunited the band for a boxed set retrospective of three CDs and a tour. ELO's version of "Xanadu" reached number one in England. With an album titled *Zoom,* Jeff Lynne returned to the ELO melodic pop form with a record that let go of much of the band's former penchant for orchestration. Ringo Starr makes a guest appearance on two cuts on the album ("Moment in Paradise" and "Easy Money"). A new cast of musicians joined Lynne and longtime associate Richard Tandy (keyboards): Rosie Kela (vocals), Marc Mann (guitar and keyboards), Matt Bisonette and George Bisonette as the rhythm section, and Peggy Baldwin and Nancy Ross on cellos.

Jeff Lynne used the spaceship logo for his 2016 tour, which followed the album *Alone in the Universe.* Lynne developed the record with Tandy and it was released November 13, 2015, the first ELO album in more than a decade. The single "When I Was a Boy" has an almost McCartney Beatlesesque sound. Clearly, Jeff Lynne's revisiting ELO with a new sound continues a personal statement and suggests a sense of something cosmic and universal at the center of musical creativity.

FIVE

David Bowie

From Major Tom to Ziggy Stardust

David Bowie will always be associated with science fiction. Soon after signing his contract with RCA Records, David Bowie became Ziggy Stardust. This was a transformation of his image that was intended to be outrageous and compelling while consistent with his artistic vision. Each of Bowie's reconfigurations drew him into the spotlight of rock criticism and contributed to making him one of the most studied of rock performers.

Bowie frequently transformed himself into a mythical creature. He remade his sound and his image over several times. In November 1971 RCA Records released *Hunky Dory*, with the single "Changes." It was an album that some executives at RCA did not especially like. In January 1972 some fourteen concert dates were set for February and March. Bowie's management, led by Dennis Katz, sought to develop publicity for Bowie in the United States. During this time, Bowie's band, led by guitarist Mick Ronson, was becoming the Spiders from Mars. Their act was artifice, cosmetics, and costuming; it was intended to be theatrical. The band was outfitted in gold suits and Bowie developed his androgynous character of Ziggy: an otherworldly hermaphrodite, a gender bending guitar playing creature somewhere in between male and female. His team thought about merchandising Ziggy dolls and boots. He drew upon his respect for Lou Reed and the Velvet Underground as the band played "White Light, White Heat" and "Waiting for the Man" alongside Bowie singles like "Suffragette City." He took cues from Marc Bolan, Iggy Pop, the New York Dolls, and Alice

Cooper's shows. He created an act, a science fiction persona that his art could speak through. *Melody Maker* called David Bowie and his band "superb parodists." Bowie told a *Rolling Stone* magazine photojournalist that his character of Ziggy was a cartoon. Yet, there was uniqueness and drama to this otherworldly character, this comic book creation. There was also in Ziggy Stardust an expression of Bowie's creativity and the malleability of the artist.

Space Oddity, in 1969, suggested Bowie's interest in other worlds and science fiction. The release of the record coincided with the Apollo mission's launch to the moon in 1969. Re-released in 1972, the single about Major Tom became a popular hit and a signature song for Bowie. The listener is immediately drawn into reflection upon humanity's ventures to outer space. In March 1972, "Starman" was the first single from *The Rise and Fall of Ziggy Stardust and the Spiders from Mars*. "Five Years" begins the recording ominously with a note of world crisis, the news that the world has only five years of existence left. In "Starman" the narrator is a child who sees a UFO. He tells his friends and he contacts the Starman. At the center of the record are the songs "Ziggy Stardust," "Suffragette City," and the record's closer "Rock 'n' Roll Suicide." Underlying this recording is a critique of art and the recording industry, of creation, construction, and manufacture. Bowie appears to reflect upon his own constructed image and upon the ways in which the industry and society creates pop stars. We hear about Ziggy, who played guitar and who seems to be a figure caught up in what some commentators on Bowie have called a "self-destruct mechanism."[1]

Bowie experimented with constructions of identity and character throughout his career. Bowie's characters represent the "periodic ecstatic self-annihilation" and rebirth of a Dionysian figure, a Phoenix that renews himself, critics have pointed out. "His other great inspiration is mythology," stated Gordon Coxkill, an early interviewer. The interviewer said that Bowie had a need to believe in legends like Atlantis and that "he has crafted a myth of the future," of a superior race. He placed Bowie within rock's history of "shock and outrage."[2]

"It's a brave new world and either we join it or we become relics," Bowie told another music critic.[3] He spoke of his music and art as participating in "a wave of the future." He acknowledged his bisexuality in a *Melody Maker* interview and this became news. His sexual orientation had been part of the life of David Jones before he became David Bowie, or the character of Ziggy Stardust. Bowie rejected any labels regarding the sexual orientation of individuals. Meanwhile, his management capitalized on the press swirling around him and announced a tour of England for summer 1972. That would be followed by an eight city tour in the United States. Capping this tour was a successful sold-out concert in Cleveland in the 3,500 seat Cleveland Music Hall. Ziggy Stardust was now a headliner, a rock "star." David Bowie had arrived.

A great deal has been written on Bowie. The writer of *Hallo Spaceboy*, Dave Thompson, calls Bowie "the biggest thing in the 1970s consciousness."[4] Frith and Horne see Bowie as creating "a blank canvas on which consumers write their dreams." Bowie is "a modern heroic figure."[5] In his introduction to *The Man Who Sold the World: David Bowie in the 1970s*, Peter Doggett calls him "popular culture's most reliable guide to the fever of the seventies."[6] Some analysis of that "fever" might be called for. One commentator, Christopher Lasch, called the decade "the age of narcissisism."[7] Doggett recognizes Lasch's book and Tom Wolfe's phrase "the me-decade." He calls the sixties an "era of progress" and no doubt strides were made in civil rights, women's rights, and environmental awareness but was the 1960s a period of more "progress" than the 1970s, which the author describes as a time of "dread and misgiving," of "hedonism and power failures."[8] Doggett proceeds to make a fine case for seeing Bowie as an important voice in the 1970s (and in the revivals of his career beyond this). Other critics have frequently seen reflections of contemporary culture throughout his work. However, to call Bowie the "the biggest thing in the 1970s consciousness," as Thompson does, or the "most reliable guide" to the 1970s in all of popular culture, as Doggett asserts, are claims that have to be qualified.

Bowie brought together rock with pantomime and with science fiction. The ongoing science fiction motif is a constant in Bowie's career, appearing in Major Tom, Ziggy Stadust, *The Man Who Fell to Earth*, and Earthling. Bowie was interested in the possibility of extraterrestrial life and UFOs. He liked science fiction films like Stanley Kubrick's *2001* and *A Clockwork Orange* and Ridley Scott's *Blade Runner*. In 2002 Bowie also mentioned a surrealist influence from the artists Man Ray, Dali, Bunuel, and the film *Un Chien Andalou*. Bowie was visually oriented and he once called his some of his songs "paintings in words." He was consciously an actor and performer. To Gordon Coxkill, Bowie spoke of his need for an audience's response and his desire to entertain. In that interview he recalled meeting Marc Bolan and having recently been on tour with Humble Pie as their opener. He spoke of the value of clubs and cabarets.

David Bowie has fascinated audiences and critics because he has continually revised and recast himself. He has been called "a manipulator of pop tastes."[9] but he also was always an artist engaged in self-discovery. David Buckley refers to Bowie as an imaginative autodidact: that is, a person who is self-educated. Early on his book on Bowie he refers to the musician's "melismatic, creaky, almost asthmatic saxophone playing."[10] He quotes Paul Buckmaster saying that Bowie was moved by "the whole sci-fi vibe which had invaded popular culture."[11] Buckmaster's talks with Bowie concerned aliens and UFOs, figures recalled from comics and science fiction literature. This was "a sort of pop science fiction mysticism mixed with a bit of metaphysics and spiritualism." Meanwhile, Bowie's friend Lesley Duncan talked about UFOs.[12]

As a child, David Jones became fascinated with science fiction. He lived at 40 Stansfield Road in Brixton. His family then moved to Bromley, the town in which H.G. Wells was born. The BBC science fiction series *Quatermass Experiment* had an impact on Bowie. Paul Trynka observes that David Jones's absorption in the series "sparked a lifelong fascination with science fiction."[13] Marc Spitz says that the *Quatermass Experiment* probably "introduced David Jones to the concept of outer space" and encouraged Bowie to imagine space exploration. He argues that this image offered him a sense of potential to break out of the repression he experienced in his environment.[14] Wendy Leigh points out that his parents thought that the *Quatermass II* series was "too adult" for him.[15] Early on in his music making, his band The Lower Third, formed at Margate near Kent in 1964–65, did the "Mars" theme from Gustav Holst's *The Planets*, which he had heard on *Quatermass*.

Bowie's science fiction references in his songs appear to relate to metaphysical questioning and reflections on identity and rock music stardom. Bowie told the *Los Angeles Times* that he used "science fiction patterns because I was trying to put forward concepts, ideas, and theories but this album hasn't anything to do with that. It's just emotional drive."[16] He was talking about a future recording, *Diamond Dogs*, on which appears "1984." He told the interviewer that "Space Oddity" was quite personal. In his discussion of the song, Michael Mooradian Lupro observes that Bowie "inhabits discrete and contradictory spaces" that we can all travel to "the brightest star in space and rock." He developed "alternative spaces." While "playing with stardom," Bowie was using space "as a place to locate difference." Lupro notes that "space technology themes" are "a consistent source of empowerment through which marginalized voices are given a safe forum for the exploration of new modes of identity."[17]

Bowie's value lies in drawing our attention to "transformations of the self," observes Richard Fitch. His art is engaged in "a postmodern politics of fluid identity."[18] Bowie's personas invite postmodern reflection on just what it means to be human. Ellen Willis wrote: "A lot of nonsense has been written about Bowie—ubiquitous comparisons to Alice Cooper can only be willful incomprehension." She concluded that Bowie was glitter and not at all troubling. "There is nothing provocative, perverse, or revolting about Bowie. He is all glitter, no grease." The bi-sexuality is "not that big a deal," Willis added. Androgyny has always been present in British rock. Bowie is a "polished pop surface," not decadence. Underneath the Day-Glo he is a folkie who likes Jacques Brel. His dyed red hair, makeup, dresses are theatrical.[19]

The science fiction framework chosen for the figure of Ziggy Stardust, with his band the Spiders from Mars, welcomes us to think about aliens and alienation and about the reinventions of the human that run through science fiction stories. Bowie calls us to give thought to media constructions of celebrity and to the disintegration and eclipse of some of these figures. He carried this mythical mode from the height of his acclaim with records like *Aladdin Sane* and *Young Americans* in the 1970s into other phases of his career. This mythical mode was present in the revival of his work in the 1990s and the farewell that he created for his final album when he knew that his death was imminent in 2016.

In Bowie's last recording he pours himself out with a final affirmation of a life dedicated to creativity. The poet Rainer Maria Rilke, in his *Sonnets to Orpheus* (1966), encouraged the artist to never "shut himself in abiding" but "to pour himself out as a spring" and to "will transformation," like a flame that will change and gain power. Bowie again faced the changes, as he declared in one of his early singles. In his final recording he embraced dying and transformed this into art. This was what the poet Keats once called negative capability. It was an affirmation, giving himself to the creative force. Bowie's farewell was, in every sense, the gift and last testament of a multi-faceted artist.

A Space Oddity

With "Space Oddity" (1969) Bowie was signed to Mercury Records and his song about Major Tom was connected with the July 1969 Apollo space mission to the moon.[20] The song emerged after Bowie's father's death from pneumonia, August 5, 1969. Zager and Evans' hit single "In the Year 2525" was on the charts a few weeks earlier than "Space Oddity." Bowie's song was re-released in 1972 and became a hit single and one of his signature songs.

"Space Oddity" has drawn considerable commentary. Critics have seen Stanley Kubrick's adaptation of Arthur C. Clarke's *2001* as one source for Bowie narrative. Carmen Paglia has viewed "Space Oddity" as "a requiem" for the age of hippies and "flower power." Major Tom was Bowie's "psychedelic astronaut." Wendy Leigh observes that the song along with "Life on Mars" and "Starman" "insured that he would be forever associated with the planets, space, the moon, and the stars." In her view, Bowie "punctured the global admiration for the Apollo mission to the moon." This seems like a rather large claim. Van Cagle sees Major Tom as a Luddite who is suicidal. Phil Auslander views "Space Oddity" as a technophobic response of the counterculture. "Tom is helpless to address the world's ills," he says. Michael Mooradian Lupro, in contrast to this, sees Major Tom as "an active participant in altering the conditions of his labor." He cannot be controlled. Lupro argues that Major Tom is resistant to the control of Ground Control; he is transgressive and breaks free. Yet, perhaps Major Tom's attention is drawn away from his mission simply by his wonder at the stars.

Linking Bowie's song to Kubrick's film *2001: A Space Odyssey*,

Marc Spitz conjectures that the song was inspired by a scene of the astronaut responding from space to his daughter on her birthday. Of course, Bowie's song was likely inspired by many more things than this particular scene. Spitz attempts to psychoanalyze Bowie, suggesting that scenes like this suggest a family connection that appealed to David Bowie who lacked security and attention in his home in childhood.[21] However we may read this, it does appear that Major Tom finds liberty in drifting away, even if one sees in this a doomed floating forever in space.

The Spaceman Enters

Bowie used the rock star as outsider and extra-terrestrial theme in *The Rise and Fall of Ziggy Stardust and the Spiders from Mars*. The androgynous figure raises questions about the construction of gender. Bowie's acoustic guitar playing is heard throughout the album: a twist on the notion of folk music authenticity. Bowie clearly can rock. "Rock 'n' Roll Suicide" brings the album to a strong conclusion.

So, who was Bowie now? In October 1972, Ellen Willis wrote: "In England Bowie may already be "a red star" but in the American context he looks more like an aesthete using stardom as a metaphor." Yet, she notes that she is "not entirely happy" with this perspective. She had quickly become a fan. At Bowie's Carnegie Hall debut she stood on her seat.[22] *Hunky Dory* (1971) was a favorite of hers. The song "Life on Mars" was on that album but the science fiction motif was not conspicuous. She expected "a soft, vague sensibility" from the cover photograph. "Instead, Bowie turned out to be an intelligent, disciplined, wry Lou Reed freak," she wrote.[23]

Then along came the Ziggy persona to disrupt that view further: "But the idea of a pop star from outer space (read pop star as explorer, prophet, poet of technology, exotic on the outside but merely human on the inside and so on) just doesn't make it—except maybe as a spoof."[24] Peter Doggett notes that Bowie beamed "the smile of the spaceman" in a BBC television performance, indicating that he was "not taking any of this seriously."[25] Willis, however, notes that Ziggy Stardust "seems to take it seriously." She points out "Bowie's flash and

Mick Ronson's crackle" and says that "Bowie is best at doing other people's songs—Lou Reed's 'Waiting for the Man,' 'White Light, White Heat,' 'I Feel Free.'"[26]

To William S. Burroughs in a *Rolling Stone* interview Bowie spoke about his creation of his Ziggy Stardust character. "Ziggy is advised in a dream by the Infinites to write the coming of Starman"[27] This is a spaceman who will come to earth as a sign of hope. The Infinites are "black hole jumpers." "Star" is about rock music ambition. The title song has a theme of a science fiction man in space. Bowie wrote it during his February 1971 promotional visit to the U.S. Ken Scott mixed the record. Mick Ronson's guitar solo is mostly improvised. Bowie adds baritone sax and piccolo in the instrumental break.

Not long after becoming Ziggy Stardust, Bowie was asked in an interview about black holes and responded that "there is one just outside New York."[28] "I've always felt like a vehicle for something else," he said, although he added that he had not sorted out what it was. Some critics questioned Bowie's pose. The authenticity critique turned upon the question of whether Bowie was merely an actor. Simon Frith, arguing for Bowie's musicality, called upon Bowie's listeners to consider "the sound of the voice."[29] Frith opposed the view of critic David Laing: "take away Bowie's image and there's nothing left." He wrote: "I know who Bowie's sold out to; I don't understand what he's sold out to. From where is this authentic rock tradition, pose-less and glamour-free? The question is whether it illuminates its situation."[30]

At this time, Bowie was creating a new album that was a departure from his previous one. *Aladdin Sane* focuses on sanity and madness with its title, which may be read as "A lad insane." The album starts with "Watch that Man" with Mike Garson on piano, playing dissonant runs and arpeggios. The *Aladdin Sane* cover shows Bowie with a mannequin look with his one eye that sees clearly and his other eye that was injured. Of the dark eye, Marc Spitz says that "in myth and legend, it implies mystic powers."[31] The dilated eye looks inward and the other looks outward. Spitz calls this "dual vision," a capacity to see the spiritual world. Camille Paglia suggests that this is a Homeric image, "a mysterious Nefertiti look" that reflects a "hallucinatory part of his imagination."[32] On Bowie's final album both eyes are blindfolded, perhaps turning attention to the inward or the oracular.

Diamond Dogs *and* 1984

David Bowie's *Diamond Dogs* emerged from his reading of George Orwell's *1984*. For many months, Bowie imagined a musical based upon Orwell's novel. Sonia Orwell, who had disliked the 1955 film adaptation of the novel, rejected any adaptations into other media and refused to allow rights for a musical. Bowie wrote "We Are the Dead," "Big Brother,'" and the "1984/Dodo" theme with Ken Scott producing and his band, the Spiders from Mars, accompanying him. ("Dodo" appeared on a reissue nearly 20 years later.) On "1984" and "Dodo," which were linked, one hears cinematic scoring and the incorporation of fragments of reference to the novel. "Dodo" at first is focused on Winston and Julia, the would-be lovers of *1984*. It then turns to the character of Mr. Parsons, their neighbor who was betrayed by his own child. Bowie's science fiction interests inform the project, along with his rejection of conformity and totalitarianism.

We can chart Bowie's movement toward *Diamond Dogs* from October 1973 to February 1974. In late 1973, David Bowie met William S. Burroughs. It was during a time when, on a personal level, Bowie appeared to be reflecting pessimistically on his sense of civilization falling apart. Perhaps Bowie was not alone in this, given the unraveling of sixties dreams. *Diamond Dogs* was a Bowie universe, a vision of a future world facing the collapse of decadence. Unlike Orwell's *1984*, it avoided political comment. Bowie's palette of musical colors lived in fragments, envisioning a dystopia. The album explored Pop Art from the 1950s and the contact between science fiction, consumerism, and Western society's potential for catastrophic events. Bowie dreamed something filmic in which cyborg punks moved through apocalyptic visions. On the final track of the album the chant of humanity is comparable to the "Two Minutes Hate" in George Orwell's novel, when the citizens of Oceania vent their anger at the enemies of Big Brother.

Alienation

Bowie's Ziggy Stardust and his Spiders from Mars raise questions about alterity, or "the other" and alienation. In what ways do we project aspects of ourselves onto the alien? How does the alien represent the unknown, or what we don't understand, or a figure to place our prejudices upon? In these scenarios the question arises: Is the alien friendly, or a monster and a symbol of fear? Is the alien "other," or is it a reflection of us?

Some critics have asserted that Bowie's alien figures reflect his own sense of alienation. Bowie said in a 1977 interview: "They were metaphysically in place to suggest that I felt alienated."[33] This otherness defined Bowie's work, says Nicholas Pegg, who observes that "time, mortality, and oblivion ... runs like a seam through Bowie's songwriting."[34] At times, early in his career, Bowie appeared as an image of urban alienation. Ian Chapman points out that Bowie addresses alienation of British youth and offers dreams. He focuses on alienation in the urban environment. He points to the cover of *The Rise and Fall of Ziggy Stardust*: industrial brick walls and cloudy, rainy sky. Bowie is the other, an outsider. Simon Frith calls this his "sense of difference" that connects him with his fans.[35] He is liminal, transitory, a reflection of estrangement. Cities may be this, Chapman adds; they have positive and negative attributes. In the bottom right of that cover photo we see boxes, torn paper in a plastic bag. L.I. CO. LONDON NO. 2005 and a sign: K. WEST. There are yellow lights in the windows, a streetlight over Bowie's head (more fancifully, an urban flying saucer?). He is "urban industrial." Chapman considers the city at night, a time when workers are out of their daily roles and all are equals. Bowie is "the mysterious man from nowhere who disrupts the city flow from within," says Lehan.[36] Raymond Williams once wrote that the city offers the "excitement and challenges of its intricate processes of liberation and alienation, contact, and strangeness, stimulation and standardization."[37] For Chapman, Bowie strikes a figure of alienation in this urban nexus.

Aliens, Monster Figures and Communication

Science fiction is filled with life forms from other galaxies that are quite different from humanity. Aristotle once held that humanity is a rational animal comprised of what he referred to as the material cause, formal cause (body or substantial form), efficient cause (having action), and final cause (a teleological unfolding of potential). Non-human life in science fiction challenges our ideas of the human. The monster figure induces terror because of its strangeness, or its powerful expression of forces of the unknown. Monsters emerge unexpectedly, when one enters an unfamiliar region, or experiments dangerously. They break through the familiar and create chaos and fear. If science and technology seek to understand and order nature, the monster is where something arises that breaks forth out of those boundaries, assuming dreadful shape and provoking a sense of vulnerability. These figures have a distant lineage extending from ancient mythology.

Indeed, one of the most often repeated plots of literature is that of overcoming the monster. The disturbing monster figure may be alien, mysterious, and threatening. However, as Christopher Booker points out, "the monster can always in the end be outwitted."[38] One may recall how Odysseus fools Polyphemus. Or, as Booker notes, we can remember how David overcomes Goliath and Perseus uses a reflecting shield to overcome the Medusa. In *The War of the Worlds*, H.G. Wells's Martians are foiled by bacteria.[39] Christopher Booker, an archetypal critic, sees a process in genre stories that includes the call of the character, or anticipation stage, the initial success of the dream stage, confrontation and the frustration stage, and the nightmare of the final ordeal. If the monster creates awe and terror the film succeeds, observes Gary K. Wolfe.[40]

Bowie, who created a recording he titled *Scary Monsters* (1980), continued to probe alienation and communication. He was curious about language, music, and interpretations of his work. In an interview with Charles Shaar Murray he pointed out that the same sentence could mean different things to different people. His songs, likewise, would "give people their own definitions."[41] He probably suspected that academics would soon be writing about him also. He told his interviewer that "America is made up of academics.... The level to which rock music has become an academic subject is just incredible." In another interview, he insisted that "the concept and the atmosphere created by the music" was more important than he was.[42]

So, if humanity ever made contact with aliens could we communicate with them? The question must have intrigued David Bowie, just as it has aroused the curiosity of science fiction readers. Writers have speculated that math or logic may be a common language, or that engineering might be one, if the alien society has built a spaceship. However, we might also wonder if our science and mathematics are the same as theirs. There may be no shared language, no shared cultural patterns. Could the first contact problem be solved through science? How does one communicate? This is a problem we find in Arthur C. Clarke's *Childhood's End*. The notion of "first contact" with alien communications appeared in the title of Murray Leinster's story of that title in 1945. The contact with another life form or society from space raises questions about whether it is possible to communicate. Does a series of signals express itself as a language? Must one be suspicious of such signals and question the intentions of aliens who would communicate with Earth? Leinster's story tells us of a spaceship's crew who encounters another spaceship. This crew does not know whether the crew on the other spaceship is a potential friend or a potential enemy. When aliens arrive on earth in the *Twilight Zone* episode "To Serve Man," humans cannot determine whether they are a threat or a hope. The aliens pose as potential benefactors to humanity who will take people on an excursion to their planet. The story hinges upon the word "serve." The last scene shows a line of people boarding the alien's spaceship. A female researcher has finally identified the writing in a book the aliens have left behind. Hurrying to the spaceship, she cries out to her associate with her discovery: "It's a cook book!"

Solaris by Stanislaw Lem raises the question of whether we could ever understand alien intelligence and communication. Scientists have set their research station on the floating water-like substance of this world, which itself seems like an intelligence. A new scientific team casts X-rays into the deep of this ocean and from it emerge images of human beings that come from the crew's memories.

There is also the question of what model of science a society is operating according to. In *The Structure of Scientific Revolutions* (1962) Thomas Kuhn theorized that science developed by successive paradigms in which new scientific knowledge advances beyond the normal science of a period (as those older views reveal anomalies). Peter Barker notes the problem raised by scientific revolutions. Which science is one functioning within? Science is often seen as cumulative building upon past knowledge. However, science undergoes noncumulative changes, when there is some incompatibility and a new perspective changes it: a paradigm shift. For example, we have seen the movement from the perspective of Ptolemy to that of Copernicus and the shift from a Newtonian world-view to the perspectives of Albert Einstein. Science encounters noncumulative changes. If our science and that of an alien culture are fundamentally different then communication may become difficult.[43]

As Bowie absorbed the BBC *Quatermass* series as a child, Cold War scenarios were appearing in science fiction. Some postwar science fiction novels tapped into the public's collective anxiety about nuclear weapons. Carl Jung in his reflections on the 1950s in *Flying Saucers: A Modern Myth of Things Seen in the Sky* (1959) connected ideas about UFO sightings with post-war anxiety about nuclear arms. Jung wrote: "Projections have what we might call different ranges, according to whether they stem from merely personal conditions or from deeper collective ones."[44]

Bowie was an inventive songwriter who drew upon the unconscious and upon the music of the Velvet Underground, Iggy Pop, the Rolling Stones and many other artists whose work he absorbed. He explored visual art, mime, theatre, and dance, film, and pulp science fiction, comics, and literature.[45] "Literary tradition ... is the collective unconscious writ large," observes James T. Jones. The art that incorporates myth is one that he describes as "a poetics of integration of archetypal imagery within individual expression."[46] This reflects the work of David Bowie.

The year 2016 was a year of remembering David Bowie, a time of honoring his contribution at the Grammy Awards and in concert and recordings. Bowie's individual expression across the many phases of his career was like the collective unconscious writ large. He was himself at times like a mythical creation. At the intersection of gender, art and artifice, his creativity extended across music, culture, fashion, film, and theatre. Bowie was not actually from outer space but his creative gifts were evidently as significant as any that his space characters could bring to make the earth a brighter and more interesting place.

Six

Pink Floyd
On the Dark Side of the Moon

Space is conveyed by Pink Floyd in their remarkable textures of sound. Pink Floyd's first recordings were evocative. The psychedelic, hallucinatory creativity of Syd Barrett, in pieces like "Astronomy Domine," was carried over into aural panoramas by Roger Waters (bass guitar), Richard Wright (keyboards), David Gilmour (guitar), and Nick Mason (drums). Pink Floyd are artists: composers, interrogators of consciousness, careful technicians of the recording studio and creators of soundscapes. One may associate Pink Floyd with science fiction simply from the title of their classic album *The Dark Side of the Moon* (1973). When we hear Rick Wright's spacey synthesizers and Dave Gilmour's deeply reverbed and echoed guitar, Pink Floyd's sonic qualities, sound effects, and impressionistic compositions may sometimes suggest space. There is a philosophical quality to many of the songs of Rogers Waters, who eventually took on the bulk of the band's songwriting. Waters often has brought a sociopolitical edge to his songs. Pink Floyd has conveyed wonder through music and spacious settings. The Pink Floyd Sound (as the group was originally called) was early on tagged as being space oriented. "We don't deliberately try to make everything come out like that," David Gilmour told interviewer Roy Shipston (November 22, 1969). "We all read science fiction and groove to *2001*."[1] The band's goal was to improve the world, he added. "There's a great revolution taking place at the moment," Gilmour said.[2]

Syd Barrett was the band's original creative source of songs. Barrett embraced concepts of science fiction and mythology as fervently as he did music and drugs. Pink Floyd's sound ranged from the sixties pop sounds of Barrett's "Arnold Layne" and "See Emily Play" toward his innovative "Astronomy Domine." After Syd Barrett's deterioration into mental illness, Roger Waters became largely responsible for the development of the band's sound and lyrics in the early 1970s. Waters' shaping of Pink Floyd's music characterized albums like *Meddle* (1971) and *The Dark Side of the Moon* (1973). Waters and Rick Wright contributed to that sound through their interest in electronics. Wright played harpsichord, harmonium and some cello as well as piano, organ, and synthesizer. The clever drum patterns and fills of Nick Mason and the virtuoso guitar playing of David Gilmour were merged in this sound.

In the first years of Pink Floyd, Syd Barrett's lyrics were mythical and the music was playful and hallucinatory. He enlisted images of unicorns and gnomes in his song lyrics and a quadraphonic PA was used by the band in playing the music. Barrett expressed his enthusiasm for "childhood fairy stories, pulp sci-fi, and J.R.R. Tolkein's tales of Middle Earth," Nicholas Schaffner observes.[3] In those early years, Barrett's roommates John Whiteley and Anna Murray, a painter, listened with him to John Coltrane's *Ascension* and Ravi Shankar records. Murray told John Canavaugh that "Syd was very interested in mythology. He thumbed through Robert Graves' *The Greek Myths* and Fraser's *The Golden Bough* between painting and writing songs."[4] Syd Barrett was drawn to older English poetry and to childhood ballads and folklore about heroes, romance, and the supernatural. "Barrett loved ballads about fairies, elves, water spirits, enchantment, and ghostly apparitions, in addition to tragic love ballads."[5] He used the moon image long before Pink Floyd's *The Dark Side of the Moon*. In "Jugband Blues" (1967), Syd Barrett refers twice to the moon, once to the sun, and once to the Queen: possibly another lunar image. "Arnold Layne" collects clothes and moonshine. Barrett's song "Bike" (1967) concludes with a reference to musical tunes as clockwork.[6] A look at the band's early catalogue of songs shows that Pink Floyd's orientation toward myth and science fiction was set early by the speculative creativity and experimentation of Syd Barrett.

The Pink Floyd Story

Back in 1966, the Pink Floyd Sound played their experimental music at the London Marquee Club, the UFO Club, and Roundhouse.

Early Pink Floyd played on Sunday afternoons from February through April at the Spontaneous Underground at the Marquee in London. Then they played at the UFO Club, which opened two days before Christmas in 1966. The Soft Machine also played there. Peter Jenner and John Hopkins had started DNA Records and sought the Pink Floyd Sound. Jenner became their first manager. In February 1967 Pink Floyd signed with EMI with an advance of 5,000 pounds (about $3,500). Their first single, "Arnold Layne," was recorded by Joe Boyd, an arranger for UFO, and was released March 11, 1967. The single "See Emily Play" followed. Richard Cromelin wrote about Barrett's "psychedelic fairy tale rock" in his notes for Capitol/Harvest Records. He called the Pink Floyd sound amorphous and compared Barrett's wit with that of Ray Davies of the Kinks. He said that the first album (September 1967) was "a product whose point of origin could as easily be the bowels of an insane asylum as a recording studio."[7]

With producer Norman Smith, Pink Floyd began to record *The Piper at the Gates of Dawn* (1967). Pink Floyd's first single, Syd Barrett's song "Arnold Layne," was followed by "See Emily Play," which climbed up the charts alongside Procol Harum's "A Whiter Shade of Pale" and the Beatles' anthem "All You Need Is Love." "Interstellar Overdrive" was placed in a documentary film. The band's third single "Apples and Oranges" (November 1967) did not survive for long. However, the mysterious album cut "Astronomy Domine" continues to shine as one of the band's classics.

In "Astronomy Domine" (1967) Syd Barrett mentions Jupiter and Saturn. These are references to planets whose names derive from the gods. Immediately these names are linked with Titania and Oberon, mythical characters in Shakespeare's *A Midsummer Night's Dream*, and with the young girl Miranda, daughter of the magician Prospero in *The Tempest*. References to the colors lime green and blue and a surrealistic pattern of surrounding sounds may suggest the imagery of a LSD trip, while the musical setting and sound effects suggest outer space. "Astronomy Domine" begins with a pulse that is immediately followed by voices that sound as if they were recorded in space command communications circa 1968–69. This introduction is followed by a beeping of code and signals. Drums enter on the left channel and guitar chords strike forth on the right in a figure which is repeated and lands on a dissonance. Then chorus vocals come skipping in on the verbal sounds "–een" and "–oun" and there is a circling pattern with drums and bass playing steadily. This comes to a stop, which is followed by a reverbed guitar. We are back to drums and bass and Nick Mason's interesting drum pattern. The space center voices from the beginning return and move into choral vocals and a descending harmonic pattern at 3:40. Vocals chant as the song comes to an end.

We hear one fan's response to the song in comments from pop music writer John Cavanaugh, who tells us how he reacted to "Astronomy Domine."[8] He calls the song a personal discovery. It did not sound to him like *The Dark Side of the Moon* or *Meddle*, which he had listened to first. He was coming indoors from the starry night sky and heard voices on the recording "like the sound of Apollo astronauts."[9] That is exactly how it sounds before the intriguing layered sound of the song develops. The song appeared on *The Piper at the Gates of Dawn* (1967), which took its title from Kenneth Grahame's *The Wind in the Willows*. The album was recorded at the Abbey Road studios at the same time as The Beatles' *Sgt. Pepper's Lonely Hearts Club Band*.

During that same period, Pink Floyd toured England with another fan of science fiction, Jimi Hendrix, in late 1967.[10] Meanwhile, Syd Barrett's time with the band was coming to an end, as he spiraled out of control in erratic behavior, LSD intake, and mental illness. He later showed up at Pink Floyd gigs at Middle Earth and he created two solo recordings. Then he withdrew from sight, for more than thirty years.[11]

In January 1968, Dave Gilmour was brought into the band. (The colloquial knick-name was formalized to his given name David in the 1980s.) By now Pink Floyd was heavily identified with space music and psychedelia. They produced multimedia shows, created music on electronic equipment, and created work that some critics called free form. "It is interesting that they share Jimi Hendrix's interest in space and astronomy," Richard Middleton wrote. He commented that on *Saucerful of Secrets* (1968), "Man is all but swallowed up in the vastness of space." The aural texture of the recording also suggested space and the reviewer suggested that the music could be "a randomly programmed computer after the end of the world."[12] A reviewer for *International Times* (who simply signed his review as Miles) took exception to the album. He found its electronic effects falling short of the now largely forgotten "Metamorphosis" by Vladimir Urrachevsky, a recording which he praised. Pink Floyd's effort, he wrote was "poorly handled and it does not add up to music.... It is too long, too boring, and totally uninventive."[13] However, other listeners disagreed with that assessment. Anyone who listens carefully to the seemingly spontaneous improvisation on that 1968 album will hear the roots of subsequent Pink Floyd recordings. These are records that have a strong basis in composition and planning.

The live recording that followed, *Ummagumma* (1969), had many fans. On "Sisyphus," Richard Wright recalled the myth of Sisyphus in which a rock is rolled uphill only to come toppling back down in a kind of eternal recurrence. A critic, Mick Favreu, writing in *International Times*, described it as having a dignified theme that developed in strange piano progressions and then went on into harpsichord, Mellotron, and organ. He praised Roger Waters' experimental piece on the album. The last piece on the record, one by Nick Mason, had a baroque flute that was followed by Mason's percussion in stereo and then returned to the opening musical theme.[14]

As Pink Floyd moved into the 1970s the band was still engaged in much experimentation. Some musical innovations happened accidentally, as Gilmour noted in his November 1969 interview with Roy Shipston.[15] Elements of their sound were changing and Waters and Gilmour and Wright were increasingly mapping out their sonic territory on *Meddle* (1971). The lyrical contributions of Roger Waters were also becoming what might be considered more profound.

Pink Floyd began to create intertextual associations across their albums. The band exercised great care about quality in their recording process. We hear complexity and structure: something more than improvisation. The science fiction and mythology of Syd Barrett fell away. Roger Waters influenced the concept album ideas the band developed in the early 1970s. The concept album *Dark Side of the Moon* (1973) played with notions of the cosmos. *The Dark Side of the Moon* and *The Wall* were Pink Floyd's strongest concept albums. *The Dark Side of the Moon* sold more than 30 million units and spent 724 week on the U.S. charts.

Pink Floyd's moon symbolism includes the lunatic in the grass of

The Dark Side of the Moon. The moon provides illumination but has to be lit by the sun. It is involved with the tides, time, and psychic states. The record alludes to women and birthing and the lunar cycle. These cycles and patterns are set within a cosmic framework.

The Dark Side of the Moon has generated many interpretations, including many misreadings that Roger Waters has found irritating. He thought that the lyrics were fairly straightforward.[16] Listeners derived different interpretations from the words and the images the band created. Critics, likewise, had a variety of responses to the record. Robert Cristgau, looking back at Pink Floyd's *The Dark Side of the Moon,* commented that the record was one that was "taken too seriously—but not without charm." He also made remarks on how effects enhanced David Gilmour's guitar sound and how Dick Parry's saxophone offered moments that "bring its clichés to life."[17]

Wish You Were Here (1975) was a bright, well-received recording that is said to refer to Syd Barrett and to reflect upon Pink Floyd's popular success. Tensions had entered the band between *Dark Side of the Moon* and *Wish You Were Here.* Listeners can hear a change in tone on *Animals* (1977), which responds to the rise of punk. Pink Floyd explores and critiques their own success and issues of technocracy, with Waters writing most of the material. On *Animals,* Waters' lyrics deride hypocritical "pigs," sycophantic and conforming "sheep," and ambitious, greedy "dogs" of business. The album is more "bilious," observes John Harris, and Waters' tone is more sarcastic than on previous albums.[18] *The Wall* (1979) explores conformity, separation, abandonment and loss, and numbness of feeling. Roger Waters' narrative of this concept album follows the loss of a father in the war, becoming a musician, and building a wall of self-protection from the world. In concert, across 29 shows, the band played behind a wall that was gradually built on stage while inflatable pigs floated above them. *The Wall* carried a theme of intentional separation, in which Waters expressed his desire to distance himself from the audience and from the music industry. Public life had taken over private life. With intense irritation, Waters had spit at a fanatic (a more crazy variety of the word "fan") at a concert. Now he wanted to build a wall to shut distance himself from the craziness. He then utilized this concept to tie together songs that ranged from the loss of his father in the war to issues of social control and conformity.

The Wall was one of the band's strongest albums. It is an album one critic calls "bitterly misanthropic," in contrast with the "melancholy with redemptive optimism" of *The Dark Side of the Moon.*[19]

The Final Cut (1983) interrogates Britain's colonial past. Waters expresses an apparent loss of faith in the band and explores issues of social violence. Pink Floyd's *The Final Cut* signaled the beginning of the end to Waters' involvement with Pink Floyd. He cited the band's "spent creative force." By the time of *A Momentary Lapse* (1987), Waters was no longer part of the band.[20] Waters had released his second post–Pink Floyd album, *Radio K.A.O.S.* There was tension, if not acrimony, between Roger Waters and David Gilmour. Gilmour had created what was essentially a solo release under the band's name, while utilizing Rick Wright and Nick Mason. Their tour lasted for nearly two years and grossed some $135 million. Waters expressed irritation that some listeners could not tell the difference between the sound of the band in the 1970s and the early 1980s sound on *A Momentary Lapse.*

This was a different Pink Floyd: one projecting fewer suggestions of space, mythical ideas, or science fiction. Pink Floyd's *Division Bell* (1994) tour, without Waters, included an eight-piece band. There had been little contact between Gilmour and Waters since 1987. However, James Guthrie, a recording engineer, was a mediator between them and helped to forge a reconnection. Pink Floyd reunited in 2005 for the Live 8 concert in London that was committed to attempting to move world leaders to act on relieving world poverty. They performed at Hyde Park, July 2, 2005 ("Breathe/Breathe Reprise," "Money," "Wish You Were Here," and "Comfortably Numb"). Their anthology *Echoes* showed strong sales following their concert appearance. That double album and classics like *Dark Side of the Moon* and *Wish You Were Here* continue to provide an intriguing introduction to the band for new listeners worldwide.

Pink Floyd was inducted into the Rock and Roll Hall of Fame in 1996. Syd Barrett, who did not attend the ceremony, died in 2006. Rick Wright died in 2008. Roger Waters performed songs from *The Wall* after his time with Pink Floyd and has produced several solo recordings. David Gilmour, who continued to make use of the band's name, has been the most active and still performs. Nick Mason is the only Pink Floyd member to date who has written his memoirs.

The Songs

Pink Floyd, with their unique sound and songs like "Astronomy Domine" and albums like *The Dark Side of the Moon*, has sometimes been associated with space, science fiction, or the cosmic. The nostalgia some critics have heard in their lyrics at times evokes a sense of loss and the recollection of wonder. In the final verse of "Comfortably Numb" on *The Wall* (1979) we hear about a fleeting glimpse that the singer caught as a child. In "High Hopes" on *The Division Bell* (1994), David Gilmour recalls a boundless childhood world of miracles and magnets before the world took those dreams away. When he sings of a glimpse of something he knew as a child he sounds like the poet William Wordsworth in his "Prelude" and "Intimations of Immortality," recalling a fleeting memory of wonder as a child. There were dreams and the world seemed greener and brighter before it all became filled up with ambition and business. An inner tide of memory pulls one back to a time when there were friends, things were sweet, and dreams flowed like this river of music that is accompanied by an orchestra.

"Musicians seem to have no fear of the unknown world that is the unconscious," writes Jenny Boyd in *Musicians in Tune*, as she addresses her subject of musicians and creativity. She quotes psychologist Carl Jung: "A characteristic of childhood is that, thanks to its naivete and unconsciousness, it sketches a more complete picture of the self."[21] In Pink Floyd's first single, "See Emily Play," Emily, who plays and borrows dreams, is this child. The piper, raver, and seer of visions of "Shine On You Crazy Diamond" is also this childlike spirit of creativity. He is the mythic, story-making impulse.

In Pink Floyd's work, the mysterious place of the unconscious is accessed by music, by drugs, by dreams. Pink Floyd creates a mythical space of caves and echoes, waves and light. The fantasy of "Echoes" brings patterns of sound that meet with images of a majestic landscape. The speaker invites the listener to a place that is submarine-green and that in a moment is rising toward light. This appears to be a description of the unconscious awakening to morning's ambassadors: the light streaming through the window, an opening of the mind.

"Set the Controls for the Heart of the Sun" (*A Saucerful of Secrets*, 1968) sounds rather like a science fiction journey. Yet, the song begins with a pastoral image of night breaking into dawn, trembling leaves, lotuses, and swallows in the eaves. The sun is personified as a watcher, a Dionysian energy that makes ripe the wine. We are given the image of a man who questions heaven, or the sun-god Helios. He is encouraged to set controls for the heart of the sun and seems to be urged to aspire toward better things. In Roman mythology, in Ovid's telling, the boy Phaeton takes the chariot of his father, the sun-god, and flies it across the sky. Pink Floyd's song suggests similar aspiration and daring.

On *A Saucerful of Secrets* the following song remains more secret than this. Will this questioner remember the secret lesson of giving? The song begins in a bass guitar figure with drums behind it and bell-like chimes on the keyboards. The vocal is whispery at first and we are told of the watching of the watcher. There are no explicit references to space, although the keyboards drift as if out to space and offer effects like a xylophone sound and sounds like the calls of gulls. There is the repetition of a musical phrase and percussion like a mantra, as in an Indian raga, and a repeating bass figure which responds to the vocal line.

"Echoes" (*Meddle*, 1971) begins with distant signals, like water drops, and with gentle keyboards that provide an ambient atmosphere. A guitar enters, with pulled strings that ping notes high on the guitar neck to a slow four rhythm. Drums enter and the guitar comes forward. The singer points to an albatross in the sky overhead, then to a labyrinth of caves and the sea below. The music builds and there is a guitar run that the drums match in rhythm. Later, in an instrumental section, bass and drums join in a march pattern and, surrounded by Wright's keyboards, Gilmour's guitar leads begin to rise above the rhythm. The pattern continues for more than a minute and fades. A windy, eerie space music takes over and high-pitched soundings call out like whales at sea. The synthesizer leads us back to the single water-drop like signals at 12 minutes, as synthesizer chords alternate. The tune breaks into a guitar reel that circles with sliding chords and a pulse on the tom-toms and bass drum that pulls out into the vocal at 13:40. The vocals of David Gilmour and Richard Wright join together on this section of "Echoes" and there are sound effects, spaciousness, and a sense of movement as the music fades.

Pink Floyd's concept album *The Dark Side of the Moon* (1973) suggested space, wonder, and lunacy. A quartet of vocalists was brought in to sing on "Us and Them," "Brain Damage," "Time," and "Eclipse": Liza Strike, Doris Troy, Lesley Duncan, and Barry St. John. The pensive "Us and Them" laments the division that occurs between people and when humanity divides into conflict and factions. Pink Floyd suggests in this song an idea similar to that of psychologist Carl Jung, who reflected upon the need for self-awareness of the projection of one's shadow onto another person or group. Listeners will also be immediately familiar with "Time," which begins with a variety of clocks chiming followed by the regular pulse of a heartbeat. There is the entry of the guitar on the E chord with a drum roll, light bell-like keyboards, and the vocal bursts in. Rick Wright sings the lead vocal and the vocals wind through a Frequency Translator, shifting pitches. He sings of running to catch the sun and how time has passed by. Dick Parry adds his memorable saxophone parts. Clare Torry contributes her amazing vocal to "The Great Gig in the Sky."

The songs on *Wish You Were Here* add a new dimension to Pink Floyd's creative venture. A long, intriguing instrumental plays for several minutes before the vocal begins on "Shine on You Crazy Diamond" (*Wish You Were Here*, 1973). The song is in seven parts and begins in the keyboards. A keyboard melody emerges in a setting like the sound of a French horn sustained by airy vocals. Two minutes into the instrumental, we hear David Gilmour's guitar. This sounds like a hollow body electric played high on the neck with some effects. The melody traces over the keyboard chords. Once the lyric begins there is a reference to the sun and to eyes like black holes. The guitar figure is bathed in reverb and echo, with keyboard sounds of strings and wind chimes behind this. The song, which might be considered a suite, has been described as a tribute to Syd Barrett. More broadly it is an affirmation of individuality and creativity.

Pink Floyd's song lyrics provoke enough reflection in listeners to merit a recent book titled *Pink Floyd and Philosophy*. Certainly, Roger Waters' lyrics provide many ideas for reflection. The institution of church or religious structure is critiqued in a song like "Sheep" (*Animals*, 1977). George Orwell's *Animal Farm* lingers behind Pink Floyd's *Animals*, where "Sheep" follow the leader. Roger Waters displays his artistic kinship with the cryptic imagination and satire of William Blake's *Songs of Experience* when he uses the 23rd Psalm and interjects references to knives and hooks that turn conforming sheep to lamb chops. This is sociopolitical commentary about dehumanization and another call for creativity and freedom.

Clearly, "The Happiest Days of Our Lives" and "Another Brick in the Wall" (*The Wall*, 1979) speak out against repression, control, and limitation in education. After all, ought not education to free the human spirit rather than incur memories of sarcasm, hurt, or exposing a child's weaknesses? Waters vigorously attacks what he calls thought control with a chorus of schoolchildren in regional dialect. As the song begins, a helicopter sound is followed by a mad voice and rhythmic stops are punctuated by the bass. From the tonic of D minor, this moves into a march and the vocal reference to schoolteachers and the kind of education that is not needed. There is a return of the mad voice and the thrash and roll of the drums sets up a prominent bass pattern that marches along under a chorus that protests against educational control.

In "Hey You" (1979) the speaker calls to someone, wondering if his listener can hear him. He admonishes the listener to not let anyone bury the light. As Dylan Thomas once called for rage against the dying of the light, this lyric asks for communication, for touch, for a sign of life. In the bridge of this song the singer laments the tragedy of the wall being too high for a shattered soul. The lyric is oblique, the music spacious, and Roger Waters concludes with a call for hope in unity and connection: don't tell me about hopelessness; we will hold on together.

The desire for freedom and transcendence appears as a constant theme across several Pink Floyd songs. "Learning to Fly" (*A Momentary Lapse of Reason*, 1987) may recall the flight of Icarus toward the sun. In this song, as the speaker rises and circles in flight, he wonders at the sky ice that forms on his wings. He realizes that for all his aspirations toward transcendence he is too earthbound. Yet, this desire for transcendence seems to be at the root of Pink Floyd's great experiment in sound. It is this sense of wonder that Syd Barrett sought in mythology and science fiction and his quest for a high that took him spiraling down. As in stories of science fiction, Pink Floyd's creativity was a search across society and space: a journey in wonder.

SEVEN

Blue Öyster Cult

Collaboration with Science Fiction Writers

Blue Öyster Cult formed in 1967 in Long Island, New York, as a band that first called itself Soft White Underbelly. Playing at bars and clubs, they developed a guitar-driven sound with a touch of eerie reverb. Sandy Pearlman became their manager and prodded them toward their proto-metal band sound.[1] "Workshops of the Telescopes" signaled their interest in science fiction and fantasy. Their album *Spectres* (1977) offered some energetic novelty with "Godzilla" and "Nosferatu." "Transmanicon MC" offered their take on a John Shirley science fiction novel title. *Agents of Fortune* brought their listeners their most well-known single, "Don't Fear the Reaper," with its airy atmosphere, moody vocals, sizzling guitar lines, and creepy lyrics. In that song the searing guitar arpeggios surrounded by harmonies became part of the band's signature sound. On "ETI: Extra Terrestrial Intelligence" there are "men in black" who stop the narrator from talking about his experiences of UFOs. This eclectic mix of science fiction and horror genre themes combined with the band's blues and hard rock/quasi-metal sound.

Listening to Blue Öyster Cult may bring us back to heavy metal's origins, although there are many metal fans who would not consider BOC a metal band. The blues based rock of the late 1960s met with the rise of heavy metal. Blue Öyster Cult layered guitars and brought the rhythm section up and made it more propulsive. The band's first records vaguely suggested something mythological or that they were engaged with demonology. The melodic leads and pop edge of their compressed tunes veered away from anything that could be called heavy metal. Sandy Pearlman evidently hoped they could be the American answer to Black Sabbath. However, they were too unique and different for that to be an adequate comparison.

Psychedelic rock had a popular phase on Long Island in the late 1960s. Blue Öyster Cult joined forces in the area near Stony Brook. In the early days, Les Braunstein and Andrew Winters were members of Soft White Underbelly. They recorded for Elektra in 1968 but Braunstein left the band and the recording was not released. Eric Bloom was working as the band's recording engineer and he replaced Braunstein. They became Oaxaca and the Stalk-Forrest Group before settling upon the name Blue Öyster Cult in 1971. It was a name that derived from a poem by their manager, Pearlman. They suggested that they were a group of aliens who had arrived to guide the earth's future.

Aliens or not, they trained their sights on New York City. There has always been a close association of Long Island bands with Manhattan. Lou Reed was from Freeport, Long Island. Elliott Murphy was from Garden City. The Rascals rehearsed their music on Long Island. Billy Joel, from Hicksville, put out his first solo album and called it *Cold Spring Harbor.* Dee Snider of Twisted Sister came from Baldwin, New York, a town from which also came some members of the Good Rats. Eddie Money was from Levittown. Pat Benatar hailed from Lindenhurst. Vanilla Fudge was a link from psychedelia to heavy metal that spent time on Long Island. The Long Island musicians of Blue Öyster Cult were obviously in good company. Yet, it is hard to tell what Long Island has to do with science fiction or horror other than the scientific studies at the Cold Spring Harbor labs, or a speeded-up Billy Joel album.

Tyrrany and Mutation, produced by Murray Krugman and Pearlman, opened up the band's sound, adding echo to Eric Bloom's vocals. The record has a bit of a punk rock edge and categorizing it as heavy metal does not quite ring true. In May 1976 *Agents of Fortune* saw the single "Don't Fear the Reaper" break onto the pop charts. The song was written by Donald Buck Dharma Roeser. At the time, Albert Bouchard was also writing more of the band's tunes. Patti Smith co-wrote two songs and performed on "The Revenge of Vera Gemini."

"Don't Fear the Reaper" is arguably the band's most familiar hit song. It was used in the famous *Saturday Night Live* sketch "More Cowbell." (David Lucas played the cowbell part during the recording session at the Record Plant in New York.) The song was used in director John Carpenter's film *Halloween* and in a mini-series adaptation of Stephen King's *The Stand*. Lines from the band's songs were used in the Robert Galbraith (J.K. Rowling) novel *Career of Evil*. These uses underscore Blue Öyster Cult's association with the horror genre and the vaguely mythical and esoteric features of the band's output. Their other big hit was "Burning for You." By the time that single appeared, their personnel was Joe Bouchard (bass), Albert Brouchard (drums), Allen Lanier (organ), Donald Buck Dharma Roeser (lead guitar), Eric Bloom (vocals/guitar). That roster of musicians has changed across the years.[2] While the lineup has since changed the band's interest in myth and science fiction has remained.

The iconography for the band draws upon mythology. The hook and cross symbol designed by Bill Gawlik in 1972 appears on all of their albums. This figure is related to Kronos, the king of the Titans and father of Zeus in Greek mythology. It is also the alchemical symbol for lead, which is a heavy metal. This was also associated with the sickle ("Don't Fear the Reaper.") and is related to the astronomical symbol for Saturn, an agricultural symbol.

Several Blue Öyster Cult songs have titles which appear to be science fiction oriented but are not at all science fiction in content. "Stairway to the Stars" is about fans seeking autographs from the "stars." "Flaming Telepaths" has no telepathy. "Astronomy," from the same album, *Secret Treaties* (1974), is a love song that barely looks at the stars.

Collaborations

Blue Öyster Cult has worked directly with science fiction writers. Eric Bloom turned to science fiction film for his song "Godzilla," which became something of a novelty hit. In the late 1970s, Bloom, an avid reader of science fiction, sent a fan letter to science fiction writer Michael Moorcock. The author wrote back saying that he liked Blue Öyster Cult. He began to send along some possible lyrics for songs.

This began a unique collaboration. The collaboration resulted in three key songs for the band: "Black Blade," "Veterans of the Psychic Wars," and "The Great Sun Jester."

Mirrors (1979) began to show the fruits of this collaboration. The album, produced by Pearlman, included "The Great Sun Jester," a Moorcock lyric based upon his novel *The Fireclown*. "The Great Sun Jester" establishes a vocal narrative that intersects with guitar and keyboards and a prominent guitar lead. The universal joker has danced between stars but his manhood is at stake. Bloom and John Trivers also contributed to this song. "Dr. Music" by Joe Bouchard opened the album. "The Great Sun Jester" followed this, playing for 4:48. Next came "In Thee," "Mirrors," and Bouchard's "Moon Crazy."

Blue Öyster Cult's association with science fiction-fantasy writer Moorcock continued with *Cultosaurus Erectus* (1980). This album opened up with "Black Blade," which was about the Moorcock character Eric of Melmbone.[3] "Black Blade" opens on power chords and drums and a single lead vocal. The chorus brings reverb-enhanced echoing background vocals. There is a strong guitar lead, a percussion break, and the return of the lead guitar. "Veterans of the Psychic Wars" appeared on *Fire of Unknown Origin* (1981) and gives us keyboard chords over a drum pattern like a tribal march. The vocal comes to center upon the story of one who has been scarred in the psychic wars. *Fire of an Unknown Origin* was a strong comeback record. Some critics had written the band off. The songs for this album were drawn from the band's work on the film *Heavy Metal* (1981). Patti Smith wrote "Career of Evil" for Blue Öyster Cult during the time of her relationship with keyboardist Allen Lanier. Rock critic Robert Metzger, a friend of the band, also contributed lyrics.

Moorcock obviously felt a creative connection with rock musicians. He first began collaborating with the psychedelic hard rock band Hawkwind. Blue Öyster Cult's haunting and gritty sound must be distinguished from the space music of Hawkwind. The Elric concept album by Hawkwind was built upon Moorcock's Elric figure. Hawkwind developed songs with science fiction themes, including "Psychosonia," "Coded Language," and "Lost Chances." Moorcock's Eternal Champions stories became significant resources for the band. In these stories his heroes appear in a battle between law and chaos and focus on maintaining cosmic balance. Moorcock's Jerry Cornelius character's adventure from the late 1960s and early 1970s also engaged the interest of the members of Hawkwind. They welcomed references to Moorcock's character Eric Melnibone with his sword Stormbringer. Moorcock appeared on two solo albums with Hawkwind lyricist Robert Calvert: *Lucky Leif* (1975) and *Hype* (1981). Hawkwind produced psychedelic rock on *The Search for Space* (1971), the double album *Space Ritual*, (1973), *Doremi Fasol Latido* (1974), *Hall of the Mountain Grill*, and *Warrior on the Edge of Time* (1975). Moorcock wrote the lyrics for "Sonic Attack" on *Space Ritual*. His contributions also included the lyrics for "Black Corridor," "Kings of Speech," "The Wizard Blew His Horn" and "Standing at the Edge."

Moorcock's connection with Blue Öyster Cult came at a time when Pearlman persisted in his dream of shaping Blue Öyster Cult into an American version of Black Sabbath. The band members wanted to go their own way. In 1981, came "Psychosoma," "Sonic Attack," and "Coded Languages" for the album *Sonic Attack*. Moorcock wrote the lyrics for the title track and to "Black Corridor," based upon his 1969 novel. His Elric novels were used through *The Chronicle of the Black Sword* (1985), which featured "Sleep a Thousand Years." Moorcock lyrics included "The Wizard Blew His Horn," "Warriors," "Standing on the Edge," and "Kings of Speed," to which he added vocals. Moorcock appeared once with Blue Öyster Cult, in Atlanta, Georgia. Otherwise, he remained behind the scenes. Later, Blue Öyster Cult welcomed the ideas of author Eric Van Lustbader, who wrote lyrics for "The Shadow Warrior."

Some rock critics have suggested that Blue Öyster Cult's releases during the 1980s declined in creative power and quality. The *Imagina* (1988) album appeared to get lost amid the popular music of that year. Blue Öyster Cult had some resurgence in the 1990s and beyond, especially with live performances. For *Heaven Forbid* (1998) and *Curse of the Hidden Mirror* (2001) many of the songs were co-written with science fiction writer John Shirley, who, according to the band's website, returned them to "a horror influenced tone."[4] The typical John Shirley character is anarchic. Shirley writes imaginative stories across both the horror and science fiction genres. Thus, he is a perfect match with Blue Öyster Cult's sensibility.

John Shirley first heard Blue Öyster Cult after they released their first album and he saw them perform in Central Park in Manhattan. He gave his lyrics to a friend of Pearlman. This became the songs "Demon's Kiss" and "The Horsemen Arrive" for *Bad Channels*. Shirley brought his imagination to Blue Öyster Cult beginning with songs like "Transmaniacon" (January 1972). This song, named after his novel, starts with a minor chord followed by a descending guitar run by Roeser, to which Lanier adds the sound of the organ. The mythic center of the song is its underworld references.[4] Shirley's dystopian novel carries a dedication to Blue Öyster Cult, Patti Smith, literary critic Leslie Fiedler, and Aleister Crowley. Since then he has written many more lyrics, writing more than the band can set to music or use. He will fax lyrics to Roeser, who creates much of the music. Among the songs that Shirley has collaborated on are "Eve of the Hurricane" and "Out of the Darkness." Bloom, who has long been fascinated with science fiction, has found collaboration with Shirley across the years interesting and productive.

When science fiction writers like Moorcock and Shirley have penned lyrics for rock bands they have entered into working relationships with the bands. Ursula K. Le Guin once recognized that "Music is a cooperative art, organic by definition, social."[5] The music and lyrical collaborations of Michael Moorcock, John Shirley, and Eric von Lustbader with Blue Öyster Cult reflect the essence of this collaborative dimension of rock music.

Symbolism, Myth and Ritual

Blue Öyster Cult's name itself evokes the arcane mysteries of a cult. Horror fantasy, science fiction, and myth meet with symbolism. Rock performances may engage in symbolism. Symbols are capable of "transforming things into something other than what they appear to profane experience to be," says Mircea Eliade.[6] There is a logic of symbols, Eliade has said. "What we may call symbolic makes it possible for man to move freely from one level of reality to another."[7] Symbols, he tells us, "unify diverse levels and realities that are to all appearances incompatible."[8] Eliade suggests that once one is in touch with this symbolic expression of the dimensions of his or her being a person one "no longer feels himself to be an air-tight fragment, but a living cosmos open to all the other living cosmoses by which he is surrounded."[9] The myths reveal this person's own destiny. The individual does not lose himself or herself in myth but comes to find the self "because those myths and rituals express cosmic realities which ultimately he [or she] is aware of as realities of his [or her] own being."[10]

If we put pop novelties like BÖC's song "Godzilla" aside, it is obvious that some aspects of Blue Öyster Cult are psychedelic and hypnotic. Their engagement with horror fantasy and science fiction corresponds with rock's reach into the imaginative, unconscious, and mythopoetic dimensions of the human mind. With their collaborators, they are creators of myth and fantastic dreams.

"It is not that modern man has become any less mythic," writes Stanton Marian, "but that he has unconsciously lived the myths of logic and science. These myths unduly restrict the deepening of human consciousness and help foster the feeling of alienation and exile so common in modern times."[11] If this is so, there may be a tension between science and myth that has to be worked through in our age. Positivism once heralded the coming of a scientific age that would do away with myth, which it classified as primitive superstition. The problem with that view is that it denies the power of the mythopoetic imagination of humanity and the capacities of art. It neglects to recognize that a myth is a story that articulates meaning in our lives. Science fiction may be an important resource in our modern dialogue between science and myth. It may interrogate "the Promethean struggle for technological control by rationalistic modes of consciousness," or may imaginatively beckon toward new possibilities.[12] Indeed, attention to science fiction and to science as quest and discovery may enable a new story, a new narrative about humanity and the cosmos, to emerge in the twenty-first century.

Stories, including myths of adventure, return and renewal help modern people to balance mythic consciousness with the technological consciousness of our time. The fantasies of rock music artists or of science fiction writers inject symbolic vision and imagination into the dialogue with science. In the realm of psychology, Sigmund Freud took seriously the symbols of the unconscious and developed his own perspectives in *Interpretation of Dreams* (1900) on dream symbols and free association. Carl Jung recognized the value of daydreaming or dream play and dreams were not reduced to the symbolic expression of libidinal drives as in Freud. Rather, Jung posited that dreams gestured toward the mysteries of the collective unconscious. Jung made use of mythopoeic narration and visualization to connect his client's personal imaginations with this transpersonal collective imagination. Rock musicians have offered dream play and music as a means to break through ego-consciousness. Their music affirms the power of imagination. It also urges us to reclaim emotion, passion, feeling, intuition, body, and our sense of wonder.

You can still hear Blue Öyster Cult at concert venues around the United States. In the winter, they are indoors at small theaters. In summer they play outdoors. Seasonal transitions and the marking of time appear in many myths, which have been documented by Sir James Frazer and other mythologists. Eliade describes the "seasonal ritual drama" as involving purifications, purgations, or the driving away of demons, the extinguishing of fires, and masked processions in which the masked figures represent the dead, fights between opposing teams, and festivals like Saturnalia or carnival that reverse the normal order of things.[13] This, he says, is a movement into darkness, an interval between times, in which the old year passes into the new. After this, the cycle of regeneration will repeat. The old time is past. It is time to "start a new life, a new creation."[14] Eliade calls this a "longing to destroy profane time and live in sacred time."[15] Eliade's suggestion is that acquaintance with myth and ritual enlivens and restores a person. "For, thanks chiefly to his symbols, the real existence of primitive man was not the broken and alienated existence lived by civilized man today."[16]

Perhaps rock concerts, as communal events, are ritual dramas that partially restore this link. The rock music experience may seek to restore, through symbols and ritual, this contact with the depth dimension of the human spirit. This would suggest that rock music fantasy is not merely a flight from reality but may well be a search for alternatives to the realities of a world otherwise entranced by materialism, positivism, and reductionism. Rock challenges the common sense and accepted attitudes of the social context by re-mythologizing the world.

EIGHT

Rush to Other Realms

A Band's Genuine Love of Science Fiction

Rush was inducted into the Rock and Roll Hall of Fame in Cleveland a few years ago. This innovative band has never fit into neat rock music marketing categories. The Canadian trio—Geddy Lee (Gary Weinrib), Alex Liveson (Alex Zivojinovich) and Neil Peart—has earned respect for their musicianship and has built a broad fan base despite resistance from some rock critics to their unique progressive rock and their quirky songs. The progressive rock of Rush is characterized by musical virtuosity, tempo changes, lengthy instrumental passages, transitions of drum fills and guitar riffs, unexpected chord progressions, and the high-pitched vocals of Geddy Lee. Science fiction is near to the heart of the band. The concepts and lyrics of drummer Neil Peart and the music composed by Rush frequently explore science fiction. With the input of science fiction writer Kevin J. Anderson, science fiction ideas appear prominently in their latest albums.

What a listener hears throughout Rush's catalog is an abiding interest in science fiction and a creative rebellion against convention. From the band's inception in the early 1970s, Rush worked in a spirit similar to progressive rock art bands like King Crimson and Gentle Giant. When an article in *Time* magazine about black holes appeared in 1975 it sparked lyricist Neil Peart's interest in science fiction and the result was Rush's "Cygnus X-1: The Voyage," a wide ranging, spacious tune that enchants listeners with its changing rhythms that may be likened to an operatic overture.[1] More recently, Kevin J. Anderson's *The Saga of the Seven Suns* science fiction series has stirred Peart and

Geddy Lee, the band's lead vocalist, to new heights of imagination. Anderson has recognized Rush as a particularly strong influence upon his fiction. His novel *Resurrection, Inc.* (1988) drew upon Rush's music and lyrics from their album *Grace Under Pressure* (1984). Recently, Peart has co-written fiction with Anderson and has brought the science fiction writer's vision to bear upon two recent album projects, *Clockwork Angels* and *Clockwork Lives*. In 2013, Rush was inducted into the Rock and Roll Hall of Fame after decades of progressive rock innovation. The three Canadians have entertained thousands of listeners with their musical dynamics and have achieved a hard-won critical acceptance from rock music writers.

In Rush's recordings the sound, the music, and the "feel" are more important than the lyrics. Peart's lyrics are always couched within the musical flights of the band. Sometimes they are not understandable upon a first listening, given Geddy Lee's shrill vocals and loud bass and the dynamics that Peart and Lifeson bring to the music. Obviously, Peart reads science fiction, mythology, and ancient history and his science fiction concepts are important to Rush. However, his drumming is more crucial than this, for Rush's focus is always the music. The bass line and the kick drum must always match to hold the tempo together, even as time signatures shift. Much of a listener's attention goes to Peart's skill as a drummer, Lifeson's guitar playing virtuosity, and Geddy Lee's versatility. Geddy Lee's ability to sing while playing bass and keyboards is itself an extraordinary phenomenon. To sing while playing guitar may include some challenges, depending upon how intricate the guitar playing is. However, to sing lead vocals while playing bass is quite an accomplishment. The bass part generally lies under the melody and sometimes works against it and it has to match the rhythm.

Science fiction and Rush coalesced in the mid–1970s. Mystical and supernatural symbolism had become something of a mainstay of heavy metal bands and some progressive rock bands in the late 1970s. Rock music would bring mystery and wonder back to the world. Rush drew upon this trend with its own imaginative creations. Most significantly, they turned toward science fiction and fantasy. Lee and Lifeson were arguably much more interested in the music than in writing lyrics and Peart, an avid reader and writer, took over that role. Science fiction ideas emerged in his lyrics and merged with the band's attention to studio technology.

Caress of Steel *and* The Twilight Zone

Rush dedicated the album *Caress of Steel* (September 1975, Mercury) to Rod Serling, the creator of *The Twilight Zone*, who died in 1975. The album was filled with Rush's complex rhythms and lyrical fantasies. Before this, Rush's song "Fly By Night" had been commercially accessible for its audience. Their self-titled album *Rush* had done reasonably well commercially. Now *Caress of Steel* emerged as an esoteric venture. Michael Moorcock's science fiction fantasy lay behind their song "Necromancer." The song tells of three travelers, no doubt the members of Rush, "men of Willowdale," who go to unknown places. This recording signaled Rush's new ventures in imagination. From Willowdale, a suburb of Toronto, they travelled across the United States and Canada with their music. "The Necromancer" is suggestive of the rest of the album. The songs that follow are imaginative musical journeys into science fiction inspired realms of thought. "The Fountain of Lamneth" is followed by "In the Valley" and "Didacts and Narpets." (Narpets is an inversion of letters for "parents" and didacts are teachers.) "No One at the Bridge" sends up a call for assistance, which is followed by "Panacea" and "Bacchus Plateau." (Bacchus, of course, is the god of wine and revelry in Roman mythology.) The album is concluded by the musical explorations of "The Fountain." The album was not well-received by rock critics but within it were the seeds of much of what was to come in future Rush recordings. In the songs on *Caress of Steel*, Rush's initial musical efforts and their excursions into science fiction established a style, offered innovative musicianship, and suggested remarkable creativity.

2112

The band's subsequent album, *2112* (March 1976, Mercury), marked Rush as a rock band with a vivid imagination and an ongoing science fiction orientation. The record further established the Rush sound. The album *2112*, like its title, is futuristic. The science fiction fantasy takes a listener into a place of anger at establishment structures. Rush's album challenges the idea of an egalitarian society where individuality is consumed. Reflecting upon the thoughtful concepts on *2112*, Deena Weinstein has called Rush's *2112* an example of the turn toward "serious rock" by rock acts like Rush, Pink Floyd, Bruce Springsteen and others.[2]

In Rush's *2112* an idealistic youth faces a monolithic social structure that controls people. The individual confronts a society that finds its reason for being in technology. The iconography of the album cover of computer circuits and man against star itself indicates this.[3] The song's protagonist finds an electric guitar from the twentieth century and he learns how to play it. Naively, he believes that the controllers will be interested in his discovery. They are not pleased. The priests of the culture consider the guitar a threat and they destroy it and any chance this individual has for personal expression. There is a great difference between the use of technologies for freedom of expression and simply being plugged into the machine.

The record immediately signals that a science fiction narrative in a context of progressive space music will present concerns about a dystopian future society. The overture to *2112* starts with high-pitched electronic glissandos and sustained notes that rise over bass tones. The sounds evoke space, in the same way that much of the genre of space music or science fiction film scores have often done by utilizing sustain and echoed tones, slow tempos, high pitches and low bass tones that convey a sense of the vastness of space. Rush's lyrics on *2112* present what Chris McDonald has called "a vision of society that is divided between a pessimistic portrayal of it as a conformist social order which the individual should resist and an optimistic view of it as an environment in which the exceptional stands out and flourishes."[4]

Neil Peart's lyrics turned for inspiration toward Ayn Rand, who vigorously opposed communist totalitarianism by asserting "the virtue of selfishness" and a libertarian view of individual choice. Some listeners wondered why the band was creating lyrics that sounded like they had come from the novels of Ayn Rand. The reason for that was Neil Peart's conscientious reading of *Atlas Shrugged* and *Anthem* (1938).

He and Alex Lifeson and Geddy Lee had adopted something like a libertarian stance against all systems that would diminish individuality and autonomy. Neil Peart was writing lyrics that contested the system or structure of Western material society and asserted themes of individualism. Critics who had not read Ayn Rand were tipped off by Peart's reference to her work when he added a mention of Ayn Rand in the album's liner notes, crediting her work. Critics began to note how the vigorous independence and libertarian stance in Ayn Rand's work appealed to the band.

In *2112*, Peart devises a tale in which the priests of the Temple of Syrinx control a collectivist society. One might hear in this some echoes of dystopian fiction like Aldous Huxley's *Brave New World* or Yvgeny Zamyatin's *We*. Thinking on one's own is discouraged in these societies as it is in the society of Rand's novel and in the society presented in Peart's song. The priests of Syrinx are not able to impede human creativity altogether, however. In Rush's story, the protagonist discovers a guitar left over from the twentieth century. He learns to play the instrument and offers his gift to the controllers, who fear and reject it. Whereas Ayn Rand's character in *Anthem* discovers electric light and this leads toward change, Peart's character's discovery of the electric guitar leads to its destruction and his dismissal because it is "not part of the plan." Rand's dissident questions collectivism and discovers a past technology that enables hope to be regained. However, in Peart's version, the guitar playing dissident does not flourish. He is a captive in a demeaning, soul-diminishing maze. He remains nameless and his dream fades. Peart's lyric is one of romantic pessimism rather than libertarian optimism.

2112 marked Rush as an album oriented band: one not inclined toward producing short radio friendly singles. Mercury Records, which had recently been purchased by Polygram, did not view *2112* as a commercial album. However, the recording attracted and built Rush's following, which Rush further developed as a touring act. The album sold an estimated 160,000 copies by June 1976. In October, it reached #61 on the *Billboard* charts. Across the years, the record has reached the platinum mark in album sales.

2112, like its title, is futuristic. A synthesized "overture" opens the album's second song, based upon Rand's *Anthem*. The discovery of electricity in Rand's novel is related to the electric guitar in Rush's song. A key figure on this album is the anonymous narrator's discovery of the guitar: a relic of the twentieth century. (Indeed, his story might have been different if he had found the tiniest guitar on earth in existence today. With experiments in nanotechnology, Cornell University scientists have made a guitar of crystalline silicon that is far smaller than a human hair. Played by an atom force microscope it produces a high-pitched sound that the Priests of Syrinx would not have heard because they exceed the range of the human ear.[5]) The priests of "The Temple of Syrinx" represent music business executives and critics who did not always like what was coming from Rush into the range of their own hearing. Those music business executives insisted upon a commercial formula for the music produced for the public. Rush did not subscribe to those categories. The band insisted that they would be engaged in the discovery of musical expression on their own terms.

2112 drew a mixed response from the critics. Dan Nooger of *Circus* magazine lamented that Geddy Lee's voice was so high and raspy that it was likely to bother listeners as much as it irritated him. He said that if that vocal got any higher and raspier it would only appeal to "dogs and extraterrestrials."[6] However, Nooger observed that he had gotten a sense of the other-worldly character of the band and their inclination toward science fiction motifs.

The Pentagram Logo

At this time, Rush introduced their logo: a pentagram, a five pointed star, created by Hugh Syme for the inside cover of the album. Neil Peart had cast The Federation as an oppressive enemy to intellectual freedom and the red star was designed to reflect this. Meanwhile, some critics wondered what that Canadian band was saying with the pentagram.

The star was once a mystical symbol for the Pythogoreans, an ancient society of the Greek isles who were deeply interested in music and mathematical ratios. Most people who have heard the name Pythagoras associate him with the Pythagorean theorem in geometry. The pentagram had for the Pythogoreans musical and mathematical relevance. The five pointed star suggests the infinite and it contains a bright star within a smaller pentagon. Tucked within this design was the golden ratio. Pythogoras believed that there were ratios between the stars—much like the strings of a harp—which conveyed "the music of the spheres." Legend has it that Pythagoras actually played a box with a string stretched across it and by moving the bridge up and down he could change the notes that could be played. When the bridge was set in position one could play what would be called the tonic or root note. Move it up and parts of the string, divided by the bridge, would have different ratios and different sounds. These could be measured mathematically. Music and math and nature itself were all related. Ratio and proportion sustained and managed musical quality and beauty, as well as physical beauty.

The universe that the pentagram symbolized was orderly: one with earth at the center and the stars revolving around it, in vibration, or making a music of the spheres. Shakespeare recalls this in *The Merchant of Venice* when his character Lorenzo says to his lover Jessica that this muddy vesture of decay so closes us in that we can no longer hear this universal music. Fascination with the pentagram goes further than this, however. Because the lines of the star are divided in a way that expresses the golden ratio, this suggests that the cosmos we live in is interconnected. Rush may be suggesting an ancient insight which persisted in Western thought at least until the time of the Renaissance: that music fills the universe.

Now armed with a significant progressive rock album and a band defining logo, Rush played live and toured steadily and their audience grew. Ray Danniels and members of their management decided that a live recording would be a good idea for their next album. To title their live album in 1976, Rush made use of another Shakespearean phrase. *All the World's A Stage* (September 29, 1976) sold well and became a gold album within two months. As if to echo the phrase, the band toured widely for seven months. By now, they had assumed outsider status, as a concept album band in a music industry that remained largely focused upon producing hit singles. Their audience responded to themes of alienation and feeling disaffected. Rush were nonconformists and their message was compelling. Often their introduction of science fiction motifs suggested a struggle for freedom that connected well with their fan base.

A Farewell to Kings *and* Hemispheres

When Rush developed their album *A Farewell to Kings* a sense of mythology lay behind it. The band's sound was augmented by the bass pedals that Geddy Lee brought in. He incorporated those bass pedals into his playing so that he could accompany Alex Lifeson's guitar at live shows, while keeping himself free to either play bass or keyboards. The synthesizer sound also grew more prominent on this album. Geddy Lee had gotten a Mini-Moog. Its sound complemented the science fiction aspects of the record. *A Farewell to Kings* opens with Rush's extended version of "Xanadu," drawn from Samuel Taylor Coleridge's opiate dream poem "Kublai Kahn." The song is eleven minutes of musical ingenuity and performance. "Cinderella Man" echoes the anti-establishment tones of some of their previous work. The song is filled with Alex Lifeson guitar solos.

During this time, Neil Peart read in *Time* magazine about black holes and it moved him to write "Cygnus X-1: The Voyage." On *Hemispheres* (1978) the narrator passes through the black hole Cygnus X-1. Terry Brown, the recording's producer, spoke the introduction to Cygnus X-1. The song follows the journey of the spaceship *Rocinante*, named after Don Quixote's horse. They recorded it in South Wales at Rockfield Studios and brought the product for mixing to Advision Studios in London.

Fans of Rush are often drawn to the band by the complexity of musical passages in pieces like "La Villa Strangiatto," on the *Hemispheres* album. The song's middle section is in 7/8 time. The principal theme recedes into Lifeson's guitar solo when he moves into an arpeggio pattern after the lead peaks at about 5:14. Such musical transitions in the band's compositions increasingly called for Lee to work at the intersection of pre-recorded, processed material and the performance he created uniquely each night on bass and keyboards. Lee is primarily a bass guitar player rather than a keyboardist. However, beginning in 1976, Rush began to make increasing use of synthesizers on their recordings, so that five of the six songs on *Permanent Waves* (1980) and all seven songs on *Moving Pictures* (1981) incorporate synthesizers.[7]

One of Rush's signature songs, "YYZ," the third track from *Moving*

Pictures, is a song filled with transition and asymmetrical meter. The song opens in Morse code and soon guitar, bass, and drums unite in 5/4 time. However, a half-minute into the song a quick passage of sixteenth notes in 6/8 time creates a change. Bass and guitar play the melody in counterpoint out to about a minute and a half into the piece, at which point Peart's drum fills bring us into the next section which features solo guitar work by Lifeson. The song expresses the virtuosity of the band well, with features like a 32-note tom fill by Peart and dazzling guitar and bass work by Lifeson and Lee. For the members of Rush "YYZ" is the aviation code for Toronto's Pearson International Airport. The song signals for them airports, travel, and homecoming to Toronto. It has been adopted for a home video game on Guitar Hero. So too has their song "Tom Sawyer," for Rock Band. People have found Rush songs fun to play on Rock Band but this has little to do with real musicianship. The members of the band "failed" when challenged to play the game's version of "Tom Sawyer" in 2008 on *The Colbert Report* on television.

Technology

Peart's ongoing interest in technology appears on *Permanent Waves* (1980), in the song "Natural Science." Here he reflects upon the social impact of technology. A scientist may look toward the future and speculate on where a technology might take our society. However, one cannot always be sure of that technology's effects. In "Natural Science" we hear that causes can't see their effects. What can be accomplished with science and technology must be balanced and care must be taken when it is applied to human beings, who have free will. (This echoes across the airwaves today in Lee's memorable declaration of free will in Rush's song "Freewill.") *Permanent Waves* continued with the science and technology theme across several songs. With "Hyperspace" comes a driving 7/8 tempo, synthesizer and heavy bass, and high vocals in brief phrases. The lyrics of these songs suggest that science can be brought into humanistic relation with humanity if science is approached with integrity.

"The Spirit of Radio," the opening song on *Permanent Waves*

(1980), affirms that music has cultural value and offers a comment on programmed radio airplay and record industry calculations. Record companies are more intent upon units sold and *Billboard* chart position than they are concerned about the enduring qualities of the art of music. "One likes to believe in the freedom of music," the song lyric says. Rush critiques the industry—its machinations, its concerts, promotions and money making engine—and asserts its right to create music that has nothing to do with studio doctored cookie-cutter singles aimed at the pop charts. Throughout the 1980s Rush repeatedly emphasized the theme of awareness and the lyrics of their songs increasingly delved into human issues. Meanwhile, their lyrics continued to draw upon science fiction motifs and figures like robots and androids and their music suggested space and technology with synthesizers and a variety of effects.

The album *Grace Under Pressure* (1984) features a Hugh Syme album cover design on which an android looks to the distance at a circuit board encompassed by liquid clouds. At this time, Rush was bringing synthesizers, sequencers, guitar and keyboard effect boxes, samplers, and pre-recorded materials into their live performances. This led some critics to question this arrangement of technology and mixture of live and processed sounds.[8]

References to science fiction, fantasy, and mythology began to drift away from Rush's records in the late 1980s. At a time when the band was drawing upon progressive rock, jazz fusion and new wave/post-punk, their song lyrics expanded to reflection on social problems and human issues like loneliness, ambition, vulnerability, war, and freedom.[9] However, they continued to draw upon their catalogue which evoked the exotic landscapes of J.R.R. Tolkein's "Rivendell" and Samuel Taylor Coleridge's "Kublai Kahn" in "Xanadu" on *A Farewell to Kings* (1977). The band's involvement with technology, in the studio and onstage, contributed to their songwriting.

Technical Innovation

Rush studiously utilizes recording technology in the spirit of *techne*, the Greek word for making. They recognize the value of artisanship over mass production. Their support of technological innovation is only qualified by their distaste for technocracy. Technology can empower or oppress. Consequently, one area of ongoing curiosity in Peart's lyrics is an inquiry into the interaction of the human and the machine. Rush's song "The Body Electric" appears to draw more upon Ray Bradbury and science fiction than upon Walt Whitman's poem. Peart's lyric creates the story of an android that can feel and that has will. The song lyric is filled with computer imagery, as Durrell Bowman points out.[10] It refers to a "humanoid escapee," an "android on the run," "data overload," "memory banks unloading ... bytes breaking" and a binary code that is sung during the song's chorus.

"The Body Electric" explores the increasing interface between the human and the machine that poststructuralist critic Mark Poster has called "the mode of information." As Poster points out, in several Philip K. Dick stories a symbiotic merger between human and machine appears: "What may be happening is that human beings create computers and then computers create a new species of humans."[11] Poster's concern is with electronic mediated communication and language and its impact upon people and society. "Information has become a privileged term in our culture," he says. "[...] Each method of preserving and transmitting information profoundly intervenes in the network of relationships that constitute a society."[12] Peart, likewise, appears to have a lively curiosity about where computer technology is taking us and where we are taking that technology.

Musical reproduction provides an example of how "electronic mediation changes the language situation," Poster points out. "The case of recorded rock music presents a quite different configuration of language. Many studio recordings of rock are from the outset structured for reproduction in the home."[13] What follows from this, he says, is a simulacrum: tracks that have been assembled into performances that exist only in their reproductions. Rush has regularly blended elements of studio accomplishment with onstage performances. That is, they perform new information. Lee sings lyrics that are sometimes his own but more often they are lyrics that Peart has written down. These lyrics have become vocalized orally and recorded electronically.

Rush is engaged in the transformation of knowledge/information by communication in songs. Digital sampling, sequencing, synthesizers, and hours spent in front of computer monitors in studios have become part of Rush's art. Technology deeply intersects with their music-making, songwriting, and performances. Reflections upon robotics, Artificial Intelligence, and how human and machine are interacting clearly interest Peart in his lyric writing.

Scientists point out that AI in robots is at present not possible. A robot cannot yet think and feel, as in Stephen Spielberg's film *Artificial Intelligence: AI*, or in the case of HAL in Arthur C. Clarke's *2001*. However, scientists are thinking about it. In the year 2001, at the Massachusetts Institute of Technology, the director of the MIT Artificial Intelligence laboratory, Rodney Brooks, paused in building humanoid robots and began asking about the difference between the organizing systems of living beings and nonliving matter.[14] He pointed out in 2008 out that at MIT people were working to build robots that can repair themselves and seek energy to maintain themselves and that a new approach had emerged to creating intellectual robots based on perception and language. Those researchers have been steadily at work on this ever since.

Humanity has been adapting conceptually and neurologically to the information age and to electronic media. Computers are now part of our everyday life and an integral part of contemporary music making in recording studios throughout the world. Communication has extended our nervous systems. We are virtually in other places in the world besides the geographical location in which we stand. The mode of information is dispersed. This, observes Mark Poster, affects "the very shape of subjectivity, its relation to the world of objects, its perspective on that world, its location in that world."[15] Rush's music, intertwined with technology, participates in this space, sending out signals that affect their listeners.

Clockwork Angels

Rush has revisited science fiction on their recent albums. Peart has returned to science fiction motifs and has collaborated with science fiction writer Kevin J. Anderson on *Clockwork Angels* (2012). With *Clockwork Angels*, a science fiction adventure novel, he repeated the dystopian issues of *2112* with new variations. Peart's life has been a process of rebuilding, healing, and expansion for the past twenty years. In 1997, he was deeply shaken when his daughter died in a car accident. His wife succumbed to cancer shortly thereafter. With his world having fallen apart, Peart pulled away from music and went on a long motorcycle journey, which he has written about in *Ghost Rider Travels on the Healing Road* (2002). He wrote letters, a journal, and lyrics to let go of hurt and anger, to free and create meaning in a life shattered by the loss of close relationships.[16] Peart has been amazingly productive since that time of tragic loss. He has remarried, had a child, lived in Los Angeles, and joined Rush for several tours and albums. *Clockwork Angels* was followed by a sequel, *Clockwork Lives*, which develops the story with airships, alchemy, and pirates.

Clockwork Angels had been anticipated for quite some time when it was released on June 12, 2012. It was recorded at Blackbird Studio in Nashville in April 2010 and at Revolution Recording in Toronto between October and December of 2011. Lee and Lifeson mentioned the project in a March 19, 2010, interview and Lifeson confirmed it in another interview on March 26 of that year. Peart announced that Nick Raskulinecz would produce the album and that they had six tunes for the record. "Caravan" and "BU2B" were recorded in Nashville and Richard Chekyi later mixed the tracks in Franklin, Tennessee. These songs were made available online. "Headlong Flight" and "The Wreckers" were launched as singles from the album. The recording included string arrangements with six violins and two cellos. The album cover, designed by Hugh Syme, showed a clock with alchemical symbols and the number 9:12, or 21:12 in twenty-four hour time, recalling the band's *2112* recording. The story-line for the concept album reflected the social dystopia of that previous album and developed a new scenario. The novelization in which Kevin J. Anderson's hand was involved appeared in February 2012.

In *Clockwork Angels* we meet with Owen Hardy who grows up in a small town in a world controlled by the Watchmaker. Owen dreams of being an assistant in the apple orchard. He misses his girlfriend and is pulled aboard a train bound for the city in Albion, where the Watchmaker rules through alchemical creations of gold and manipulations of the time and the weather. All things need order and fall under his control. On the train, Owen has no money and he is given a loan by the Anarchist. (We hear of him in the fourth cut on the record, "The Anarchist.") The Anarchist faces off against the Watchmaker, who asserts that "the universe has a plan: all is for the best." Owen gets caught up in a plot that might remind one of the anarchism in Joseph Conrad's *The Secret Agent*. The anarchist implicates him in a bombing and Owen is on the run.

Clockwork Angels sold well. It received Canada's Juno Award for best album of the year in 2013 and led Peart to explore writing "2113," as a sequel to *2112*. He imagined a new recording: *Clockwork Lives*. Peart also wrote another memoir: *Far and Near: On Days Like These* (October 2014.)

Rush's entry into the Rock and Roll Hall of Fame was a peak of public recognition for the band's a long career of innovative musicianship and fiercely independent thinking. Science fiction has figured significantly in their journey. They have brought science fiction concepts, images, and social critique into connection with their idiosyncratic style of progressive rock. The imagination of Rush has embraced technology fervently, while warning against excesses of scientism or political control and asserting the dignity and rights of individuals to be as unique as they choose to be.

NINE

The Alan Parsons Project
Robots and Telepathy

Mystery, science fiction, and drama converge in the smooth, lush sound produced by the musicianship and technological skills of the Alan Parsons Project. Ten studio albums and a string of hit singles that might be classified as easy listening rock came from this musical collective in which the studio recording talents of Alan Parsons were matched with the songwriting skills of Eric Woolfson. They brought together a cast of vocalists and musicians to create some of the most memorable pop music of the 1970s and early 1980s.

The Alan Parsons Project, at first, was never quite what we would call a rock band. It consisted of two very talented studio-minded musicians, Parsons and Eric Woolfson, who created many gold and platinum albums and utilized guest vocalists. Woolfson was the songwriter, coming up with a string of easy listening light rock hits and several science fiction concept albums. Parsons was a renowned recording engineer and producer, who was an assistant recording engineer for the Beatles' *Abbey Road* and *Let It Be* and the recording engineer for Pink Floyd's *The Dark Side of the Moon* (1974). He had produced albums for Ambrosia, Al Stewart, and Pilot. Woolfson and Parsons displayed a technological mastery of the recording studio and a penchant for exploring the mysterious and a variety of science fiction themes. They offered speculations on robots, time, and electronic and satellite surveillance. The Alan Parsons Project scored several radio friendly singles on their first albums and broke out commercially with the vocal by Woolfson on his song "Eye in the Sky" in 1982. The song remotely reflects Philip K. Dick's novel *Eye in the Sky* (1957). Its haunting melody and arrangement captures a creepy surveillance theme in an atmosphere enhanced by smooth vocal harmonies.

154

Parsons and Woolfson met in the early 1970s, when Woolfson pursued music management to supplement his career as a songwriter. Parsons, a talented music arranger and studio engineer, became one of his first clients. Alan Parsons began his career by working at the EMI tape duplicating facility at Abbey Road. There he met The Beatles and worked as an assistant, studying their remarkable work on *Sgt. Pepper* and the Beatles' subsequent recordings. His work continued with Paul McCartney on *Wild Life* and *Red Rose Speedway*, and, most significantly, he recorded Pink Floyd's *Dark Side of the Moon.* Parsons also recorded three albums with Pilot, with Ian Bairnson on guitar, Stuart Tosk on drums, Billy Lyell on keyboards, and David Paton's vocals. He developed three albums with Al Stewart, including the singles "Time Passages" and "The Year of the Cat," jazzing up Stewart's folk-based music and adding the familiar saxophone part. With the Hollies, Parsons produced five albums, including their hit recording of the Neil Diamond song "He Ain't Heavy, He's My Brother" and their recording of "The Air That I Breathe." He mixed Ambrosia's first album and was involved with their recording *Somewhere I've Never Traveled.* Parsons declined to work on Pink Floyd's *Wish You Were Here* because he was beginning work with Woolfson on the Alan Parsons Project.

Woolfson was born in Glasgow on March 18, 1945. He was fascinated with science fiction and mystery stories. His uncle played piano and that encouraged Woolfson to take piano lessons as a child. He abandoned formal lessons and was mostly self-taught. He eventually became a session pianist and spent time on London's Denmark Street, a music center. He met Jimmy Page and John Paul Jones in the years before their formation of Led Zeppelin. He then met Andrew Oldham, the manager of the Rolling Stones, who was impressed by his songs and gave him a publishing deal with Immediate Records. Woolfson's songs were recorded by Marianne Faithful, Frank Field and others. His early recordings included a Chris Farlowe B-side on "Out of Time." Woolfson met Tim Rice and Andrew Lloyd Webber at Southern Music, as they were turning their attention to the musical theater. Attempting to make a living in the music business, Woolfson he became an independent record producer and he tried out artist management. Carl Douglas, whose "Kung Fu Fighting" reached the pop charts in 1974, became one of his clients. However, more important for his future was his new association with producer Parsons. The Alan Parsons Project emerged from that partnership. Woolfson was deeply involved with all of the group's hits. In the late 1980s Woolfson focused on musical theater.

The science fiction concepts of Woolfson were often expressed on record with spacious effects and synthesizers. They were enriched by with the masterful studio technology of Alan Parsons. In 1976, Woolfson had recently finished adapting four of Edgar Alan Poe's stories and two of Poe's poems. Parsons produced and engineered the *Tales of Mystery and Imagination* (1976) album, bringing lush instrumentation to an album based in themes that were largely conceived of by Woolfson.[1]

The Image of the Robot

For their second album, the Alan Parsons Project turned to Isaac Asimov's novel *I, Robot* for inspiration and explored the potential of artificial intelligence. *I Robot* (1977) is often considered the masterpiece of the Alan Parsons Project and it has been re-released in an extended version titled *Legacy*. Eric Woolfson spoke with Isaac Asimov as he prepared the songs for this recording. Asimov approved of the project. The rights for *I, Robot* had been given to a television movie company. At the same time that Eric Woolfson arrived at the idea for a concept album, Harlan Ellison was adapting the nine stories for a screenplay. *I Robot* used the title of Isaac Asimov's book but dropped the comma in that title. In Asimov's novel, Dr. Susan Calvin tells stories to the narrator, who is a reporter in the twenty-first century. Woolfson seized upon this scheme for a narrative pattern for his songs. The album offers a narrative about robots and human wills in conflict with each other.

According to the album liner notes, Woolfson structured the album thematically around the idea of "The story of the rise of the machine and the decline of man."[2] This occurred when the human "tried to re-create the robot in his own image." The record ends with "Genesis, Chapter 1, Verse 32," a speculation that takes us beyond the text, since the written biblical document of *Genesis* has 31 verses. Woolfson created an eclectic weave of songs and instrumentals and brought together a collective of musicians from the bands Pilot and Ambrosia, whose recordings Parsons produced at the time. The musicians included David Paton on acoustic guitar and bass, Stuart Tosh on drums, Ian Bairnson on guitars, B.J. Cole on steel pedal, John Leach on cymbalon and kantele, and Duncan Mackay, who added keyboards.

On the album cover, the Alan Parsons Project is featured in a hazy photo of band members crossing the escalator tubes of circular Terminal 1 at Charles De Gaulle Airport near Paris. Over this is superimposed a painting of a robot. The singles "I Wouldn't Want to Be Like You" and "Don't Let It Show" became hits that are still often played on classic rock and album oriented rock (AOR) stations. "Day After Day (The Show Must Go On)" also reached the charts. The song "Breakdown" has had a long life in radio play on AOR stations. The album's opening cut is the instrumental "I, Robot." The vocal on "I Wouldn't Want to Be Like You," which follows, is by Lenny Zakatek, a vocalist often featured among the Parsons revolving cast of singers. The musical journey continues with Peter Staker's vocal, along with Jaki Wittren singing on "Some Other Time." "Breakdown" features the singing of Allan Clarke, a key member of the Hollies. Dave Townsend's vocal on "Don't Let It Show" ends the first side of the LP. When listeners turned the vinyl record over they heard Steve Harley singing on "The Voice." "Nucleus," with its obvious science derived title, provided an instrumental break before "Day After Day" with Jack Harris' vocal. The instrumental of "Total Eclipse" provided further musical atmosphere from composer Andrew Howell. Its title and the music suggested something cosmic, or at least astronomical. Then the album came to a conclusion with "Genesis Ch.1 v.32." Woolfson was involved with writing every one of the songs, except for the Howell composition. Parsons assumed the role of director-producer. He recorded and engineered the tracks, assisted with arrangements, and produced the album.

The work of Parsons and Woolfson was acclaimed by Stephen Holden in *The Village Voice* on August 29, 1977. In his article, "Alan Parsons' Robot: Sci-Fi Cinerama," he observed the album's theme. The decline of man "came with the discovery of the wheel" said the liner notes. "I flinched when I read it," Holden wrote. But the theme was not pretentious, he concluded. He called *I Robot* "the head album of the year. While it offers warnings about humanity's imminent technological self-destruction," he wrote, it stands as "a stunning demonstration of its creator's control over technology": This is "massive, richly textured music," Holden said. He insisted that *I Robot* reflects our culture's "love-hate relationship with technology." Holden then added his view that Alan Parsons is responsible "for some of the grandest montage in rock." He referred to their music as "Mahlerian." *I Robot* lyrics are "based on a riddle rather than a narrative idea," he suggested. Parsons and Woolfson had achieved a remarkable fusion of their talents. Holden wrote: "But the scope of the sound is so majestic and the melody to graceful that mysticism eclipses dread." He asserted that "Breakdown" can stand next to the Who's *Tommy*, and he noted that the Alan Parsons Project recognizes and refers to R&B influences on "I Wouldn't Want to Be Like You."[3]

Certainly, the image of the robot has developed across the years, even as robots themselves have further developed. They have been tools and slave labor, or service robots that can take over human work functions. However, androids and cyborgs imitate human functions and develop toward artificial intelligence. That is, they transcend the capacity to perform assigned work tasks and begin to imitate human consciousness. Computers and robots merge to become artificial forms that may appear humanlike. Some science fiction writers have pushed this further, suggesting that all human functions are to be replaced by advanced robots. Bill Gates told Charlie Rose on PBS in February 2016 that he believes that robotics and computerization will advance to exceeding human capacity in about fifty years.

Robots force us to think about what it means to be human. What happens when a computer chip is inserted into a person, or an individual is reconstituted by technology to become the six million dollar man? What is an artificial person? What will happen if studies in artificial intelligence at MIT, or other research facilities in technological innovation, produce robots with keen artificial intelligence? As medical technology and computer technology advance, these questions, once posed by science fiction, arise more often and have to be taken quite seriously. As the public is given films like *AI: Artificial Intelligence* and *Ex Machina*, the inquiry into artificial intelligence by scientists proceeds like a mythical quest into the unknown.

The mythological ancestor of the robot is Talos, the giant that

Jason and the Argonauts must contend with as they seek the Golden Fleece. Talos is made of bronze and he guards the island of Crete. In the 1963 film *Jason and the Argonauts,* Talos creaks, like a door on a rusty hinge. He is a monstrous figure with sword in his hand and with his feet on the rocks on either side of the passageway through which the Argonauts must travel. This figure of Talos is decidedly mechanical.

Robots, however, have increasingly been conceived of as something beyond mechanical creatures of human invention. The modern idea of a robot appeared in Czechoslovakian writer Karel Capek's 1920 play *R.U.R.:* initials that designated Rossum's University Robots. These were organic beings, rather than mechanical ones. They were made from living tissue at the Rossum factory. These robots would serve mankind as cheap labor. However, in Capek's story they become more advanced and revolt, killing the humans, except for one. Fritz Lang's film *Metropolis* (1927) followed with an image of a robot. In 1938, Lester Del Rey created a domestic robot in his story "Helen O'Loy." Her name is derived from the metal alloys used to construct her. Two characters in the story want to find a way to humanize her and they succeed. She falls in love with one of them. O'Loy becomes a housewife in a marriage and the fact that she is a robot is hidden from view. When her husband dies she asks his friend to dismantle her and bury her with him.

Soon afterward, Isaac Asimov was writing his stories featuring robots. He asserted that robotics could develop in ways genuinely beneficial to humanity. He wrote *I, Robot, The Naked Sun, Caves of Steel* and featured some robots with humanlike qualities. The robots of Asimov are efficient, sometimes brilliant, and well-governed. They show robots as a positive benefit to mankind, in contrast with the labor-rebellion of Capek's robots, who ultimately threaten humanity. These images circulated through dozens of science fiction stories and became familiar figures in television and film. Helper robots were introduced to children in the 1960s on the television program *Lost in Space,* which featured a loveable robot who signaled any threat with a cry of "Danger, danger Will Robinson." In Ira Levin's 1972 satire *The Stepford Wives* (and its 2004 film remake) speculation arises that the women in a Connecticut community are robots. The robot as potential enemy, which hearkens back to the alienated creature of Mary Shelley's *Frankenstein,* can be seen in the robots and computers of the television series *Battlestar Gallactica* (2004) that would take over humanity, or in the cybernetic organism played by Arnold Schwartzenegger in James Cameron's film The *Terminator* (1984). The robots that appear in Asimov novels suggest a helper, more like C3PO and R2D2 in *Star Wars*.

Asimov's laws of robotics in *I, Robot* (1950) became a standard that other science fiction writers responded to: A robot must not injure a human being. A robot must obey orders given to it by human beings except when such orders conflict with the First Law to not harm human beings. A robot is required to protect itself while not violating either of the first two laws. Science fiction writer Stanislaw Lem opposed this view and stated that Asimov's laws of robots "give us a wholly false picture of the real possibilities."[4]

Eye in the Sky: *Surveillance and Telepathy*

Parsons and Woolfson followed *I Robot* with *Pyramid* (1978) and *Turn of a Friendly Card* (1980). With *Pyramid*, they imagined Egyptian mythology. *Turn of a Friendly Card* emerged from their time in Monaco and their fascination with the world of gambling. On the title song they explore the human tendency toward greed. The song is developed in five parts and features vocals by Chris Rainbow. The ballad "Time," with Eric Woolfson's vocal, is the closest thing to science fiction of the six songs offered on this album. "Games People Play," the album's other single, is sung by Lenny Zakatek. A reference to Edgar Allan Poe slips back into the picture with "The Gold Bug," an instrumental.

The Alan Parsons Project burst into full public view with their best-selling *Eye in the Sky* (1982), of which millions of copies have been sold. For this album they borrowed a title from a 1957 novel by Philip K. Dick and explored a dystopian world of surveillance. Woolfson was an avid science fiction reader but because of copyright he never took anything from either Asimov or Dick other than the general atmosphere of science fiction. Instead, he created his own narrative and set it to harmonic, smooth music that seemed much less edgy than the topics he had chosen. The clear, crisp, almost crystalline mastering of *I Robot* by Woolfson, produced with his daughter Sally and with Parsons, is a sign of the perfectionism in another musical era. "Nucleus" makes use of analog keyboards, a precursor to 1980s digital sampling, layering chords upon chords to create its distinctive sound. Their film-like music and radio friendly singles marked them as a progressive art band that recorded concept albums deeply identifying with science fiction.

Eye in the Sky (1982) opens with the spacey instrumental "Sirius." The popular distribution of the title song, "Eye in the Sky," which reached #3 of the Billboard charts, brought attention to the album's opening piece. "Sirius" has been used by the Chicago Bulls basketball team, when announcing its players before a game. The bass keeps playing at the end of this instrumental and brings us into the title track. "Eye in the Sky" may be about satellites, or about hidden cameras in a casino. The narrator may be spying on his lover, or the song may suggest Orwell's *1984* theme of "big brother is watching you." For some listeners today the lyric might anticipate more recent concerns about government monitoring of Internet use and phone conversations, given increased concerns about terrorism. The lyrics to "Eye in the Sky" speak not only of looking at someone but also about being able to read someone's mind. Thus, the song carries the suggestion of telepathy, which has remained a persistent theme in science fiction.[5]

"Children of the Moon" follows, with a choir, string and brass orchestration, and David Paton's vocals. The song continues a vaguely science fiction theme on this album. Yet, it soon becomes clear that with this record the Alan Parsons Project was moving away from the concept album approach. A suggestion of science fiction remains and a sense of mystery still lingers in the ethereal vocals. "Gemini" follows, with a title that may call up associations with space travel and the cosmos and the evocative vocal by Chris Rainbow. The symphonic effects by Parsons on "The Silence" and the 95 orchestral pieces conducted by Andrew Powell have a quality of airiness and suggest an expansiveness of space. This last song on the first side of the vinyl LP begins and ends with a ballad sung by Eric Woolfson. Its center is filled with Powell's rich orchestration. If one is listening to a CD remix of the album "The Silence" easily transitions into "You're Gonna Get Your Fingers Burned" and Lenny Zakotek's vocals. "Psychobabble" follows with a strong bass line and vocals from Elmer Gantry (Dave Terry). "Psychobabble" is energetic and pulses forward. In his review of the album Stephen Thomas Erlewine described the song as having "a bright propulsive edge."[6] "Mammogamma," which follows, was created on and by computers. "Step by Step" features a guitar solo from Ian Bainston. On this song a guitar is played directly into the mixing deck with no amplification. Zakotek contributes the vocal. "Old Wise" concludes the album. *Eye in the Sky* drew comparisons from critics with the work of 10CC, an English pop/rock band of producer-songwriters with an art-rock sensibility. Erlewine compared "Children of the Moon" to "Heart to Heart" by Kenny Loggins. He added the often repeated view that this album is not about a theme but is focused upon creating "a lushness of sound" with "sweet melody," textures and pop hooks.

The hit song "Eye in the Sky" may be about surveillance. However, it also raises the topic of telepathy with its lyric about reading one's mind. Telepathy makes group mind possible. "Most group mind stories, for instance, suggest the appearance of group mind is a function of the dynamics of evolution," writes Stan McDaniel.[7] He notes *Childhood's End* by Arthur C. Clarke as an example. He refers to the orthogenetic view of Teilhard de Chardin, which would not require telepathy. Teilhard coined the term *noogenesis* for mental evolution.[8] Teilhard de Chardin wrote: "The more complex a being is the more it is centered in itself and therefore the more conscious does it become."[9] The priest-paleontologist asserted that matter and life itself is a dynamic process emerging within consciousness and that the orientation of the evolutionary axis of development can be empirically determined.

Olaf Stapledon's *Last and First Men* (1930) presented a group mind of 96 individuals. In the story we read that this would not be possible "did not the temperament and capacity of each differ appropriately from those of the others."[10] Stapledon identifies evolutionary advancement with brain size but beyond past biological limits he posits the idea of group mind. The telepathic connection does not constitute group mind but a mode of association. In Clarke's *Childhood's End* first language must be removed. Clarke's narrator says that the group mind "will be a single entity as you yourselves are the sums of myriad cells."[11] In *Strangers in a Strange Land*, Robert A. Heinlein suggests group mind will be better than what came before it.

Musical Theatre

When Woolfson left Parsons to pursue musical theatre the Alan Parsons Project went into suspended animation for a few years. Woolfson began pursuing writing musicals with *Freudiana* (1990), which was based upon the life and works of Sigmund Freud. His songs from this became the basis for the last Alan Parsons Project recording. Parsons returned with of his own three songs, two of which were science fiction themed. Ian Bairnson and Stuart Elliott worked out the songs for *Time Machine* (1999). Professor Frank Close, an Oxford based physicist, narrates on the idea of the universe on "Temporalis." Dr. Close is a noted particle physicist who has served as vice-president of the British Association for the Advancement of Science and has been awarded the Kelvin Medal of the Institute of Physics for his contributions, through many books, lectures, and interviews, to public understanding of physics.

Through all of the years that they recorded as the Alan Parsons Project the group members never played live in concert. Parsons made up for that during the 1990s as he started a touring band and played music that has been described as by some rock music critics as symphony-rock. Woolfson was involved in the creation of *On the Air* (1996), which was about flight, from Daedelus and Icarus to the Apollo mission's flight in space. *On the Air* (1996), recorded by Parsons, was followed by *The Time Machine* (1999), an album using the title of H.G Wells's classic novel.

Woolfson's second musical, *Gaud*, was staged at Aachen, Germany, in 1994. The play went on to Alsdorf in 1995 and to Cologne in 1996. *Gambler* (1996) recalls the time he lived in Monte Carlo and utilizes songs from *Turn of a Friendly Card*, *Eye in the Sky*, and other Alan Parsons Project albums. *Dancing Shadows* (2007) was based upon a Korean play, *A Forest Fire*, and it played to audiences in South Korea. With his next musical, *Poe*, the songwriter revisited his interest in Edgar Allan Poe's works. He composed "Wings of Eagles," "Train to Freedom," and "Angel of the Odd," from a Poe story. The musical was staged at the Abbey Road Studios with Steve Balsamo, Anna-Jane Casey, Juliet Caton, David Burt, and James Gillan. The Halle Opera House produced *Poe* in Germany from August 2009 to March 2011, a time during which Woolfson passed away.

In 2010 Parsons' band changed members and again transformed into a live band. Alan Parsons turned his considerable recording talents in the direction of electronica. His son Jeremy made significant contributions to the recording. *A Valid Path* featured David Gilmore of Pink Floyd. Alan Parsons has recently developed a series of informative recording arts videos that are narrated by actor Billy Bob Thornton. There is an accompanying book in which studio techniques are discussed. Meanwhile, Parsons has worked with Lichtmond, a German electronic band and recorded ukulele player Jake Shimabukoro. He has contributed vocals to a recording project by Billy Sherwood and Chris Squire of Yes and he sang with Mexican pop music performer Aleks Syntek. The science fiction motifs that were such an important aspect of the Alan Parsons Project have faded into the past. The songs remain, with their richly produced sound and their images of robots and an eye in the sky.

Coda

Since David Bowie released his song "Changes" in January 1972 rock music has gone through many changes, breakthroughs, and reinventions. The mythic imagination has always stayed alive amid the transitions of culture and Bowie was one of rock's great experimenters with its possibilities. Bowie's passing in January 2016 was yet one more change. As a central figure in any discussion of rock, myth, and science fiction, he appears as one of those key performers whose work and mutating image may be called postmodern. His art, often in conversation with myth and with science fiction, was one of mime, theatre, and visual expression as well as one of music. On almost anyone's list of science fiction rock songs, Bowie's songs appear at the top. He made of himself a mythical figure. Bowie was involved in efforts to represent alienation, stardom, and culture through a play of signs that included science fiction imagery.[1] David Bowie was a rock cultural icon who played with myth.

Rock's devotion to the mythical may remind us that mythic imagination is ever at play in contemporary culture: in our art, our politics, our public rituals, and our entertainment. Postmodern fantasy, play, and the fusion of media (including rock music, print, and visuals) have an affinity with popular cultural forms, including the science fiction we see in films and on our TV screens. Science fiction is alive and well across print, electronic, and recorded media. In connection with rock music, science fiction offers open-ended, genre-bending possibilities. Gerald Alva Miller reminds us that "science fiction extrapolates beyond our present condition to imagine the potential transcendence of those limits."[2] Science fiction enables us to see things anew. It "destabilizes our normal conceptions of reality" and "inserts the marvelous into our reality," observes Miller. Consequently, our sense of stability may "prove to be nothing more than fantasies."[3] This has been the underlying message of rock songs and performances from artists like Bowie, Pink Floyd, Rush, or Iron Maiden. Creativity casts the world in new ways.

Rock music fantasy also calls to mind cyberpunk's recent ventures. Larry McCaffrey has connected the postmodernist philosopher Jean Baudrillard's thought with cyberpunk and he has proposed that technological changes can be linked with the postmodern condition. McCaffrey observes that artists who are "instinctively or intuitively" aware of this "have relied on themes and aesthetic modes previously associated with [science fiction]."[4] Rock music artists seem to have this instinctive response. Carlen Lavigne has pointed out that cyberpunk addresses technological issues in society. There are few aliens, space battles, or foreign planets in this fiction. Rather, there is attention to post-industrial society. She quotes science fiction writer Bruce Sterling's assertion that cyberpunk in the 1980s recognized social issues: "Technical culture has gotten out of hand," Sterling asserted." The advances of the sciences are so deeply radical, so disturbing, upsetting, and revolutionary that they can no longer be contained. They are surging into culture at large."[5] This surge of science into the culture is captured imaginatively in science fiction novels, films, television shows, and rock songs.

Despite all the dire observations of the music industry's decline in our digital age, rock music is very much alive. Rock music is fun. It is expressive play. Rock music speaks to us in a visceral way and it is not always as serious as a critic might make it seem. Rock is seriously expressive. When marketed, it becomes seriously commercial. Rock music was first theorized by practitioners rather than academics, by journalists, musicians, by record companies and their public relations departments, by radio producers and deejays. Rock criticism, as Simon Frith has said, is an investigation into a popular form of entertainment that is also "compelled to draw from high theory."[6] This reminds us that one of the features of postmodernism is the blending of high art and popular art. Like Frith, we can study material culture: how popular music is made, distributed, and consumed. But, also like Frith says, we also have to add that rock "in its mass cultural form" is engaged in "the struggle for fun."[7] Ultimately, reading science fiction and listening to rock music is about fun and imagination.

I hope that you have found some of this book fun and informative. Rock is to be welcomed as fun, even while it is subjected to criticism in the music press, by fans, or by others who choose to analyze its cultural impact. For anyone who pursues a study of rock music, myth, and science fiction further, listening is central. That is where you and I need to begin our interpretations. In *Rocking the Classics* Edward Macan observes: "Most popular music studies tend to be more sociologically than musicologically oriented."[8] This continues to be largely the case. Many early studies of rock focused on verbal messages in lyrics or on visuals rather than the music itself. Yet, to talk about music, as Luciano Pavorotti once observed, is like making love by chain mail. It is better to tune in with our feelings, to "be there," to listen and be moved.

Rock music manifests in culture and it offers fertile ground for cultural studies. Greil Marcus, for example, has brought rock into conversation with a consideration of American culture.[9] A critic like this offers keen perspectives on how rock speaks about our lives and our world. Likewise, we have much to gain from the inquiries and speculations of science fiction writers and critics. If we can still say that philosophy begins in wonder and seeks wisdom, they might be among the best popular thinkers of our time.

Science fiction has to contain some realism to appear rational and communicate with readers. Yet, it might be seen as a game "for grappling with issues of post-modern identity," as Gerald Alva Miller suggests.[10] This appears to be a feature of science fiction that David Bowie employed with his Ziggy Stardust persona and in testing the boundaries of gender and human identity. Science fiction of this sort, in Miller's words, destabilizes "our traditional definitions of self and society."[11] Miller reminds us that science fiction is a genre that allows us "to explore the human in new ways."[12] He points to Hayden White's emphasis upon narrative and White's view that story functions as humankind's most basic tool for making sense out of reality. Today we encounter "streams of data" that continually "emanate from media sources," he observes. To be human is to tell stories that "build our images of the world."[13]

Science fiction may speculate about the future. It may reflect the open-endedness and fragmentation in the postmodern condition. Critics note the genre's unique value. Science fiction looks at "material reducibility and at least implicitly, utopian possibility," observes Carl Freeman. Science fiction presents concepts that "have not yet been worked out," says Steven Shaviro. Miller describes science fiction as a space for "the fantastic, the marvelous, and the uncanny." Gary K. Wolfe points to science fiction's emergent literary respectability and a climate of increasing diversity.[14]

The appeal of science fiction for creative rock musicians and their audiences lies in its drive to know, its magic and drama, and its engagement with myth and the capacity for wonder. Readers and listeners are invigorated by the challenge of new and different worlds and characters. For Miller, "texts inscribe virtual spaces" and "science fiction is in a liminal space between realism and fantasy."[15] As reader response critics point out, the reader actualizes the text. Similarly, it is the listener to rock music who brings a song to life with his or her unique sensibility. So, with this coda, I encourage you to listen again and repeat that phrase. A listener like you, participating in the experience of music, is an interpreter of the sounds, patterns, and signs of a song. So, in an investigation of science fiction and myth in rock music, our best approach is to listen with open minds and hearts and to make up our own minds about the passionate, spacey, or mind-stretching sounds that we are hearing.

Chapter Notes

Introduction

1. See C.G. Jung, *The Collected Works of C.G. Jung*, Bollingen Edition (Princeton: Princeton University Press, 1970–1979).

2. Damien Cave, winter 1976.

3. Johannes Kepler, *Mysterium Cosmographum* (Tubingen, 1596, 2d ed., 1628).

4. Usula LeGuin, Introduction, *Norton Book of Science Fiction and Fantasy*, ed. Brian Attlebery and Ursula Le Guin (New York: Norton, 1997).

5. Robert Scholes is quoted by Raymond M. Olderman, *Beyond the Wasteland: A Study of the American Novel in the 1960s* (New Haven: Yale University Press, 1972), 26.

6. Mircea Eliade, Introduction, *Rites and Symbols of Initiation* (New York: Harper Torchbooks, 1965), ix.

7. Carl Sagan, *Cosmos* (Norwalk, CT: Easton), 196.

8. Joseph Campbell, *The Hero with Thousand Faces* (Princeton: Princeton University Press, 1949).

9. In his criticisms of rock music, Alan Bloom, in *The Closing of the American Mind* (1985), argued that rock was distracting the best and brightest of America from higher pursuits, like listening to Mozart, or the study of Plato. He called Mick Jagger of the Rolling Stones "Nietzsche's Nihiline." Bloom's concern was a variation on Plato, who would throw the poets out of his Republic and banish certain modes of music because of their presumably detrimental effect upon people and thus upon society. See Allan Bloom, *The Closing of the American Mind* (New York: Simon and Schuster, 1987).

10. Friedrich Nietzsche, Letter to Erwin Rohde, *Selected Letters of Friedrich Nietzsche*, trans. Anthony Ludovici (London: Heinemann, 1921, reprint 1923), 58.

11. Friedrich Nietzsche, *Works: The Birth of Tragedy from the Spirit of Music*, vol. I: 135–36.

12. *The Nation*, March 28, 1987: 16.

13. Norwood Russell Hanson suggests this in *Patterns of Discovery: An Inquiry into the Conceptual Foundations of Science* (Cambridge: Cambridge University Press, 1972).

14. Albert Einstein, *Ideas and Opinions* (*Mein Weltbild*), trans., ed. Sonja Bargmann (Norwalk: Easton, 2004), 64–65.

Chapter One

1. See *Led Zeppelin and Philosophy*, ed. Scott Calef (Chicago: Open Court, 2009). Pop music listeners have heard of mythical places like Atlantis from Donovan and Avalon from Kenny Loggins. The mythical bird that rose from the ashes has appeared in "Phoenix" by Wishbone Ash and in the song and album *Phoenix* by Dan Fogelberg. In the mid–1970s listeners heard of the Celtic

moon-goddess of inspiration, night and death, "Rhiannon," from Fleetwood Mac. More recently radio pop brought Katy Perry's extraterrestrials and Lady Gaga's Venus.

2. Mike Pinder is quoted in Gary James's interview, www.classicbands. com.

3. Denny Laine was a member of Paul McCartney and Wings in the 1970s.

4. Mike Pinder interview with Gary James, www.classicbands.com.

5. Leon Hendrix and Adam Mitchell, *Jimi Hendrix: A Brother's Story* (New York: Thomas Dunne, 2012). Michael Moorcock's "Dead Singers" revives Jimi Hendrix (*Factions*, ed. Giles Gordon and Alexander Hamilton, 1974). See Michael Moorcock, *Book of Martyrs*, 1976. See also Gregory Benford, "Doing Lennon" *Analog* (April 1975) and Michael Swanwicj, "The Feast of St. Janis," *New Dimensions* 11 (1980).

6. Ian Abrahams, *Hawkwind: Sonic Assassins* (London: SAF, 2004).

7. C. Clerk, *The Saga of Hawkwind* (London: Omnibus, 2004).

8. Clerk, 8.

9. Edward Macan, *Rocking the Classics* (Oxford and New York: Oxford University Press, 1997), 41.

10. Abrahams, 83.

11. Abrahams, 38.

12. This included Moorcock's appearance on Hawkwind's *Earth Ritual* tour in 1984.

13. With Hawkwind in mind, M. Butterworth wrote science fiction novels *The Time of the Hawklords* (1976) and *Queens of Deliria* (1977) that depict the survival of a nuclear holocaust. The enemy attempt to affect the minds of the survivors by playing them the music of the Carpenters, Elton John, and Simon and Garfunkel.

14. Macan, *Rocking the Classics*, 73.

15. The Moody Blues produced no studio albums from 1972 to 1978.

16. Marianne Tatom Letts, *Radiohead and the Resistant Concept Album:* *How to Disappear Completely* (Bloomington: Indiana University Press, 2010), 19. Hawkwind's psychedelia preceded the formation of Radiohead. Letts points to the use of Mellotron and Moog on Radiohead's *OK Computer* and calls the album one of "enormous scope," noting its artwork and its "dense subject matter."

17. Letts, 22.

18. Macan, 60.

19. Macan, 63.

20. Macan, *Endless Enigma: A Musical Biography of Emerson, Lake, and Palmer* (Chicago: Open Court, 2006), 59.

21. See Marianne Tatom Letts's discussion of concept albums in *Radiohead and the Resistant Concept Album*.

22. Letts, 14.

23. Yet, one may wonder if the Beatles album has the same "tonal and motivic coherence" that Shaugn O'Donnel hears on Pink Floyd's *The Dark Side of the Moon*. The Beatles' *Sgt. Pepper* recording comes under some scrutiny in Letts' discussion of concept albums. Letts considers the cohesive unity ascribed to the songs as perhaps "a function of commerce" (Letts, 17).

24. Macan, 59.

25. Macan, 60

26. Macan, 61.

27. Macan, 4.

28. Brian Stableford, *Science Fact, Science Fiction* (London: Routledge, 2006), 316.

29. For Edward Macan, as for Davin Seay and Mary Neely, the counterculture was religious or spiritually oriented. It was not primarily an ideological or oppositional movement. As Macan puts it, this "mirrored a generation's quest for some metaphysical depth" (*Rocking the Classics*, 6).

30. Macan, *Rocking the Classics*, 4.

31. John J. Scheinbaum, "Progressive Rock and the Inversion of Musical Values," in *Progressive Rock Reconsidered*, ed. Kevin Holm Hudson (London and New York: Routledge, 2002), 21–42.

32. Robert Walser's discussion appears in *Running with the Devil: Power, Gender, and Madness in Heavy Metal Music* (Middleton, CT: Wesleyan University Press, 1993). Walser examines the correlation between classical music and guitar solos by Ritchie Blackmore, Eddie Van Halen, and Randy Rhoades. In *Endless Enigma*, Edward Macan investigates the relationships between classical repertoire and the music of Emerson, Lake, and Palmer.

33. Andy Greene, "William Shatner on His New Prog Rock Album and *Star Trek*," *Rolling Stone*, September 11, 2013. Also see Tony Kaye, Rick Tierney, Scott Connor, *Spoken Word*.

34. Paul R. Kohl, review of Edward Macan, *Endless Enigma: A Musical Biography of Emerson, Lake and Palmer* (Chicago: Open Court, 2006).

35. Macan, *Endless Enigma*, 648.

36. Macan, *Endless Enigma*, 164.

37. Macan, *Endless Enigma*, 196.

38. Macan, *Endless Enigma*, 198.

39. Macan, *Endless Enigma*, 33.

40. Macan, *Endless Enigma*, 24.

41. Rick Wakeman and Marin Roach, *Grumpy Old Rock Star and Other Wondrous Stories* (London: Preface, 2008), 47.

42. Wakeman and Roach, 41.

43. Bill Martin, *Music of Yes: Structure and Vision in Progressive Rock* (Chicago: Open Court, 1997), 133.

44. Bill Martin, 134.

45. Stuart Chambers, *Yes: An Endless Dream of '70s, '80s, '90s Rock Music* (London: General Store Publication House, 2002), 135–36. Also see Interview with Steve Howe, www.bondgezou.com.

46. Jennifer Rycenga, 148. See "Tales of Change Within the Sound" in Kevin Holm-Hudson, *Progressive Rock Reconsidered* (London and New York: Routledge, 2002).

47. Paul Myers, *A Wizard, a True Star: Todd Rundgren in the Studio* (London: Jawbone, 2010), 118.

48. Myers, 140. The record includes "Space War." David Bowie attended Utopia's concert at Carnegie Hall and Neal Peart of Rush attended several shows (126).

49. Brian May's first band was named *1984*, after George Orwell's novel.

50. Brian May interview with Terry Gross, "Queen Guitarist Rocks Out to Physics," *The Guardian*, August 3, 2010, www.theguardian.com.

51. See Brian May, *Bang! The Complete History of the Universe* (London: Carlton, 2006).

52. May interview with Terry Gross, *The Guardian*, www.theguardian.com.

53. See Harris M. Berger's Foreword to the 2014 edition of Robert Walser, *Running with the Devil* (Middleton: Wesleyan University Press, 1993), vii.

54. Berger, xx.

55. Deena Weinstein also points to the apocalyptic strain of Christianity, especially *Revelation in Heavy Metal: The Music and Its Culture* (New York: Da Capo, 2000), 129.

56. Berger, vii.

57. Walser, 1.

58. Walser, 3–4.

59. Walser, 6–7. Robert Walser quotes Dickinson, 7.

60. Weinstein, 124. William Blake, in one of his poems, had a similar argument with the priests who exhausted all of the wonder and mystery from the garden.

61. Walser, 14.

62. Weinstein, 38.

63. Weinstein, 39.

64. Weinstein points to Van Halen's "Running with the Devil," Judas Priest's "Saints in Hell," AC/DC's "Highway to Hell" and "Sin City" among others. She notes how Iron Maiden made use of Poe's "Murders in the Rue Morgue" and how creators of heavy metal have drawn upon horror films, 40.

65. Weinstein, 40–41.

66. Robert Palmer, "Dark Metal: Not Just Smash and Thrash," *New York Times*, November 1990. See Weinstein, 43.

67. Chris Welsh interview with Jimmy Page, www.therockbackpages.com/ article.

68. Theodore Gracyk, *Listening to Popular Music: Or, How I Learned to Stop Worrying and Love Led Zeppelin* (Ann Arbor: University of Michigan Press, 2007), 32.

69. Chris Welsh interview with Jimmy Page. Mick Wall, *When Giants Walked the Earth: A Biography of Led Zeppelin* (London: Orion, 2008), 263.

70. Theodore Schick, *Led Zeppelin and Philosophy: All Will Be Revealed*, ed. Scott Calef (Chicago: Open Court, 2009), 97.

71. Susan Fast, *In the Houses of the Holy: Led Zeppelin and the Power of Rock Music* (Oxford: Oxford University Press, 2001), 50.

72. Fast, 50.

73. Fast, 52, 57.

74. Fast, 52.

75. Fast, 53.

76. *Ibid.*

77. See *Led Zeppelin and Philosophy*, 105–09. "Achilles Last Stand" is on *Presence* (1976).

78. Randall E. Auxier, "Magic Pages and Mythic Plants," 117–27, Calef, *Led Zeppelin and Philosophy*, 118.

79. Auxier, 127.

80. Auxier, 123.

81. Fast, 54, 56.

82. Fast, 50, 56.

83. Calef, *Led Zeppelin and Philosophy*, 136–39.

84. Martin Popoff says the tuning down began with the album *Master of Reality, Black Sabbath: Doom Let Loose* (Toronto: ECW, 2006), 57.

85. Walser, 148.

86. Deena Weinstein notes that some heavy metal lives in the same universe as tabloid news and the "prole" leanings of fans of pro wrestling, 294. Black metal was heard in Norway in the 1990s with Burzum and Mayhem. It featured keyboards as well as guitar, bass, and drums, piercing vocals, and visuals that called upon an array of Western imagery representing the demonic. A disturbing byproduct of black metal was the burning of old churches or the desecration of cemeteries.

Chapter Two

1. C.G. Jung, *The Theory of Psychoanalysis and Integration of the Personality*. In his study of symbols, Carl Jung was "grappling with the endless proliferation of mythical fantasies" (*Symbols*, Part II, 220). In 1934, Dr. Joseph Henderson observed a trend in Jung's work. Deirdre Baer writes: "There is a clear, discernible trend in his writings from mid-decade onward, as he recounts fewer and fewer of his patients' personal problems and his own technical methods of dealing with them. More and more, he directs his attention toward the non-personal, the objective, the psychic, and all those concepts he would eventually gather under the rubric of the 'archetypes of the collective unconscious,'" Deirdre Baer, *Jung: A Biography* (New York and Boston: Little, Brown, 2003), 395.

2. Jenny Boyd and Holley George Warren, *Musicians in Tune*, New York: Fireside, 120.

3. Jung writes: "The forms we use for assigning meaning are historical categories that reach back into the mists of time" (*Collected Works*, 9.1: 32–33). Archetypes have potential that is actualized when engaged within a particular culture and time. See Joseph Campbell, "Imprints of Experience," *Primitive Mythology: The Masks of Gods* (Princeton: Princeton University Press, 1973), 50–131.

4. Deena Weinstein, 214. Weinstein cites Aldous Huxley's comments on theatre, in which lighting and effects bring spectators into that "other world, which lies at the back of every mind, however perfect its adaptation to the exigencies of social life, 217. Aldous Huxley, *The*

Doors of Perception and Heaven and Hell, 165.

5. Weinstein, 214–15.

6. Weinstein 232; Durkheim, *The Elementary Forms of Religious Life*, 470.

7. Weinstein, 232.

8. Ernst Cassirer, *An Essay on Man* (New Haven: Yale University Press, 1944, reprint 1967), 32.

9. Cassirer, 73.

10. Cassirer, 25.

11. Cassirer, 27.

12. William J. Broad, *The Oracle: The Lost Secrets and Hidden Message of Ancient Delphi* (New York: Penguin, 2006), 13. See Anthony De Curtis, "Myth and Commerce in the Music Business," in *Stars Don't Stand in the Sky: Music and Myth* (New York: New York University Press, 1999), 32.

13. David Buckley, *Strange Fascination, David Bowie: The Definitive Story* (London: Virgin, 1999), 60. Buckley notes that Bowie talked with producer Tony Visconti about "Bradbury, Asimov and Sturgeon, as well as some obscure writers," including the Julian Jaynes book. See *Strange Fascination*, 60.

14. For other examinations of creativity, you might consult the work of psychologist Frank Barron. See also Brewster Ghiselin, *The Creative Process* (1952) and Rollo May, *The Courage to Create* (New York: Norton, 1993).

15. Erich Fromm, *The Forgotten Language of Dreams, Fairy Tales and Myth* (New York: Grove, 1951).

16. Robert Walser, *Running with the Devil: Power, Gender, and Madness in Heavy Metal Music* (Middleton, CT: Wesleyan University Press, 1993), 108. Examples of the uses of myth in classical art music are numerous. Orpheus appears in Monteverdi *L'orfeo* (1607); Christoph Gluck, *Orpheus Ed Euridice* (1763); and Jacques Offenbach, *Orphee Aux Enfers* (Orpheus and the Underworld). We meet the story of Troy in Hector Berlioz's *Les Troyens* (1858), a five-act opera. Virgil's *Aenead* appears in Henry Purcell's *Dido and Aeneas* (1689). Also notable is Mozart's *Ideomeneo* (1781). Richard Straus wrote many operas with mythic settings: *Elektra* (1909), *Ariadne and Naxos* (1912), *Die a Gypsche Helena* (1927), *Daphne* (1938).

17. T.S. Eliot, "Tradition and Individual Talent," (1919) in *The Sacred Wood*. London: Faber and Faber 1923. *Selected Essays*, New York: Harcourt Brace, 3–11.

18. Leigh Brackett, Introduction to *The Best of Planet Stories*, vol. 1 (New York: Random House, 1975).

19. Paul F. Ford, *Companion to Narnia: A Complete Guide to the Magical World of C.S. Lewis' Narnia* (New York: HarperCollins, 2005), 295.

20. John Cawelti, *Six Gun Mystique* (Bowling Green: Bowling Green University Press, 1970), 31.

21. Joseph Campbell and Bill Moyers, *The Power of Myth* (New York: Anchor, 1991), 183.

22. Mircea Eliade, *Myth and Reality*, trans. Willard Trask (New York: Harper Torchbooks, 1968), 141.

23. Neil Peart interview, June 13, 2012, *The Objective Standard*, www.theobjectivestandard.com.

24. Herbert Wells, in *H.G. Wells, the Critical Heritage*, ed. Patrick Parrinder (London: Routledge, Kegan, Paul, 1972), 260.

25. See Nicholas Pegg, *David Bowie* (London: Reynolds and Acorn, 2002; reprint, London: Titan, 2011).

26. *Los Angeles Times*, September 1974.

27. Wendy Leigh, *Bowie: The Biography* (London and New York: Gallery, 2014), 15.

28. Buckley, 39.

29. Gary K. Wolfe, *The Known and the Unknown: The Iconography of Science Fiction* (Kent State: Kent State University Press, 1979), 15.

30. C.S. Lewis, *Of Other Worlds: Essays and Stories*, ed. Walter Hooper and Geoffrey Bles (London: Bles, 1966), 111–12. Hard science fiction has focused

upon rigorous and accurate scientific findings and technical details. It is one way of categorizing science fiction stories. Asimov's short story "Evidence" is one example.

31. Ursula Le Guin, Introduction, *Norton Book of Science Fiction* (New York: Norton, 1997).

32. Leigh Brackett is cited by Rosemary Arbur, 11.

33. Alfred I. Tauber, *Science and the Quest for Meaning* (Waco: Baylor University Press, 2009), 139. Tauber writes that science acts upon presuppositions: the view that "The world is material and ordered; we might discern this order by detached empirical observation, neutral rational description, and objective analysis; laws will emerge from this inquiry and they will remain inviolable; why nature corresponds to our human mathematical and objective descriptions remains mysterious, but the empirical product of that method has been highly successful and thus approximates a depiction of the real as truth," 218, n. 4.

34. Walser, 26.

35. Pat Cadigan, *Ultimate Cyberpunk*, x. The term cyberpunk originated from a 1985 *Washington Post* article by Gardner Dazois who drew the term from the title of Bruce Bethke's 1983 short story "Cyberpunk." See Carlen Lavigne's excellent study: *Cyberpunk Woman, Feminism and Science Fiction: A Critical Study* (Jefferson, NC: McFarland, 2013).

36. Richard Maltby views popular culture as "Escapism that is not an escape from or to anywhere, but an escape of our utopian selves," 14.

37. *Ibid.*

38. Alvin Toffler, *Future Shock* (New York: Random House, 1970), 384.

39. Raymond Williams and Pierre Bourdieu, both cited in *Popular Culture*, 5.

40. Raymond Williams, analysis, in *Popular Culture*, 32.

41. Williams, 36.

42. Wolfe, 13.

43. Samuel R. Delany, *The Jewel Hinged Jaw* (New York: Berkeley Windhover, 1978). See Nicholas D. Smith, *Philosophers Look at Science Fiction* (London: Burnham, 1982), 12.

44. Michael Berman, *Everyday Fantastic: Essays on Science Fiction and Human Being* (Cambridge: Cambridge University Press, 2008), 18.

45. Robert A. Heinlein, *Nature, Faults and Virtues*, 22. Heinlein's "Future History" series looks at potential problems in the future. "Universe and Common Sense" in *Astounding*, 1941.

46. William Atheling, Jr. (James Blish), *More Issues at Hand* (Chicago: Advent, 1970).

47. Joanna Russ, "Speculations: The Subjunctivity of Science Fiction," *Extrapolation* 15.1 (December 1973): 52.

48. See Henry Jenkins, "Strangers No More, We Sing: Filking and the Social Construction of the Science Fiction Fan Community," in Lisa A. Lewis, *The Adoring Audience: Fan Culture and Popular Media* (London: Routledge, 1992). This article explores consumers who also produce (212) and fan music making. Jenkins offers the example of *Star Trek* as fan culture, 214–16.

49. Stuart Hall and Paddy Wannel discuss the interactions between text and audience and social relations in popular music "youth" culture. They assert that exposure to the work contributes to the shape of one's mental image of the world, *The Popular Arts* (London: Hutchison, 1964), 281.

50. The signs that appear in connection with progressive rock, heavy metal, or other rock genres are rooted in culture. This semiology, Robert Walser points out, is best approached through ethnography, historical analysis, and argumentation about culture (31). Music is a social activity in which the use of myth and symbols can be productive of new meanings for listeners. An inquiry into this can help us to understand the consciousness, thoughts, desires, and

dreams of a culture and its rock-influenced subcultures (34).

51. Robert Scholes, *Structural Fabulation: An Essay on Fiction of the Future* (University of Notre Dame Press, 1975), 29. The fan of progressive rock, for example, knows codes to which the uninitiated are oblivious, observes Edward Macan in *Rocking the Classics* (Oxford: Oxford University Press, 1997).

52. See Brian Atteberg and Veronica Hollinger, *Parabolas of Science Fiction* (Middletown: Wesleyan University Press, 2013), 8. Samuel R. Delany uses the example of a huge red sun and a blue one (1978), 26.

53. William Tenn is the science fiction writing pseudonym for Philip Klass.

54. Atteberg and Hollinger, 9.

55. Science fiction offers us a way to overcome the separation of the two cultures of science and literature that was of concern when C.P. Snow delivered his Rede Lectures in 1959. Snow wrote at a time when science was still something of a cultural outsider. The study of science was then an intellectual pursuit that was only beginning to break into the curriculum at the British universities. Scientific study had first been offered at the "brick" universities in northern England and only later became part of the curriculum at Oxford and Cambridge.

56. Aldous Huxley was quite aware of J.B.S. Haldane's essay "Daedelus, or Science and the Future" (1923), in which Haldane wrote: "The scientific worker of the future will more and more resemble the lonely figure of Daedelus as he becomes conscious of his ghastly [enterprise] and proud of it" (London: Kegan Paul, 1923), 93.

57. Wolfe, 15.

58. Neil Gaiman, Foreword, Samuel R. Delany, *Einstein Intersection* (Middletown: Wesleyan University Press, 1998), vii.

59. Gaiman, viii, ix.

60. Larry McCaffrey, *Storming the Reality Studio* (Durham: Duke University Press, 1991), 3–4.

61. Scholes, 24. Robert Scholes begins his book writing about metafiction, or fiction that is about other fiction.

62. Kingsley Amis, *New Maps of Hell: A Survey of Science Fiction* (London: Gollancz, 1961), 54.

63. See Brian Aldiss's comments in the first chapter of *The Billion Year Spree: The True History of Science Fiction* (New York: Schocken, 1974). Aldiss points to sources in the Gothic novel and points out that Ann Radcliffe's *Mysteries of Udolpho* continually explained the apparently unnatural phenomena.

64. Aldous Huxley, Letter to Ketheran Roberts (May 18, 1931). *Letters of Aldous Huxley*, ed. Grover Smith (New York: Harper and Row, 1969).

65. Wolfe, 125.

66. Aldiss, *Billion Dollar*, 246–47. Gary K. Wolfe provides a list of some apocalyptic science fiction stories, 127.

67. Robert Bloch in Basil Davenport's symposium of the science fiction novel in 1959 called it an unconscious social criticism.

68. David Wragg, "Or Any Art at All: Frank Zappa Meets Critical Theory," *Popular Music* 20, no. 2 (May 2001): 217.

69. Michael Polyani and Harry Prosch, *Meaning* (Chicago: University of Chicago Press, 1975), 25. The Nobel Prize winning biologist Julian Huxley wrote: "It is the merest ant and twaddle to go on asserting, as most of our press and people continue to do, that increase of scientific knowledge and power must in itself be good" (238). See "The Tissue Culture King," *Time Probe: The Sciences in Science Fiction*, ed. Arthur C. Clarke.

70. Lewis Mumford, *The Pentagon of Power, The Myth of Machine* (New York: Harcourt, Brace, Jovanovich, 1974), 27.

71. Victor Ferkiss, *Technological Man: The Myth and Reality* (New York: New American Library, 1970), 255.

72. Dave Grohl and the Foo Fighters celebrate the musical character of American cities on their album *Sonic Highways* (RCA, 2014). In "Running on

Empty" (1978), Jackson Browne suggests that he and the band can't even remember which city they are in because they've done so many shows in a row.

73. Raymond Williams, *The Country and the City* (London: Chatto and Windus, 1973), 72–276.

74. Ketterer (102) is cited by Gary K. Wolfe, 86.

75. Theodore Roszak, *Where the Wasteland Ends* (Garden City, NY: Doubleday), 10.

76. Gary K. Wolfe, *How Great Science Fiction Works* (Chantilly, VA: The Great Courses, 2016), 169.

77. Wolfe, *How Great Science Fiction Works*, 105.

78. Wolfe, *How Great Science Fiction Works*, 88–91.

79. Wolfe makes these observations and cites parallels, *How Great Science Fiction Works*, 95.

80. Wolfe, *How Great Science Fiction Works*, 97.

81. See Raymond Williams, *The Country and the City*, 276–280.

82. Northrup Frye, *Anatomy of Criticism* (Princeton: Princeton University Press, 1957), 33. For this quote see "The Archetypes of Literature," *Kenyon Review* 1 (1951), 49. In *Anatomy of Criticism*, Frye connects myth and literary tradition intertextually and he does not refer to the collective unconscious as the source of archetypes in the Jungian sense. "Poetry Can Only Be Made Out of Other Poems; Novels Out of Other Novels" (97). The recurring images of archetypes are "Social Facts" that "Help to Integrate Our Literary Experience" (99). See George Jensen's discussion in *Post-Jungian Criticism: Theory and Practice* (Albany: SUNY Press, 2003), 6–7.

Chapter Three

1. "What united the Bay Area bands was their need to assimilate traditional American folk musics, particularly the blues, into rock" (Hall, 386). Ferdinand de Saussure provided the terms sign, signifier, and signified to describe how we use language. Roland Barthes held that myth is a system of communication. Semiotics is the study of meaning making through signs.

2. Richard King has referred to this countercultural sensibility as an effort "to create a new religion." See *The Party of Eros, Radical Social Thought and the Realm of Freedom* (Chapel Hill: University of North Carolina Press, 1972).

3. *Creem* (1974), 71. Variations on this theme have been provided by Coleman, 1992 (447), Considine (663), and Evans, 1992 (364). M. Coleman's reviews are on Barry Manilow, The Carpenters, Journey, and Neil Diamond. See Steve Jones, *Pop Music and the Press* (Philadelphia: Temple University Press, 1974).

4. See Simon Frith, *Sound Effects: Youth, Leisure, and the Politics of Rock and Roll* (London: Constable, 1983), 163. The notion that "Rock and roll has saved lives" is found in Marsh's biography of Bruce Springsteen, *Born to Run* (Introduction, xvi).

5. Ram Dass, *Be Here Now* (San Cristobal, NM: Lama Foundation, 1971). *Be Here Now* encourages presence in the moment.

6. Nancy Reid, "Clinging to the Edge of Magic: The Shamanic Aspects of the Grateful Dead," 183.

7. Reid, 184.

8. Reid, 185.

9. Graham Nash, *Wild Tales: A Rock and Roll Life* (New York: Crown, 2013), 199.

10. David Crosby and Carl Gottlieb, *Long Time Gone* (New York: Doubleday, 1988; reprint 2000), 19.

11. Nash, 204.

12. Nash, 120.

13. Nash, 186.

14. Nash, 199.

15. Michio Kaku, *Physics of the Impossible: A Scientific Exploration of Phasers, Force Fields, Teleportation and Time*

Travel (New York: Doubleday, 2008), 166.

16. Kaku, 169.

17. Kaku, 168.

18. Cited by Gary K. Wolfe, *The Known and the Unknown: The Iconography of Science Fiction* (Kent State: Kent State University Press, 1979), 22–23.

19. Wolfe, 21.

20. Wolfe, 74–75.

21. Marion Leonard points out that for some critics they both have a "tomboy image." Marion Leonard, *Gender in the Music Industry: Rock Discourse and Girl Power* (Aldershot: Ashgate, 2007), 37. There have been no science fiction references from Joan Jett, Laura Nyro, Patti Smith, Pat Benatar, Melissa Etheridge, or many other female rock performers. The B52s got as far as naming their band after a plane but no prominent female group has chosen an interstellar space vehicle to represent their band. It might be asked why female rock performers have not more extensively explored the science fiction medium as a resource for their work.

22. Patti Smith, *The Guardian* (May 2005).

23. This Lenny Kaye interview appears online.

24. Jenny Garber in *The Lost Women of Rock Music: Female Musicians in the Punk Era*, ed. Helen Reddington (Aldershot: Ashgate, 2007), 3.

25. Mircea Eliade, *Myth and Reality*, trans. Willard Trask (New York: Harper Torchbooks, 1968), 417.

26. Eliade, 421.

27. Eliade, 421–22.

28. Eliade, 423.

29. Jones (99) offers a sampling of rock critics who address a preference for "tougher, grittier, more real," "intensity," and "passion over precision."

30. Kambrew McLeod, 108.

31. McLeod, 109. For example, Dave Marsh wrote of Neil Young's *Tonight's the Night* in 1975: "The music has a quality of offhand first take crudity matched recently only by *Blood on the Tracks*," 67.

32. Harding and Nett, 60. Gottlieb and Wald, 252. Norma Coates (1998), 79. Coates' comment "ultimately fictive masculinity" appears 52–53, "Revolution Now? Rock and the Political Potential of Gender," *Sexing the Gender: Popular Music and Gender*, ed. Sheila Whitely (London: Routledge, 1997). Coates' thoughts on "stereotypical masculinity" are on 52. Mimi Schippers, *Rockin' Out of the Box: Gender Manuvering in Alternative Hard Rock* (New Brunswick, NJ: Rutgers University Press, 2002), 23, see 20–23. Sheila Whitely suggests that songs present the evil woman who ruins men's lives, *The Space Between the Notes: Rock and Counterculture* (London: Routledge, 2000), 38; Deena Weinstein, *Heavy Metal Music and Culture* (New York: Da Capo, 2000), 104; Robert Walser, *Running with the Devil* (Middleton: Wesleyan University Press, 114–17).

33. Rock has focused on being accessible and commercial by centering attention on its well-known 'classic' performers connoting an aura of "Stability." Coates gives attention to *Rocklist* to demonstrate how the gendered list indicates the masculinist discourse of rock and "replicates the social dynamics currently operative in nascent cyberspace," 81.

Chapter Four

1. In January 1970 Carl Wayne left the Move. On July 12, 1970 Wood added strings to a Lynne song that was intended as a Move B-side. The Move's final album, *Message from the Country*, was finished. The song became the first ELO single.

2. This is the number of hits in the United States. ELO had 26 UK pop singles.

3. For the Special Theory of Relativity (1905) see Albert Einstein, "On the

Electrodynamics of Moving Bodies," *Annalen Der Physiks* 17 (1905): 801–921. For the General Theory of Relativity (1914–1915) see his November 1915 publications "On the Theory of General Relativity," "Explanation of the Perihelion Motion of Mercury," and "Field Equations on the Theory of Gravitation." Also of interest are Einstein's exposition of the hole argument in *Physikalishe Zeitschraft* 15 (1914), "On the Relativity Problem" *Scientia* 15 (1914): 337–48, and "The Formal Foundation of the General Theory of Relativity" (1914). "Contributions to Quantum Theory" (1914), "The Space-Time Problem," *Koralle* 5 (1930): 486–88. The papers, originally in German, are available in English translation.

4. Other ELO records include: *Balance of Power* and *Zoom*. Band members included Mike Edwards (cello), Andy Craig (cello), Hugh McDowell (cello), Wilfred Gibson (violin), Mike de Albuquerque (bass), Colin Walker (cello), Mik Kaminski (violin), Kelly Groucutt (bass and vocals), Dave Morgan (guitar, synthesizer, vocals) Melvyn Gale (cello), Louis Clark (synthesizers, string arranger).

5. Axl Rose was quick to distinguish hard blues oriented rock from pop music at this MTV gathering in 1992. Several critics, from Dave Marsh to Robert Christgau, have argued for "authentic" rock as blues based and different from pop music. ELO has only gradually redeemed itself from the pop category among some critics.

6. Intervals of music may be consonant. Pythagoras found that ratios of 2:1, 3:2, and 4:3 sound consonant. Major thirds, major sixths, and minor thirds are consonant. Hemholtz determined that musical dissonance occurs in the greatest when partials of two tones are at 30 to 40 beats per second.

7. Jeff Lynne, who worked with ELO's array of orchestral and rock instruments as the band's primary songwriter and producer, has earned wide recognition as a fine record producer for his efforts with other musicians.

Chapter Five

1. David Bowie, *Strange Fascination: David Bowie, the Definitive Biography* (London: Virgin, 1999), 160.

2. Gordon Coxkill, interview with David Bowie, in *Bowie on Bowie: Interviews and Encounters with David Bowie*, ed. Sean Egan (Chicago: Chicago Review Press, 2015), 11.

3. Interview with David Bowie, *Bowie on Bowie*, 167.

4. David Thompson, *Hallo Spaceboy: The Rebirth of David Bowie* (Toronto: ECW, 2006), 2.

5. Simon Frith and Howard Home, *Art into Pop* (London: Methuen, 1987). See also *Enchanting David Bowie: Space, Time, Body, Memory*, ed. Tonja Cinque, Christopher Moore, and Sean Redmond (London: Bloomsbury, 2015), 276.

6. Peter Doggett, *The Man Who Sold the World: David Bowie in the 1970s* (New York: HarperCollins, 2012), Introduction.

7. Christopher Lasch, *The Age of Narcissism: American Life in an Age of Diminishing Expectations* (New York: W.W. Norton, 1979).

8. Doggett, Introduction.

9. *Ibid.*

10. Buckley, 19.

11. Buckley, 60. Bowie discussed Julian Jaynes' *The Origins of the Bicameral Mind* with Tony Visconti. Bowie was an avid reader and his adult reading has been documented by the Art Gallery of Toronto, Ontario. His reading includes R.D. Laing's *The Divided Self*, the poetry of Allen Ginsberg, *On the Road* by Jack Kerouac, works by Martin Amis, Peter Ackroyd, William S. Burroughs, Julian Barnes, Bruce Chatwin, Stephen King, Don De Lillo's *White Noise*, Colin Wilson's *The Outsider*, and many others.

12. Buckley, 60–61.

13. See Paul Trynka, *Starman* (Boston and New York: Little, Brown, 2011), Chapter One. *The Day of the Triffids* was also broadcast by the BBC.

14. Marc Spitz, *Bowie: A Biography* (New York: Crown/Archetype, 2010), 22.

15. Wendy Leigh, *Bowie: The Biography* (London and New York: Gallery, 2014), 29.

16. David Bowie interview, *Los Angeles Times* (September 1974), in *Bowie on Bowie: Interviews and Encounters with David Bowie*, ed. Sean Egan (Chicago: Chicago Review, 2015).

17. Michael Mooradian Lupro cites Ken McLeod (2003) and Taylor (2001). See "Keeping Space Fantastic: The Transformative Journey of Major Tom," *Enchanting David Bowie: Space, Time, Body, Memory*, ed. Toija Cinque, Christopher Moore, and Sean Redmond (London: Bloomsbury, 2015). Ken McLeod makes a reference to an internal space of "feelings, desires, dreaming" (337). Sheila Whiteley speaks of space as empowering. Bowie creates space sonically. Sheila Whiteley, *The Space Between the Notes: Rock Music and the Counterculture* (New York and London: Routledge, 1993), 3.

18. Richard Fitch, "In This Age of Grand Allusion: Bowie, Nihilism and Meaning," (19–34). *David Bowie, Critical Perspectives*, ed. Eoin Devereaux, Aileen Dillane, and Martin J. Power (London: Routledge, 2015).

19. Ellen Willis, *Out of the Vinyl Deeps: Ellen Willis on Rock Music* (Minneapolis: University of Minnesota Press, 2011).

20. The name of the record company, Trident, and the name of the space mission, Apollo, both recall figures from Greek mythology. So does the name of the Trident studio in which the album was recorded: a name associated with the pitchfork of Poseidon/Neptune, the god of the sea.

21. Carmen Paglia's observation comes three years earlier than Don McLean's *American Pie* in which he

sings of a generation lost in space. Wendy Leigh, *David Bowie: The Biography* (London: Gallery, 2014), 15. Van Cagle, *Reconstructing Pop/Subculture: Pop, Rock, and Andy Warhol* (Thousand Oaks and London: Sage 1995), 112. Philip Auslander, *Performing Glam Rock, Theatricality and Gender in Popular Music* (Ann Arbor: University of Michigan Press, 2006), 128. Michael Mooradian Lupro, "Keeping Space Fantastic: The Transformative Journey of Major Tom." Marc Spitz, *Bowie: A Biography* (New York: Crown/Archetype, 2010), 105–06.

22. Willis, 39.

23. Willis 38.

24. Willis, 39.

25. Doggett, 155.

26. Willis, 39.

27. "Beat Godfather Meets Glitter Main Man," William S. Burroughs' interview with David Bowie, *Rolling Stone*, February 28, 1974.

28. "Goodbye Ziggy and a Big Hello to Aladdin Sane," David Bowie interview with Charles Shaar Murray, *New Musical Express*, January 27, 1973. *Bowie on Bowie*, 31. Bowie commented in this interview that he admired John Lennon's ability to create puns.

29. Simon Frith, *Sound Effects: Youth, Leisure, and the Politics of Rock N' Roll* (New York: Pantheon, 1981), 154.

30. Simon Frith, "David Bowie," *Let It Rock*, June 1973.

31. Spitz, *Bowie: A Biography* (New York: Crown/Archetype, 2010), 39.

32. Carmen Paglia is quoted by Spitz, *Bowie: A Biography*, 39.

33. David Bowie interview, youtube.com, Broadcast Interviews, 1977.

34. Nicholas Pegg, *The Complete David Bowie* (London: Titan, 2011).

35. Simon Frith (1988, 136) is quoted by Ian Chapman in "Ziggy's Urban Alienation: Assembling the Heroic Outsider," *Enchanting David Bowie*.

36. Ian Chapman cites Richard Lehan, *The City in Literature* (Berkeley: University of California Press 1998), 98.

37. Raymond Williams, "The Metropolis and the Emergence of Modernism," in *Unreal City: Urban Experience in Modern European Literature and Art*, ed. David Kelley and Edward Timms (Manchester: Manchester University Press, 1985), 13–14, 23.

38. Christopher Booker, *The Seven Basic Plots: Why We Tell Stories* (New York: Continuum, 2004), 33.

39. Booker, 33. See Booker's discussion about science fiction, 39–45.

40. Gary K. Wolfe, 21.

41. Charles Shaar Murray interview with David Bowie, "David at the Dorchester," *Interviews and Encounters with David Bowie*, 16.

42. Interview with David Bowie, *Interviews and Encounters with David Bowie*, 31.

43. Gary K. Wolfe points out that in James Blish's story, *A Case of Conscience*, there is a catastrophe in which science has "swept away the theories that forbade" travel faster than light. "People on one side of a revolution may be quite incapable of understanding people on the other side" (Barker, 80–81).

44. Carl G. Jung, *Flying Saucers: A Modern Myth of Things Seen in the Sky*, trans. R.F.C. Hull (New York: Harcourt Brace, 1959), 10.

45. Bowie is quoted as saying that he would visually draw the direction of an instrumental solo. This one went from a flat line to sprays of broader lines. See *The Complete David Bowie* by Nicholas Pegg, under "Moonage Daydream."

46. James T. Jones, 236. Jones points out that literature helps us to experience abstract moral issues more concretely, 240. The novelist John Gardner echoes this view in *On Moral Fiction* (New York: Basic, 1978).

Chapter Six

1. Roy Shipston, "Are Spacemen Floyd on Their Way Back to Earth?" Interview with Pink Floyd, *Disc Maker Echo*, November 22, 1969, 59.

2. Shipston, 58.

3. Nicholas Schaffner, *Saucerful of Secrets: The Pink Floyd Odyssey* (New York: Dell, 1991), 35.

4. Julian Palocios, *Syd Barrett and Pink Floyd: Dark Globe* (London: Plexus, 2010), 110.

5. Palocios, 113–14.

6. In Barrett's song "Bike" he says the sound will "Ching." Barrett was familiar with the I Ching and was intrigued by his copy of Richard Wilhelm's translation of it. See Palocios, 111. On *The Dark Side of the Moon*, in "Time," clocks chime as the song begins and later we race toward a sinking sun only to have it arise behind us again.

7. Richard Cromelin, "Roger Waters: Dark Side of the Tube," *Los Angeles Times*, September 13, 1992. Also see Irwin Stambler, *Pop Rock Sound* (New York: St. Martin's, 1974), 400.

8. John Cavanaugh, *The Piper at the Gates of Dawn* (New York and London: Continuum, 2007). Cavanaugh tells his story of his first acquaintance with the song after coming indoors from a starry night. He begins his introduction with this recollection.

9. *Ibid.*

10. The "aura of science fiction and fantasy" around the band had led to "specialized gigs" such as one at an American science fiction convention," notes Nicholas Schaffner, *Saucerful of Secrets*, 136.

11. Syd Barrett released *The Madcap Laughs* (Harvest/Capitol, 1969). *Barrett* (1970) appeared the next year. There was also a record title *Opel* (1988). *The Madcap Laughs* was re-mastered in 2010.

12. Richard Middleton, "Piper at the Gates of Dawn," *Pop Music and the Blues* (1972). *Pink Floyd Through the Eyes of the Band, Its Fans, Friends and Foes*, ed. Bruno MacDonald (New York: Da Capo, 1997), 44.

13. Miles, *International Times* (July 1968): 46.
14. Mick Favreu, *International Times* (October 1969): 47. *Pink Floyd Through the Eyes of the Band, Its Fans, Friends, and Foes*, ed. Bruno MacDonald (New York: Da Capo, 1996), 44.
15. Shipston, 59.
16. Musicologist Lawrence Kramer has pointed out that interpretation cannot be controlled. It may reach toward "any association, substitution, analogy, construction, or leap of inference that it requires." Lawrence Kramer, *Music as Cultural Practice* (Berkeley: University of California, 1990), 15.
17. Robert Christgau, "Dark Side of the Moon," *Christgau's Record Guide: Rock Albums of the 70s* (Boston: Ticknor and Fields, 1989), 6.
18. John Harris, *Dark Side of the Moon: The Making of the Pink Floyd Masterpiece* (New York: Da Capo, 2006), 16.
19. Harris, Introduction.
20. Phil Rose, *Roger Waters and Pink Floyd: The Concept Albums* (Madison: Fairleigh Dickinson University Press, 2015). Waters made this comment in an interview with the author.
21. Jenny Boyd and Holly George Warren, *Musicians in Tune: 75 Contemporary Musicians Discuss the Creative Process* (New York: Fireside, Simon and Schuster, 1992), 80.

Chapter Seven

1. The band first appeared in clubs on Long Island around 1967 as Soft White Underbelly. Four albums later, their most memorable song, "Don't Fear the Reaper," appeared on *The Agents of Fortune* (1976) and received wide airplay. Sandy Pearlman who, as a rock critic, is sometimes credited with having used the term "heavy metal," went on to manage the band.
2. See Martin Popoff, *Blue Oyster Cult: Secrets Revealed*. Listen to October 30, 2012, SONY Legacy, 17-CD boxed set. This coincided with Halloween, perhaps because of the Reaper. Currently, joining Bloom and Roeser are Jules Radino (drums), Richie Castellano (keyboard and guitar/background vocals) and Kasim Sultan (bass).
3. Bloom contributed "Black Blade" and "Veterans of the Psychic Wars" with Michael Moorcock. The science fiction author also wrote the lyrics for Hawkwind. This British psychedelic hard rock band dwelled in mythic stories. Their work included *In Search of Space* (1971), *Space Ritual* (1973), and *Warrior on the Edge* (1975).
4. An interview with Alexander Laurance in 1994 John Shirley observes that he and Bruce Sterling had done "Parallel Work." http://www.blueoyster cult.com.
5. Ursula K. Le Guin, *The Dispossessed: An Ambiguous Utopia* (New York: Harper and Row, 1974), 257.
6. Mircea Eliade, *Myth and Reality*, trans. Willard Trask (New York: Harper Torchbooks, 1968), 452.
7. Eliade, 453, 455.
8. Eliade, 455.
9. *Ibid.*
10. Eliade, 456.
11. Stanton Marian (Duquesne University diss. 1981, 227) is cited in *Shamanism: An Expanded View of Reality*, ed. Shirley Nicholson (Wheaton, IL: Quest, 1987), 269.
12. *Ibid.*
13. Eliade, 398.
14. Eliade, 401.
15. Eliade, 407.
16. Eliade, 456.

Chapter Eight

1. Nicole Biamonte offers a fascinating reading of "Cygnus X-1" from *A Farewell to Kings* she points out how the music patterns the storyline. "Contre

Nous," *Rush and Philosophy: Heart and Mind United*, ed. Jim Berti and Durrell Bowman (Chicago: Open Court/Carus, 2011), 196.

2. Deena Weinstein, *The Artistic Vision of Modern Society in Rush, Pink Floyd, and Bruce Springsteen* (Montreal: New World Perspectives, 1985).

3. Timothy Smolko, "What Can This Strange Device Be?" *Rush and Philosophy*, 228.

4. Chris McDonald, "Open Secrets, Individualism, and Middle Class Identity in the Songs of Rush," *Popular Music and Society* 31 (2008): 319.

5. Michio Kaku, *Physics of the Impossible* (New York: Doubleday, 2008), 31.

6. Dan Nooger, "Rush Goes into Future Shock: Music Will Not Exist in 2112," *Circus* (April 27, 1976).

7. Durrell Bowman, "More than They Bargained For," *Rush and Philosophy*, 170. He lists Lee's instruments on these albums as Minimoog, Oberheim OBX-a, and Roland Jupiter 8.

8. Durrell Bowman comments on Paul Theberge, *Any Sound You Can Imagine*, and H. Stith Bennett, "Notation and Identity in Contemporary Popular Music," *Popular Music* 3 (1983): 231. See *Rush and Philosophy*, 177.

9. Bowman, 188.

10. Bowman, 179.

11. Mark Poster, *The Mode of Information: Poststructuralism and the Social Context* (Chicago: University of Chicago Press and Cambridge: Polity, 1990), 4.

12. Poster, 7.

13. Poster, 9.

14. Rodney Brooks, "Making Living Systems," *Science at the Edge: Conversations with the Leading Scientific Thinkers Today*, ed. John Brockman (New York: Union Square, 2008), 51.

15. Poster, 15.

16. Neil Peart, *Ghost Rider* (Toronto: ECW, 2002), 258–262. Peart offers his recommendations for adapting to difficult circumstances.

Chapter Nine

1. Following the first album they were signed to Clive Davis's new record label, Arista Records. A series of successful albums followed: *I, Robot* (1977), *Pyramid* (1978), *Turn of a Friendly Card* (1980), *Eye in the Sky* (1982), *Ammonia Avenue* (1984), *Vulture Culture* (1985), *Stereotomy* (1986), and *Gaud* (1987).

2. *I, Robot* (1977) liner notes. The robot theme appears in Styx's *Kilroy Was Here* with "Mr. Roboto." The Flaming Lips created "Yoshimi Battles the Pink Robots."

3. Stephen Holden, *The Village Voice*, August 29, 1977, 38. The album also had a song called "The Voice." It has a robotized warning speaking over the sound of the bass.

4. Cited by Gary K. Wolfe, *The Known and the Unknown: The Iconography of Science Fiction* (Kent, OH: Kent State University Press, 1979), 158.

5. "Electric Eye" by Judas Priest has a similar theme and is examined by Robert Walser (164). The song, which appears on *Screaming for Vengeance* (1982), is described as conveying music codes of power and danger with a scrambling guitar solo and syncopated choruses that attempt to defy "solid metric organization." "The song ends with feedback and echo, like a science fiction movie soundtrack accompanying a view of space—vast, mysterious, and ineffable" (164).

6. Stephen Thomas Erlewine, review of *The Eye in the Sky*, All Music Reviews, www.allmusicreviews.com.

7. Stan McDaniel, "The Coalescence of Minds," *Philosophers Look at Science Fiction*, ed. Nicholas D. Smith (Chicago: Nelson Hall, 1982), 118–19.

8. Teilhard de Chardin, *The Future of Man* (New York: Pyramid, 1966), 116.

9. de Chardin, 120. For Teilhard, the scientist-priest, who refers to evolving consciousness as *Noogenesis*, this leads, in a religious sense, toward *Christogen-*

esis, which would be the redemption of the evolutionary past.

10. Olaf Stapledon, *Last and First Men*, 1933, 224. "The More Complex the Form the More Percipient and Active the Spirit," 34. Also see 231.

11. Arthur C. Clarke, cited. in *Philosophers Look at Science Fiction*, ed. Nicholas Smith (Chicago: Nelson Hall, 1982), 122.

Coda

1. See Jean Baudrillard, *Simulacra and Simulation* (1981), Frederic Jameson, *Postmodernism and the Logic of Late Capitalism* (1991), Brian McHale, *Postmodern Fiction* (1987) and *Constructing Postmodernism* (1992), Douglas Kellner and Steve Best, *The Postmodern Turn* (1997) and *The Postmodern Adventure* (2001). The emphasis placed upon simulation and simulacra in postmodern society by a theorist like Jean Baudrillard finds a complement in an artist like this, as well as in stories of virtual reality, computing and electronic identities, and digital global networks. Fragmentation and de-centering of the subject are aspects postmodernism, as is simulation. Bowie engaged in all of this. Frederic Jameson has presented postmodernism as a crisis in representation.

2. Gerald Alva Miller, Jr., *Exploring the Limits of the Human Through Science Fiction* (New York: Palgrave, 2012), 3.

3. Miller, 12–13.

4. Larry McCaffrey, 3.

5. Carlen Lavigne, *Cyberpunk Women: Feminism and Science Fiction: A Critical Study* (Jefferson, NC: McFarland, 2013).

6. Simon Frith, 1987 essay, 461–62; see *Music for Pleasure: Essays on the Sociology of Pop* (Cambridge: Polity and New York: Routledge, 1988). *Taking Popular Music Seriously* (2007) collects some of his essays. In his essays he makes use of symbolic interactionism and Marxist theory.

7. Frith, *Sound Effects*, 1983, 272.

8. Edward Macan, *Rocking the Classics* (New York: Oxford University Press, 1997), 145.

9. Greil Marcus, *Mystery Train*, 6th ed. (New York: Plume, 2015).

10. Miller, 18.

11. *Ibid.*

12. Miller, xii.

13. Miller, 1–2.

14. Carl Freeman, 32. Miller cites Carl Freeman's assertion that "science fiction is determined by the dialectic between estrangement and cognition," pp. 16–17. Steven Shaviro (ix), cited by Miller, 7. Gary K. Wolfe, *How Great Science Fiction Works*, 175–180, 184.

15. Miller, 7.

Bibliography

Abrahams, I. *Hawkwind: Sonic Assassins*. London: SAF, 2004.

Adorno, Theodor. "On the Fetish Character in Music and the Regression of Listening" (1938). In *Essays on Music*, ed. R. Leppert, trans. S.A. Gillespie. Berkeley: University of California Press, 2002.

_____. "The Schema of Mass Culture." In *The Culture Industry*. New York: Routledge, 1991.

Aldiss, Brian. *The Billion Year Spree: The True History of Science Fiction*. New York: Schocken, 1974.

Anderson, Kevin J., and Neil Peart. *Clockwork Angels*. Toronto: ECW, 2012.

Asimov, Isaac. *The Foundation Trilogy*. New York: Avon, 1974.

_____. *I, Robot*. New York: Random House, 1950. Reprint, New York: Bantam/Spectra, 2008.

Atheling, William, Jr. [James Blish]. *More Issues at Hand*. Chicago: Advent, 1970.

Atteburg, Brian, and Veronica Hollinger. *Parabolas of Science Fiction*. Middletown, VT: Wesleyan University Press, 2013.

Auden, W.H. *The Enchafed Flood, or Romantic Iconography of the Se*a. New York: Random House, 1950.

Auslander, Philip. *Performing Glam Rock: Gender and Theatricality in Popular Music*. Ann Arbor: University of Michigan Press, 2006.

Auxier, Randall E. "Magic Pages and Mythic Plants," *Led Zeppelin and Philosophy*, ed. Scott Calif. Chicago: Open Court, 2009.

Ballard, J.G. *Crash*. New York: Farrar, Straus, 1973.

Barron, Frank. *Creativity and Personal Freedom*. New York: D. Van Nostrand, 1968.

Barthes, Roland. *Mythologies*. London: Vintage, 2009.

Basche, Philip. *Heavy Metal Thunder*. San Francisco: Chronicle, 1985.

Bassy, Pascal. *Kraftwerk: Man, Machine, and Music*. London: SAF, 1993.

Beaver, Harold, ed. *The Science Fiction of Edgar Allan Poe*. Harmondsworth: Penguin, 1976.

Beer, John. *Coleridge the Visionary*. London: Chatto and Windus, 1959.

Benjamin, Walter. "The Work of Art in the Age of Mechanical Reproduction." In *Illuminations*. London: Fontana, 1973.

Berman, Michael. *Everyday Fantastic: Essays on Science Fiction and Human Being*. Cambridge: Cambridge University Press, 2008.

Bernal, J.D. *The World, the Flesh, and the Devil* (1929). London: Cape Editions, 1970.

Biamonte, Nicole. "Contre Nous." In *Rush and Philosophy: Heart and Mind United*, ed. Jim Berti and Durrell Bowman, 189–200. Chicago: Open Court/Carus, 2011.

Bibliography

Blish, James. *A Case of Conscience, in American Science Fiction: Five Classic Novels, 1956–1958*, ed. Gary K. Wolfe. New York: Library of America, 2012.

_____. *Cities in Flight*. New York: Avon, 1970. [*They Shall Have Stars, A Life for the Stars, Earthman Come Home, The Triumph of Time*.]

Bodkin, Maud. *Archetypal Patterns in Poetry*. Oxford: Clarendon, 1934.

Bourdieu, Pierre. *Distinction: A Social Critique of the Judgment of Taste*. London: Routledge, Kegan Paul, 1984.

Bowman, Durrell. "More Than They Bargained For." In *Rush and Philosophy*, ed. Jim Berti and Durrell Bowman, 169–188. Chicago: Open Court/Carus, 2011.

Boyd, Jenny, and Holly George Warren. *Musicians in Tune: Seventy-Five Contemporary Musicians Discuss the Creative Process*. New York: Fireside/Simon & Schuster, 1992.

Bracket, Leigh. Introduction. *The Best of Planet Stories*, vol. 1. New York: Random House, 1975.

Bradbury, Ray. *Fahrenheit 451*. New York: Simon & Schuster, 2013.

_____. *The Martian Chronicles*. New York: Simon & Schuster, 2012.

Brooks, Rodney "Making Living Systems." In *Science at the Edge: Conversations with the Leading Scientific Thinkers Today*, ed. John Brockman, 250–56. New York: Union Square/Sterling, 2008.

Brown, Mack. "A Star Comes Back to Earth." *Telegraph Magazine*, December 14, 1996, 304–316.

Bruford, Bill. *Yesyears: A Retrospective*. Videocassette. Vision Entertainment/Atlantic Record Corp., 1991.

Buckley, David. *Strange Fascination: David Bowie, The Definitive Story*. London: Virgin, 1999.

Burroughs, William S. *Soft Machine*. New York: Grove, 2011.

Cadigan, Pat. *Ultimate Cyberpunk*. New York: Ibooks, 2002.

Cagle, Van. *Reconstructing Pop/Subculture: Art, Rock, and Andy Warhol*. Thousand Oaks and London: Sage, 1995.

Calif, Scott, ed. *Led Zeppelin and Philosophy*. Chicago: Open Court, 2009.

Campbell, Joseph. *The Hero with a Thousand Faces*. Princeton: Princeton University Press, 1949.

Campbell, Joseph, and Bill Moyers. *The Power of Myth*. New York: Anchor, 1991.

Capek, Karel. *R.U.R. (Rossum's Universal Robots)*, trans. Claudia Novak-Jones. New York: Penguin Classics, 2004.

Caroti, Simone. *The Generation Starship: A Critical History 1934–2001*. Jefferson, NC: McFarland, 2011.

Chapman, Ian. "Ziggy's Urban Alienation: Assembling the Heroic Outsider." In *Enchanting David Bowie: Space, Time, Body, Memory*, ed. Toija Cinque, Christopher Moore, and Sean Redmond. London: Bloomsbury, 2015.

Cherryh, C.J. *Down Below Station*. New York: DAW, 2001.

Christe, Ian. *Sound of the Beast: The Complete Headbanging History of Heavy Metal*. New York: HarperCollins, 2003.

Christgau, Robert. "Dark Side of the Moon." In *Rock Albums of the 70s*. New York: Da Capo, 1990.

Clarke, Arthur C. *Childhood's End*. (1953). New York: Del Rey, 1987.

_____. *The City and the Stars*. (1958). London: Gollancz, 2001.

Clerk, C. *The Saga of Hawkwind*. London: Omnibus, 2004.

Coates, Norma. "Revolution Now? Rock and the Political Potential of Gender." In

Bibliography

Sexing the Groove: Popular Music and Gender, ed. S. Whiteley London: Routledge, 1997.

Coleridge, Samuel Taylor. "Kublai Kahn." In *Coleridge.* London: Folio, 2003.

_____. "The Rime of the Ancient Mariner." In *Coleridge.* London: Folio, 2003.

Collins, Jon. *Rush Chemistry.* London: Helter Skelter, 2010.

Coxkill, Gordon. "David Bowie." *New Musical Express,* November 15, 1969.

Crosby, David, and Carl Gottlieb. *Long Time Gone.* New York: Doubleday, 1988, reprint 2007.

Curtis, Jim. *Rock Eras: Interpretation of Music and Society, 1954–1984.* Madison: University of Wisconsin Press, 1984.

Davenport, Basil. *The Science Fiction Novel: Imagination and Social Criticism.* Chicago: Advent, 1969.

Delany, Samuel R. *City of a Thousand Suns.* New York: Ace, 1965.

_____. *Dahlgren.* (1975). New York: Vintage, 2001.

_____. *The Einstein Intersection.* Middletown: Wesleyan University Press, 1998.

_____. *The Fall of the Towers.* New York: Ace, 1971.

_____. *The Jewel Hinged Jaw.* New York: Berkeley Windhover, 1978.

Delville, Michael. "The Moorcock/Hawkwind Connection." *Foundation* 62 (Winter 1994–95): 64–69.

Dick, Philip K. *The Eye in the Sky.* New York: Mariner, 2012.

_____. *The Man in the High Castle.* New York: Mariner, 2012.

Doggett, Peter. *The Man Who Sold the World: David Bowie in the 1970s.* New York: HarperCollins, 2012.

Doyle, Peter. *Echo and Reverb: Fabricating Space in Popular Music, 1900–1960.* Middletown: Wesleyan University Press, 2005.

Egan, Sean, ed. *Bowie on Bowie: Interviews and Encounters with David Bowie.* Chicago: Chicago Review, 2015.

Eliade, Mircea. *Myth and Reality,* trans. Willard Trask. New York: Harper Torchbooks, 1968.

_____. *Occultism, Witchcraft, and Cultural Fashions.* Chicago: University of Chicago Press, 1976.

Emerson, Keith. *Pictures of an Exhibitionist.* London: John Blake, 20003.

Fast, Susan. *In the Houses of the Holy: Led Zeppelin and the Power of Rock Music.* New York: Oxford University Press, 2001.

Felix, Justin. "That Space Cadet Glow: Science Fiction Narratives in Roger Waters's KAOS and Amused to Death." *Extrapolation* 41, no. 4 (Winter 2000): 375.

Ferkiss, Victor. *Technological Man.* New York: Mentor/New American Library, 1969.

Finney, Jack. *Invasion of the Body Snatchers.* (1954). New York: Charles Scribner's Sons, 1998.

Fitch, Richard. "In This Age of Grand Illusion: Bowie, Nihilism and Meaning." In *David Bowie: Critical Perspectives,* ed. Eoin Devereaux, Aileen Dillane, and Martin J. Power, 19–34. London: Routledge, 2015.

Forrester, George, Martyn Hanson, and Frank Askew. *Emerson, Lake and Palmer: The Show That Never Ends.* London: Helter Skelter, 2001.

Frank, Pat. *Alas, Babylon* (1959). New York: Harper Perennial, 2005.

_____. *Forbidden Area.* Philadelphia: Lippincott, 1956.

Frith, Simon. "David Bowie." *Let It Rock,* June 1973.

_____. *Music for Pleasure.* Cambridge: Cambridge University Press, 1988.

_____. *Performing Rites.* Cambridge: Harvard University Press, 1996.

_____. *Sound Effects: Youth, Leisure, and the Politics of Rock.* London: Constable, 1983.

Bibliography

_____. "The Suburban Sensibility: British Rock and Pop." In *Visions of Suburbia*, ed. Roger Silverstone, 269–79. London: Routledge, 1996.

Frye, Northrup. *Anatomy of Criticism*. Princeton: Princeton University Press, 1957.

_____. "The Archetypes of Literature." *Kenyon Review* 13, no. 1 (1951).

Gaiman, Neil. Foreword. Samuel R. Delaney, *Einstein Intersection*. Middletown: Wesleyan University Press, 1998.

Gibson, William. *Neuromancer*. New York: Ace, 1984.

_____. "Rocket and Radio." *Rolling Stone* 554 (June 15, 1989): 84.

Greene, Andy. "Inside Rush's Sci-Fi Opera." *Rolling Stone* 1160/1161 (July 5, 2012): 22.

Haldane, J.B.S. *Daedelus, or Science and the Future*. London: Kegan Paul, 1923.

Hall, Stuart, and Paddy Wannel. *The Popular Arts*. London: Hutchison, 1964.

Hamilton, Edith. *Mythology*. Boston and New York: Little, Brown, 1942.

Harris, James F. *Philosophy at 33 1/3 rpm: Themes in Classic Rock Music*. Chicago and La Salle: Open Court, 1993.

Haven, Richard. *Patterns of Consciousness: An Essay on Coleridge*. Amherst: University of Massachusetts Press, 1969.

Heinlein, Robert A. *Methusalah's Children*. (*Astounding* July, August, September 1941). New York: Gnome, 1958.

_____. *Orphans of the Sky*. (1951). New York: Baen, 2001.

_____. "Science Fiction: Its Nature, Faults, and Virtues." (1959). In *The Science Fiction Novel: Imagination and Social Criticism*, ed. Basil Davenport. Chicago: Advent, 1969.

_____. *Starship Troopers*. (1959). New York: Ace, 1987.

_____. *Stranger in a Strange Land*. (1961). New York: Ace, 1991.

Herbert, Frank. *Dune*. New York: Ace, 1990.

Hicks, Michael. *Sixties Rock: Garage, Psychedelia and Other Satisfactions*. Urbana: University of Illinois Press, 1999.

Holmes, Richard. *Coleridge, Early Visions, 1772–1804*. New York: Pantheon, 1989.

Holon-Hudson, Kevin. *Progressive Rock Reconsidered*. New York: Routledge, 2002.

Homer. *The Odyssey*, trans. Robert Fagels. New York: Penguin, 1990.

Hudson, Kevin Holan. *Progressive Rock Reconsidered*. London: Routledge, 2002.

Hull, Robot A. "Sounds and Visions: Psychedelia." *Creem* (January 1981). Also in *The Sound and the Fury: A Rock's Back Pages Reader*, ed. Barney Hoskins. New York: Bloomsbury, 2003.

Hung, Eric. "Hearing Emerson, Lake and Palmer Anew: Progressive Rock as Music of Attraction." *Current Musicology* 79–80 (Spring/Fall 2005): 245–59.

Huxley, Aldous. *The Letters of Aldous Huxley*, ed. Grover Smith. Cambridge: Harvard University Press, 1969.

Huyssen, Andreas. *After the Great Divide: Modernism, Mass Culture, Postmodernism*. Basingstoke: Macmillan, 1986.

Ihde, Erin. "Do Not Panic: Hawkwind, the Cold War and 'the Imagination of Disaster.'" *Cogent Arts and Humanities* (March 2015): 1–13. http://www.cogentoa,tandfonline.com, accessed July 2, 2015.

Jensen, George. *Post-Jungian Criticism*. Albany: State University of New York Press, 2003.

Jones, James T. "Sharing a Shadow." *Post-Jungian Criticism: Theory and Practice*, ed. James S. Baumlin, Tita French Baumlin, and George H. Jensen. Albany: State University of New York Press, 2004.

Jones, Steve. *Pop Music and the Press*. Philadelphia: Temple University Press, 1974.

Bibliography

Jung, C.G. *Flying Saucers: A Modern Myth of Things Seen in the Skies*, trans. R.F.C. Hull. New York: Harcourt Brace, 1959.

_____. *Memories, Dreams, Reflections*, ed. Anelia Jaffe, trans. Richard and Clara Winston. New York: Random House, 1961. Reprint, New York: Vintage, 1989.

Kaku, Michio. *Physics of the Impossible: A Scientific Exploration in the World of Phasers, Force Fields, Teleportation, and Time Travel.* New York: Doubleday, 2008.

Kaye, Lenny. "Flying Saucers and Rock and Roll." *Locus* 5 (September 16, 1972): 6.

_____. "The Tattooed Dragon Meets the Wolfman." Exhibition of Mimeographed Fanzines. New York Book Fair, 2014. www.thoughtcatalog.com.

Kennedy, Victor. *Strange Brew: Metaphors of Magic and Science in Rock Music.* Newcastle-upon-Tyne: Cambridge Scholars, 2013.

Ketterer, David. *New Worlds for Old: The Apocalyptic Imagination. Science Fiction, and American Literature.* Garden City: Doubleday Anchor, 1974.

Knight, Damon. "To Serve Man." *Galaxy Science Fiction* (November 1961). In *Far Out.* New York: Simon & Schuster, 1961.

Knight, G. Wilson. *The Starlit Dome.* Oxford: Clarendon, 1941.

Kohl, Paul R. Review of Edward Macan, *Endlesss Enigma: A Musical Biography of Emerson Lake and Palmer. Popular Music and Society* 32, no. 3 (July 2009): 437–39.

Kramer, Lawrence. *Musical Meaning: Toward a Critical History.* Berkley: University of California Press, 2001.

Kuhn, Thomas S. *The Structure of Scientific Revolutions.* Chicago: University of Chicago Press, 1970.

Laing, Dave. *The Sound of Our Time.* London: Sheed and Ward, 1969.

_____. "The World's Best Rock Read: Let It Rock 1972–75." *Popular Music and Society* 33, no. 4 (2010): 449–63.

Laing, Dave, Marshall Lee, and Derek B. Scott. *Popular Music Matters.* Burlington, VT: Ashgate, 2014.

Larson, R.D. *Musique Fantastique.* Metuchen, NJ: Scarecrow, 1985.

Lavigne, Carlen. *Cyberpunk Women, Feminism and Science Fiction: A Critical Study.* Jefferson, NC: McFarland, 2013.

LeGuin, Ursula. Introduction. *The Norton Book of Science Fiction*, ed. Ursula Le Guin and Brian Attebery. New York: W.W. Norton, 1997.

_____. *The Left Hand of Darkness.* New York: Ace, 2000.

Lehan, Richard. *The City in Literature.* Berkeley: University of California Press, 1998.

Leigh, Wendy. *Bowie: The Biography.* New York and London: Gallery, 2014.

Letts, Marianne Tatom. *Radiohead and the Resistant Concept Album.* Bloomington: Indiana University Press, 2012.

Lewis, C.S. "On Science Fiction." In *Of Other Worlds: Essays and Stories*, ed. Walter Hooper and Geoffrey Bles. London: Bles, 1966.

Lowes, John Livingston. *The Road to Xanadu: A Study in the Ways of the Imagination.* Boston: Houghton Mifflin, 1927.

Lupro, Michael Mooradian. "Keeping Space Fantastic: The Transformative Journey of Major Tom." In *Enchanting David Bowie: Space, Time, Body, Memory*, ed. Toija Cinque, Christopher Moore, and Sean Redmond. London: Bloomsbury, 2015.

Macan, Edward. *Endless Enigma: A Musical Biography of Emerson, Lake, and Palmer.* Chicago: Open Court, 2006.

_____. *Rocking the Classics.* Oxford and New York: Oxford University Press, 1997.

MacDonald, Bruno, ed. *Pink Floyd: Through the Eyes of the Band, Its Fans and Foes.* New York: Da Capo, 1997.

Bibliography

MacLeod, Donald. "Axeman/Astrophysicist Brian May Named University Chancellor." *The Guardian*, November 17, 2007.

Maltby, Richard. Introduction. *Dreams for Sale: Popular Culture in the Twentieth Century*, ed. Richard Maltby. London: Harrup, 1989.

Marcus, Greil. *Mystery Train*, 6th ed. New York: Plume, 2015.

Martin, Bernice. "The Sacralization of Disorder: Symbolism in Rock Music." *Sociology of Religion* (1979).

Martin, Bill. *Listening to the Future: The Time of Progressive Rock*. Chicago: Open Court, 1998.

_____. *Music of Yes: Structure and Vision in Progressive Rock*. Chicago: Open Court, 1996.

Maslow, Abraham. *Religions, Values, and Peak Experiences*. New York: Viking Penguin, 1970. Reprint, 1987.

May, Rollo. *The Courage to Create*. New York: W.W. Norton, 1975. Reprint, New York: Bantam, 1985.

McCaffrey, Larry. *Storming the Reality Studio*. Durham, NC: Duke University Press, 1991.

McDaniel, Stan. "The Coalescence of Minds." In *Philosophers Look at Science Fiction*, ed. Nicholas D. Smith. Chicago: Nelson Hall, 1982.

McDonald, Chris. "Open Secrets, Individualism, and Middle-Class Identity in the Songs of Rush." *Popular Music and Society* 31 (2008): 319.

McGann, Jerome. *The Romantic Ideology*. Chicago: University of Chicago Press, 1984

McGraw-Hill Concise Encyclopedia of Science and Technology, 5th ed. New York: McGraw-Hill, 2005.

McKinney, Angus. "The Future Isn't What It Used to Be." *New Musical Express*, September 13, 1986: 102–139.

McLeod, Ken. Review of Edward Macan, *Endless Enigma: A Musical Biography of Emerson, Lake, and Palmer*. *Notes* (June 207): 874–76.

_____. "Space Oddities: Aliens, Futurism, and Meaning in Popular Music," *Popular Music* 22, no. 3, 337–55.

McRobbie, Angela. "Notes on What Happened to W- and Post-Feminist Symbolic Violence." In *The Aftermath of Feminism: Gender, Culture, and Social Change*, 124–49. London: Sage, 2009.

Meisel, Perry. *The Cowboy and the Dandy: Crossing Over from Romanticism to Rock and Roll*. New York and Oxford: Oxford University Press, 1998.

Meyer, Leonard. *Emotion and Meaning in Music*. Chicago: University of Chicago Press, 1956.

Middleton, Richard. Review, *Piper at the Gates of Dawn* (44–45). *Pop Music and the Blues* (Fall 1967).

Miles. Review of *A Saucerful of Secrets*. *International Times* (August 8, 1968).

Moorcock, Michael. *The Black Corridor*. Frogmore: Granada, 1969.

Morris, Chris. "Lynne Zooms Back to ELO with Epic Disc." *Billboard* 163, no. 4 (June 15, 2001).

Moskowitz, Sam. "How Science Fiction Got Its Name." *The Magazine of Fantasy and Science Fiction* (1957). In *Explorers of the Infinite: Shapers of Science Fiction*, ed. Sam Moskowitz. New York: Meridian, 1959.

Mullen, Richard D. "The Earthmanist Culture: Cities in Flight as a Spenglerian History." Afterword to *Cities in Flight* by James Blish. New York: Avon, 1970.

Mumford, Lewis. *The Pentagon of Power: The Myth of the Machine*. New York: Harcourt Brace Jovanovich, 1970.

Bibliography

Murray, Charles Shaar. "Goodbye Ziggy and a Big Hello to Aladdin Sane." *New Musical Express,* January 27, 1973. In *Bowie on Bowie: Interviews and Encounters with David Bowie,* ed. Sean Egan, 25–35. Chicago: Chicago Review, 2015.

Myers, Paul. *A Wizard, a True Star: Todd Rundgren in the Studio.* London: Jawbone, 2010.

Nash, Graham. *Wild Tales: A Rock and Roll Life.* New York: Crown, 2013.

Nooger, Dan. "Rush Goes Into Future Shock: Music Will Not Exist in 2112." *Circus* (April 27, 1976).

Olderman, Raymond. *Beyond the Waste Land: A Study in the American Novel of the Nineteen Sixties.* New Haven: Yale University Press, 1972.

Orwell, George. *1984.* New York: Harcourt, Brace, 1983.

Peart, Neil. *Ghost Rider: Travels on the Healing Road.* Toronto: ECW, 2002.

Pegg, Nicholas. *The Complete David Bowie.* London: Reynolds and Acorn, 2002. Reprint, London: Titan, 2011.

Polyani, Michael, and Harry Prosch. *Meaning.* Chicago: University of Chicago Press, 1975.

Poster, Mark. *The Mode of Information: Poststructuralism and Social Context.* Chicago: University of Chicago Press and Cambridge: Polity, 1990.

Power, Martin J., Eoin Devereux, Aileen Dillane. "Where Are We Now? Contemporary Scholarship on David Bowie." In *David Bowie: Critical Perspectives.* London and New York: Routledge, 2015.

Prince, Michael J. "The Science Fiction Protocols of Frank Zappa: Problems of Genre and Satire in Billy the M____, Joe's Garage, and Thing Fish." *Chapter and Verse* (Spring 2005) www.popmatters.com.

Reich, Charles A. *The Greening of America.* New York: Random House, 1970.

Reid, Nancy "Clinging to the Edge of Magic: The Shamanic Aspects of The Grateful Dead." *Perspectives on The Grateful Dead,* ed. Robert G. Weiner and Rebecca G. Adams. Westport, CT: Greenwood, 1999.

Rose, Phil. Interview with Roger Waters (February 28, 1995) in *Roger Waters and Pink Floyd: The Concept Albums.* Madison, NJ: Fairleigh Dickinson University Press, 2015.

Roszak, Theodore. *Making of the Counter Culture* (1969). Berkeley: University of California Press, 1995.

_____. *Where the Wasteland Ends.* New York: Bantam, Doubleday, Dell, 1970

Russ, Joanna. *The Female Man.* (1975). Boston: Beacon, 2000.

_____. "Speculations: The Subjunctivity of Science Fiction." *Extrapolations* 15, no. 1 (December 1973): 52.

_____. "Towards an Aesthetic of Science Fiction." *Science Fiction Studies* 2, Part 2 (July 1975): 112–18.

Sanjek, David. The Bloody Heart of Rock and Roll: Images of Popular Music in Contemporary Speculative Fiction." *Journal of Popular Culture* 28, no. 4 (Spring 1995): 179–209.

Schindler, Scott. "Pink Floyd." In *Icons of Rock: An Encyclopedia of the Legends Who Changed Music Forever,* vol. 2, ed. Scott Schindler and Andy Schwartz. Westport, CT, and London: Greenwood, 2008.

Schippers. Mimi. *Rockin' Out of the Box: Gender Maneuvering in Alternative Hard Rock.* New Brunswick, NJ: Rutgers University Press, 2002.

Scholes, Robert. *Structural Fabulation: An Essay on Fiction of the Future.* South Bend: University of Notre Dame Press, 1975.

Bibliography

Seay, Davin, and Mary Neely. *Stairway to Heaven: The Spiritual Roots of Rock n' Roll*. New York: Ballantine, 1986.

Shaffner, Nicholas. *Saucerful of Secrets: The Pink Floyd Odyssey*. New York: Dell, 1991.

Shelley, Mary. *Frankenstein*. New York and Oxford: Oxford University Press, 2009.

Shipston, Roy. "Are Spacemen Floyd on Their Way Back to Earth?" *Disc and Music Echo*, November 22, 1969.

Shirley, John. "Science Fiction and Rock Music." *Metaphores* 9–10 (April 1984).

Silverberg, Robert. *The Science Fiction Hall of Fame, vol. 1, 1929–1964*. New York: Orb, 2005.

Sinclair, David. "Station to Station." *Rolling Stone*, June 10, 1993. In *Bowie on Bowie: Interviews and Encounters with David Bowie*, ed. Sean Egan, 231–48. Chicago: Chicago Review, 2015.

Skeggs, Beverly. *Formation of Class and Gender: Becoming Respectable*. London: Sage, 1977.

Slavca, Neil. *Electric Don Quixote: The Definitive Story of Frank Zappa*. London: Omnibus, 2003.

Smith, Nicholas D. *Philosophers Look at Science Fiction*. London: Burnham, 1982.

Smolko, Timothy. "What Can This Strange Device Be?" In *Rush and Philosophy: Heart and Mind United*, ed. Jim Berti and Durrell Bowman, 225–238. Chicago: Open Court/Carus, 2011.

Snow, C.P. *The Two Cultures and the Scientific Revolution*. Rede Lecture, 1959.

Spitz, Marc. *Bowie: A Biography*. New York: Crown/Archetype, 2010.

Stableford, Bill. *Science Fact, Science Fiction*. London: Routledge, 2006.

Stambler, Irwin. *Pop, Rock, Soul*. New York: St. Martin's, 1974.

Stamp. Paul. *The Music's All That Matters: A History of Progressive Rock*. London: Quartet, 1997.

Stapledon, Olaf. *Last and First Men*. (1930). Mineola, NY: Dover, 2008.

Stenning, Paul. *Iron Maiden: Thirty Years of the Beast*. Chicago: Independent Publishers, 2006.

Stevenson, Nick. *David Bowie: Fame, Sound and Vision*. Cambridge: Polity, 2006.

Sterling, Bruce. *Tomorrow Now: Envisioning the Next Fifty Years*. New York: Random House, 2003.

_____. *Zeitgeist*. New York: Spectra, 2001.

_____, ed. *Mirrorshades: An Anthology of Cyberpunk*. London and New York: Palladin Books, 1986.

Storey, John. *Cultural Theory and Popular Culture: A Reader*. London: Pearson, 2006.

Stump, Paul. *The Music's All That Matters: A History of Progressive Rock*. London: Quartet Books, 1997.

Sturgeon, Theodore. *The Complete Stories of Theodore Sturgeon*. Berkeley: North Atlantic, 1997.

Tamarkin, Jeff. *The Turbulent Flight of Jefferson Airplane*. New York: Simon & Schuster, 2003.

Tauber, Alfred I. *Science and the Quest for Meaning*. Waco, TX: Baylor University Press, 2009.

Toffler, Alvin. *Future Shock*. New York: Vintage, 1970.

Tribbe, Matthew D. *No Requiem for the Space Age: The Apollo Moon Landings and American Culture*. New York: Oxford University Press, 2014.

Trynka, Paul. *David Bowie: Starman*. New York and Boston: Little, Brown, 2011.

Bibliography

Van Elferen, I. *Gothic Music: Sounds of the Uncanny*. Cardiff: University of Wales Press, 2012.

Wakeman, Rick, and Martin Roach. *Grumpy Old Rock Star and Other Wondrous Stories*. London: Preface, 2008.

Waldrop, Sheldon. *The Aesthetics of Self-Invention: Oscar Wilde to David Bowie*. Minneapolis: University of Minnesota Press, 2004.

Wall, Mick. *Run to the Hills*. London: Sanctuary, 2004.

Walser, Robert. *Running With the Devil: Power, Gender, and Madness in Heavy Metal Music*. Middleton, CT: Wesleyan University Press, 1993.

Watts, Michael. "Oh, You Pretty Things." *Melody Maker* 22 (January 1972).

Weinstein, Deena. *Heavy Metal: The Music and Its Culture*. New York: Da Capo, 1991. Reprint, 2000.

_____. *Serious Rock: The Artistic Vision of Modern Society in Rush, Pink Floyd and Bruce Springsteen*. Montreal: New World Perspectives, 1985.

Wells, H.G. *The Time Machine*. New York: Penguin Classics, 2005.

_____. *The War of the Worlds. A Critical Edition of the War of the Worlds: H.G. Wells's Scientific Romance*, ed. Harry M. Geduld and David Y. Hughes. Bloomington: Indiana University Press, 1993.

Westfahl, Gary. *The Mechanics of Wonder: The Creation of Science Fiction*. Liverpool: Liverpool University Press, 1998.

Whiteley, Sheila. *The Space Between the Notes: Rock and the Counterculture*. London and New York: Routledge, 2000.

Williams, Raymond. "The Analysis of Culture." In *Cultural Theory and Popular Culture: A Reader*, ed. John Storey. London: Pearson, 2006.

_____. "Base and Superstructure in Marxist Cultural Theory." In *Problems in Materialism and Culture*. London: Verso, 1980.

_____. *The Country and the City*. London: Chatto and Windus, 1973.

_____. *Culture and Society*. Harmondsworth: Penguin, 1963.

_____. "The Metropolis and the Emergence of Modernism." In *Unreal City: Urban Experiences in Modern European Literature and Art*, ed. David Kelley and Edward Timms. Manchester: Manchester University Press, 1985.

Willis, Ellen. *Beginning to See the Light: Sex, Hope, and Rock and Roll*. Jackson: University of Mississippi Press, 2012.

_____. *Out of the Vinyl Deeps: Ellen Willis on Rock Music*. Minneapolis: University of Minnesota Press, 2011.

Wolfe. Gary K. *American Science Fiction: Nine Classic Novels of the 1950s*. New York: Library of America, 2012.

_____. *How Great Science Fiction Works*. Chantilly, VA: The Great Courses, 2016.

_____. *The Known and the Unknown: The Iconography of Science Fiction*. Kent, OH: Kent State University Press, 1979.

Wragg, David. "Or Any Art At All: Frank Zappa Meets Critical Theory." *Popular Music* 2, no. 2 (2001): 205–222.

Zamyatin, Yvgeny. "Herbert Wells." In *H.G. Wells, The Critical Heritage*, ed. Patrick Parrinder, 260. London: Routledge, Kegan and Paul, 1972.

_____. *We*. (1924), trans. Natasha Randall. New York: Modern Library, 2006.

Zappa, Frank, and Peter Occhiogrosso. *The Real Frank Zappa Book*. New York: Simon & Schuster, 1989.

Zelazny, Roger. *Damnation Alley*. London: Sphere, 1971.

Zimmerman, Nadia. *Counterculture Kaleidoscope: Late 1960s San Francisco*. Ann Arbor: University of Michigan Press, 2009.

Index

Index

Index

Index

Index

Index

Index